Learning to Program
OS/2® 2.0 Presentation Manager™
by Example

(Putting the Pieces Together)

VAN NOSTRAND REINHOLD
OS/2 TITLES

OS/2 Presentation Manager GPI Graphics by Graham C.E. Winn

Writing OS/2 2.0 Device Drivers in C by Steven J. Mastrianni

Now That I Have OS/2 2.0 on My Computer—What Do I Do Next? by Steven Levenson

Integrating Applications With OS/2 2.0 by William H. Zack

The COBOL Presentation Manager Programming Guide by David M. Dill

Comprehensive Database Performance for OS/2 2.0's Extended Services by Bruce Tate, Tim Malkemus, and Terry Gray

Client-Server Programming With OS/2 2.0 by Robert Orfali and Daniel Harkey

C Programming in the OS/2 2.0 Environment by V. Mitra Gopaul

Learning to Program
OS/2® 2.0 Presentation Manager™
by Example

(Putting the Pieces Together)

Stephen A. Knight

VNR | VAN NOSTRAND REINHOLD
New York

To my wife, Allison, and my children, Eric and Christopher,
for all their patience and support.

Printed in the United States of America.

Van Nostrand Reinhold
115 Fifth Avenue
New York, New York 10003

Chapman and Hall
2-6 Boundary Row
London, SE1 8HN, England

Thomas Nelson Australia
102 Dodds Street
South Melbourne 3205
Victoria, Australia

Nelson Canada
1120 Birchmount Road
Scarborough, Ontario MIK 5G4, Canada

16 15 14 13 12 11 10 9 8 7 6 5 4 3 2

Library of Congress Cataloging-in-Publication Data
Knight, Stephen A., 1935—
    Learning the program OS/2® 2.0 Presentation Manager™ by example:
putting the pieces together/Stephen A. Knight.
       p. cm.
    Includes index.
    ISBN 0-442-01292-6
    1. Operating systems (Computers) 2. Presentation manager
(Computer program) 3. OS/2 (Computer file) I. Title.
QA76.76.063K62 1992
005.4'3—dc20   92-13080
                                                           CIP

Contents

Foreword

The introduction of the Personal Computer (PC) has changed our world in many ways. Not only has the PC revolutionized the way many people work, but it has also changed the way computer buyers assess value. Just a decade ago, masses of people were very willing to buy a personal computer with a relatively slow processor, a non-graphical display, a single diskette drive, limited memory, and a dot matrix printer. Today, for approximately the same price, consumers can buy a system with a very powerful processor, a high resolution color graphical display, both diskette drive and large hard file, several megabytes of memory, and a laser printer with color and graphic capabilities.

Today's consumer has more options available at a lower cost. Intense competition enables the consumer to be more demanding than ever before, and buyers are choosing their systems with care.

As PC hardware is available at competitive prices, and more tasks are being done by computer, it became clear to all types of users that new software needed to be developed to keep up with hardware capabilities. IBM made the commitment to develop the best possible new operating system. A robust system that would allow users at every level to perform tasks on their computers faster, easier, and more effectively than ever before. IBM believed that the time was right for an entirely new operating system, not just an overlay to improve DOS functions.

OS/2 2.0 is that new system—one that allows authors like Steve Knight to write a book and produce illustrations, use a database, and make sure he got the best deal on his contract all at the same time—and probably keep the season's scores for the local little league games to boot. It is also a system that large corporations can use for their most sensitive, mission critical operations. On the desktop, individual and corporate users will have power and function heretofore available only on large, mainframe and minicomputer systems. Users can be separated by desks, by rooms, or by continents; the power of OS/2® and networks will bring them together.

Presentation Manager for OS/2 was designed to help software developers provide a consistent user interface for all their applications. It includes a large set of functions that reduce the amount of complex specialized code usually needed to resolve device dependencies and advanced graphics techniques. The programming techniques are therefore easier, but the PM is so different from other, older systems, that new programmers, and programmers new to OS/2 2.0 Presentation Manager alike, need a guide. Knight's book, *Learning to Program OS/2® 2.0 Pre-*

sentation Manager™ *by Example,* provides an excellent introduction to learning OS/2 2.0 Presentation Manager programming. He provides information in an interesting, fun, and productive way. Once you have mastered the information in this book, you will move on to advanced topics in Presentation Manager without feeling intimidated. You will come to appreciate the function and power of OS/2 2.0 Presentation Manager and discover potential you had not imagined was available.

You will write better programs—your clients and customers will be happier, and more productive. OS/2 2.0 helps you get the most out of your PC and this book should help programmers get the most out of OS/2.

James Cannavino
General Manager
IBM Personal Systems

Preface

Operating System/2™ (OS/2®) is an extremely powerful operating system for IBM® personal computers and compatibles that have an Intel® 80286 processor or higher, a high resolution color monitor, and several megabytes of memory. Unlike its predecessor, DOS, OS/2 is designed to provide full multitasking and memory management facilities, interprocess communication support, and application protection mechanisms. These features may not mean much to the ultimate user, but they are key features and address major issues that application developers must deal with in today's PC market. Hence, as personal computers become cheaper and more powerful, OS/2 looks very attractive from a software developer's point of view.

Another striking feature of OS/2 is Presentation Manager™ (PM) which provides a highly graphical environment to the end user of the personal computer and provides an easy-to-use and consistent way to interact with applications developed for this environment. Therefore, it is a plus for applications written for the OS/2 environment to also be written to take advantage of the PM environment.

Most likely, developers who write a PM application for the first time will find working in this environment to be quite different from that which they are familiar. However, developers who learn how to write PM applications come to like it and find great satisfaction in the outcome of their efforts.

The PM Application Program Interface (API) is very rich in function, having hundreds of functions and parameters to control these functions, available to the application writer. People confuse richness of function with complexity. But actually many of these functions reduce complexity by eliminating the need for developers to write thousands of lines of code while helping to enforce a consistent appearance of the application to the end user.

Learning to Program OS/2® 2.0 Presentation Manager™ by Example was written to help application programmers new to PM learn how to write PM applications. A complete working example of a PM application written in the C programming language shows the way. It is written and compiled as a 32-bit application for the new release of OS/2 (OS/2 2.0). Because it is written and compiled as a 32-bit application, it requires at least a 80386 processor to execute.

Both the executable PM program and the C source code are provided with this book so that modification or copying parts of this application are possible. The application provided with this book uses many features of the PM Application Program Interface, while the text explains the structure of this program and how the different functions of Presentation Manager are used.

This book does not attempt to replace the PM technical references and does not use every feature of Presentation Manager. In fact, this book assumes you have accessibility to detailed information about PM functions and a good understanding of the C programming language. *Learning to Program OS/2® 2.0 Presentation Manager™ by Example* offers techniques that you can use with the PM functions provided and gives a good working example of how to put PM functions together. Also, the book is intended to provide this information in an interesting and fun way.

Acknowledgments

I thank the following people for their technical assistance and cooperation in helping me produce this book: Mark Benge, Peter Brightbill, Brad Broyles, Dick Conklin, Tom Gall, Peter Haggar, Diana Mack, Tai Nam, Bob Nelson, Jeff Robison, Curt Rose, Jeff Ryan, and Ruth Taylor. I also thank Ken Aaker and Jerry Donney for their assistance in producing some of the book's art work and Claire Riley for editing the book manuscript. Thanks also to my manager Phil Mayer and my editor Dianne Littwin for their time and support.

Thanks to all of you for helping make this book a reality.

1

Overview

A Presentation Manager (PM) application is easy to recognize in the OS/2 environment. Besides being part of the standard graphical user interface (GUI) that comes with OS/2, most PM applications look and feel very similar to one another. Some application developers find this similarity distressing because they prefer their applications to look and operate in a very distinct way. From an end user perspective, however, this consistency aids in the ability to quickly learn new applications written for this environment.

Many of the noticeable similarities between PM applications have to do with the windows in which they appear to be contained and the features and controls with which they can be manipulated. Screen 1-1 shows a typical Presentation Manager screen. From an end user's perspective, Screen 1-1 shows four windows which are owned by two applications. These four windows are the System Clock window, which is all by itself, and the Action Log window and Project Control window which are owned by the WorkFrame/2™ window. Shortly you will see that from a programmer's perspective, there are really many more windows on this screen! The relationship between the windows shown in Screen 1-1 is illustrated in Figure 1-1.

As suggested by Figure 1-1, a hierarchical relationship exists between the windows. in the Presentation Manager envrionment. The root of this relationship is called the *Desktop*, which is also a window even though it does not visually present itself as one. (You may think of the Desktop as a window that consumes the entire screen.) Figure 1-1 also implies that Presentation Manager applications are given ways to create windows as needed, and when these windows are created, parent/child relationships are established. In order to coordinate work between windows, Presentation Manager provides mechanisms that allow information to be sent and received between the

1

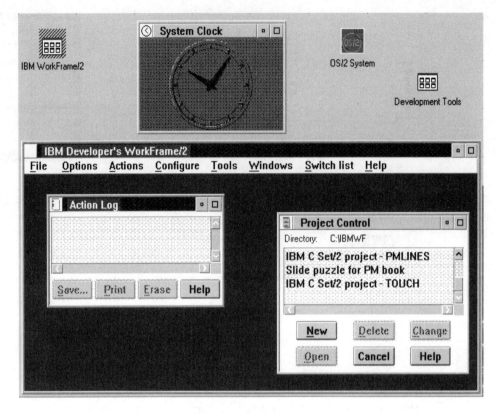

Screen 1-1. Windows.

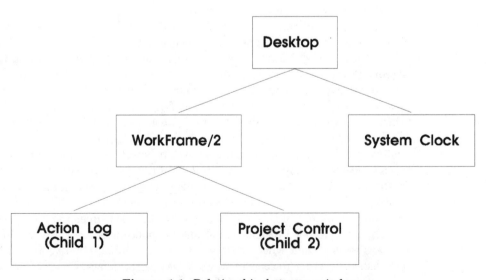

Figure 1-1. Relationship between windows.

different windows. The passing of information between windows will be discussed in more detail, but first, let's examine the different parts of a typical window.

Figure 1-2 details the basic features of an application window as seen by the end-user. Following are descriptions of each of these features and how they can be used. The descriptions given for these features are for normal use. There are, however, cases where these descriptions may not apply for some PM applications.

Title Bar contains title information for the application that controls the window. By clicking on this area with mouse button 1, this window may gain *input focus*. Input focus means this window comes to the foreground of the screen and may receive input from the keyboard. If you press and hold mouse button 1 while pointing to this area, you can move the window as you move the mouse. When you release button 1, the window will remain at the new location.

Action Bar contains keywords you can activate by clicking on the word with mouse button 1. If you activate one of these keywords, a pull-down menu containing more selectable options is produced.

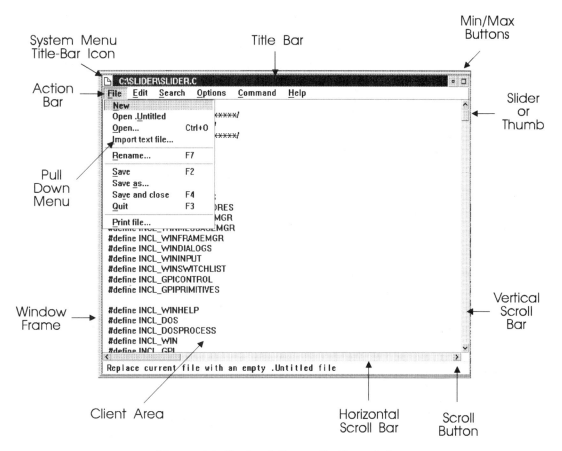

Figure 1-2. Parts of the application window.

System Menu contains system services for the application. These services can be accessed with the keyboard or mouse and include items such as close, minimize, maximize, size, and move the application window.

Size Border or **Window Frame** is the outside perimeter of the application window. This frame area changes color when the window comes to the foreground and gains input focus. By pressing and holding mouse button 1 while pointing at the border edge or corner and then moving the mouse, you can resize the window area. When you release the mouse button, the window will retain the new size.

Vertical/Horizontal Scroll Bars control the visible region of the application presentation area. Within these areas are controls called the slider or thumb and scroll buttons that let you manipulate the visible region.

Scroll Buttons allow you to shift the contents of the application client area by either one line or one character at a time. This is done by clicking mouse button 1 on the scroll button indicating the direction of the scroll action. As you do this, you will see the contents of the window shift and the corresponding slider move in the direction of the scroll.

Slider or **Thumb** is a control and indicator in the scroll bar area. The size and relative location of the slider within the scroll bar area indicates the relative location of the visible region of the application presentation area that is currently visible. By pressing and holding down mouse button 1, and then moving the mouse in the direction of the scroll, you can quickly scroll through the application's client area. The information in the window may or may not change until you release the mouse button. If you would like to page up or down through the client area by using the scroll bar controls, click mouse button 1 while the mouse pointer is in the area between the slider and the scroll button.

Minimize/Maximize Buttons allow you to quickly increase or decrease the size of the application window. If you use the maximize button, the window size will increase to the largest practical size for the application. If you use the minimize button, the window will either be reduced to an icon that remains on the desktop or will totally disappear. How you have setup Presentation Manager will determine what will happen when you minimize a window. These controls are activated by clicking mouse button 1 on the appropriate button. If you want to return an application icon to a window, double click mouse button 1 on the icon. If the icon of the application is not present on the desktop, click mouse buttons 1 and 2 at the same time in the desktop area and a list of active applications from which you can choose will appear.

Client Area is the presentation area for the application. The client area may be too small to hold all the information that the application wants to be present. In this case, *clipping* may occur. Clipping means that part of the information that you are attempting to put in the application window will not be visible due to the size of the window. Note that this is only a visual effect; the application always has the information! You may either have to maximize the window or use scroll bars to view all the application's information.

Even though the previously listed features are relatively common to most PM applications, the application developer can choose whether or not to support them. Furthermore, you will see that there are several other standard PM controls and features to help you further manage your application.

COMMUNICATION BETWEEN WINDOWS

To coordinate activity between windows, Presentation Manager provides a message passing mechanism. The messages being passed in this environment contain a wide variety of information. In fact, hundreds of message types exist and can be sent to your application. For instance, Presentation Manager will send your application keyboard and mouse movement messages as appropriate. Not only can Presentation Manager generate messages but other applications can also generate and transmit their own messages. However, the basic structure of a message in the PM environment must be the same no matter if Presentation Manager generated it or it was generated by another application. Figure 1-3 shows the basic structure of a message used in the PM environment followed by a description of each message field.

HWND is the window handle to which the message is being sent. This is a 32-bit value and is used by Presentation Manager to identify information about the destination window.

MSG is a 16-bit value that identifies the type of message being transmitted. Presentation Manager provides many symbolic names for these values to help you easily identify the message type. For instance, the symbolic name *WM_CHAR* is a message type that passes keyboard information to the window application.

mp1 and **mp2** are 32-bit values that contain parameter information associated with the message type. These parameter fields are always 32 bits in length, but the information within these fields will vary in type and

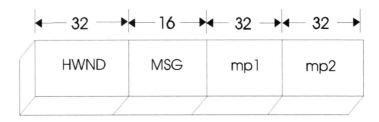

Figure 1-3. Message structure.

is dependent on the message type. Furthermore, you may find more than one type of information in a single parameter field. For instance, mp1 may contain a 16-bit word and two 8-bit characters for a certain message type; for a different message type, this same field may contain a 32-bit pointer. Several acros exist to help extract the different types of information that can be found in these fields. For instance, *CHAR1FROMMP*, *CHAR2FROMMP, CHAR3FROMMP*, and *CHAR4FROMMP* are macros that extract the first, second, third, or fourth byte from a 32-bit field. Other popular macros are *SHORT1FROMMP* and *SHORT2FROMMP* that extract the first two or second two bytes from a 32-bit field. Throughout this book you will see several other macros that provide similar assistance.

Messages are passed to your application in a structure called a message queue. In Chapter 2, Working with Messages, you will see how to generate and gain access to this message queue, but for now, let's look at how messages flow through and are used in the PM environment.

When different types of activity occur in the personal computer, Presentation Manager will generate messages and place them in message queues. Message queues are the primary source of input to PM applications. Messages are placed in the message queues in a priority and time sequence and are processed by the different PM applications one at a time. If input to a message queue is much faster than an application's ability to process it, messages may be lost. As the different PM applications receive these messages, they send them to various procedures designed to act on their content. These procedures are called *window procedures* or *WinProcs*. Your application will generate one or more of these window procedures to operate on user input and manipulate the contents of a presentation area; however, Presentation Manager also provides other window procedures in this environment that are available to your application. Many of these other window procedures are for control windows. For instance, the window frame is a window and has its own window procedure to control it. The title bar, system menu, minimize button, maximize button, scroll bars, and so on are also windows, and have their own window procedures to control them as well. In fact, most of the standard controls you see in this environment are windows with window procedures provided by Presentation Manager. Therefore, much of the work needed to manipulate this environment is provided by Presentation Manager. And as this environment is enhanced, such as the style or look of the different controls, your application is enriched at no extra cost to you. Figure 1-4 illustrates a more detailed window diagram of Screen 1-1. However, due to the number of real windows present on Screen 1-1, only a subset of them are represented by Figure 1-4.

Now that you are aware that there are many more windows on the screen than are apparent to the end user, look again at the window hierarchy of a typical PM application as shown in Figure 1-4. Notice that even though there are many more windows in Figure 1-4 than were presented earlier, the hierarchy is still maintained.

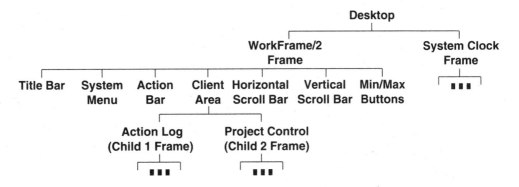

Figure 1-4. Window hierarch.

THE APPLICATION

This book will discuss in detail a slide puzzle application. A slide puzzle is a matrix of rectangular pieces with one blank or missing piece. Therefore, the pieces in the matrix can always slide either horizontally or vertically toward the blank piece but never in a diagonal direction. When the pieces are assembled in the

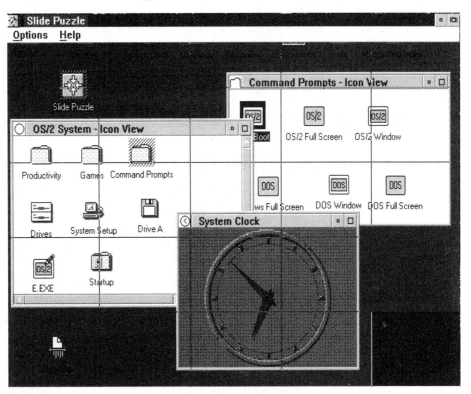

Screen 1-2. Slider puzzle application.

correct order, they form a picture. For our slide puzzle, the picture is the image of the desktop when the application is started. Screen 1-2 shows an example of a desktop image that has been captured by the slide puzzle application. Notice that a blank piece is found at the bottom right corner of the puzzle when the slide puzzle program is first started.

As you move the mouse pointer about the slide puzzle area, the pointer icon changes to indicate the direction of a valid move. When you move the mouse pointer to a region of the puzzle that would cause an invalid move, the pointer icon changes to the symbol X. To cause a move, click mouse button 1 on the piece of the puzzle you want to slide toward the blank. If the slide puzzle has input focus and you would rather use the keyboard than the mouse, use the arrow keys to move the pieces. Screen 1-3 is the result of making one horizontal and one vertical move with the mouse.

Puzzle Options

There are several options available that make the puzzle more challenging and fun. To view these options, select the Options pull-down menu from the slide puzzle action bar.

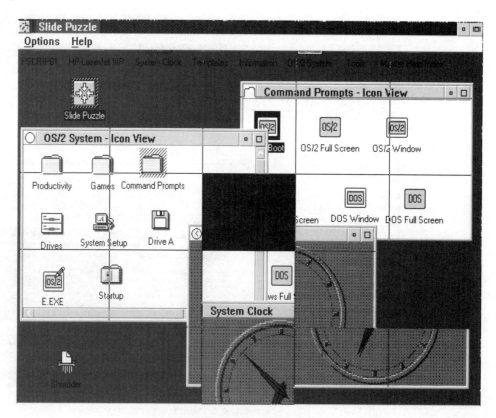

Screen 1-3. Puzzle after two moves.

One of the first visual effects you may want to turn on or off is the grid. To do this, select the Grid option from the Options pull-down menu. This option acts like a switch and either places or removes vertical and horizontal lines on the puzzle so you can better see the puzzle matrix. In the previous example screens, the grid was on. Screen 1-4 shows a puzzle with the grid off. You can also toggle this option on and off by pressing the *Ctrl-G* key sequence without accessing the Options pull-down menu.

You may also notice that the grid size on Screen 1-4 is different from the previous screens, and the puzzle image is just the desktop with no other windows on it. This was done by using the New Puzzle option from the Options pull-down menu. This option lets you choose a grid number from 4 to 25 and also lets you choose a time delay (in seconds) before the desktop image is captured for a new puzzle picture. To create Screen 1-4, this option was selected, all the applications were minimized, and icons were arranged before the delay value expired. You can also select this option with the *Ctrl-N* key sequence without accessing the Options pull-down menu.

Besides changing the grid number to make the puzzle more challenging, you can also let the puzzle perform random moves to scramble the picture. To do this, select the Random Moves option from the Options pull-down menu. You can then enter the number of random moves, from 1 to 1,000, that you want the puzzle to

Screen 1-4. Puzzle grid off.

make. The puzzle will then move pieces automatically until the count has been achieved. You can also select this option without accessing the Options pull-down menu by pressing the *Ctrl-R* key sequence. For complex pictures with a large grid number, this option will challenge even the best puzzle solver.

While the puzzle is being scrambled, you may want to do some other work. Because this puzzle is a multithreaded application, you can do anything else you want while the puzzle is operating in the background.

If you become frustrated when trying to solve a puzzle, you can undo up to the last 3,000 moves by selecting Undo from the Options pull-down menu. Just like the Random Moves option, the puzzle will start to slide pieces automatically until either the puzzle is solved or 3,000 moves have expired. Also, just like the Random Move option, you can let this activity occur in the background while you do something else. You can also select this option with the *Ctrl-U* key sequence without accessing the Options pull-down menu.

To stop the puzzle from providing random moves or undoing moves for solving the puzzle, use the Stop option from the Options pull-down menu. This option can also be selected with the *Ctrl-S* key sequence without accessing the Options pull-down menu.

There is also a bug in this application! It will appear to run across the desktop at random. This bug is an image of a grasshopper and if you look closely you'll notice its legs actually move as it runs across your screen.

WORKING WITH THE DISKETTE

This book comes with a diskette containing both the source code and the compiled slide puzzle application. By providing you with this, you can manipulate the slide puzzle application and see the effects of your actions. Furthermore, since the source code is provided, you are saved from the tedious chore of entering this information. Finally, if parts of this source code are similar to what you want to develop for your own project, you can use those parts.

Important: You should understand and test all source code used from this diskette that is used as part of your own project. There is no guarantee that this code will meet all your needs or that it contains no errors.

Before you modify any source code that came with this book, save the contents of the diskette and store it in a safe place. This will help insure that you always have the source code and executable program in case the original gets damaged.

After saving the contents of the diskette, you may choose to install the contents of this diskette on your target system hard drive. You can run the slide puzzle application from diskette by making the drive where the diskette is located the current drive and executing SLIDER.EXE; however, performance may be poor. To install the slide puzzle application on your hard file, use the following steps:

      1. Make a directory of your choice for the slide puzzle application. Then change the current directory to this new directory. If you already have a directory created that you want to put the slide puzzle in, just change the current directory to that directory.

2. Copy SLIDER.EXE and SLIDER.ICO to the hard file directory. If you want the SLIDER.HLP (help information) in the same directory as the program, copy this file also; Otherwise copy SLIDER.HLP to a directory with other help file information (\OS2\HELP\).

3. Update all path information as needed so the slide puzzle program and help information can be found by OS/2.

4. Copy a program template from the templates folder and modify it to reference SLIDER.EXE and its icon SLIDER.ICO. This step will make the slide puzzle application accessible from the OS/2 2.0 Workplace Shell.

After installing the slide puzzle application, you should run it to become familiar with its operation and functional characteristics. You will then develop a good point of reference for the slide puzzle application which will be helpful as you read the rest of this book. To start the slide puzzle application, enter the command SLIDER from a command line prompt or, if you made a template for it, double click on the slide puzzle application icon from the Workplace Shell.

There is a startup parameter for the slide puzzle application that lets you select the number of puzzle pieces. If you have a template defined for the slide puzzle, enter a number from 4 to 25 in the parameter field for this program to specify the number of puzzle pieces found on each side of the puzzle. For example, if you use the number 10, the puzzle will contain 100 puzzle pieces minus 1 for the blank piece. If you start the slide puzzle application from a command line prompt, enter the following:

SLIDER *number*
where *number* is a number between 4 and 25.

Finally, before you change any source code, make sure you can compile and build the application so it works the same as the one provided. You do not have to use the same tool set or procedure to build the application as was used for this book, but they are given as a point of reference. (Of course, at this time, I'm not aware of other 32-bit C compilers other than the one referenced in this book!) Before examining the build tools and procedure, let's review the contents of the files on the diskette.

Following is a list and description of each file found on the diskette:

SLIDER.H contains definition and include statements used during the compile step for SLIDER.C and SLIDER.RC.

SLIDER.C contains all of the C source code for the slide puzzle application. This source code is provided in one large source file so it is easier for you to find code segments. As you become familiar with the source code, you will probably want to break it into smaller pieces and then compile and link them as separate objects.

SLIDER.OBJ contains the results from compiling the SLIDER.C file.

SLIDER.ICO contains the application icon for the slide puzzle.

SLIDER1.PTR - SLIDER5.PTR contain the pointers used by the slide puzzle application.

BUG1.BMP - BUG5.BMP and **BUG1MASK.BMP - BUG5MASK.BMP** contain bit- maps used to produce an animated bug (grasshopper) for the slide puzzle application.

SLIDER.BMP contains a bit-map of the slide puzzle icon.

SLIDER1.BMP contains a bit-map of a block.

SLIDER.RC contains all the resource definitions for the slider application. Icons, bit-maps, menus, and dialog boxes are examples of resources used by a PM application.

SLIDER.RES contains the results from compiling the SLIDER.RC file.

SLIDER.IPF contains the source for the slide puzzle help text.

SLIDER.HLP contains the results from compiling the SLIDER.IPF file.

SLIDER.EXE is the executable code for the slide puzzle application.

DIALOG.DLG contains definitions of dialog boxes.

DIALOG.H contains definition statements for the dialog boxes and is used during the compile step for SLIDER.C and SLIDER.RC.

Because of things like help text and resources, you may find building a PM application to be a little different from what you may have experienced in other environments. However, the first couple steps, which involve compiling and linking the C source code, will probably be very familiar to you. Remember that the slide puzzle application is being built as a 32-bit OS/2 application.

The compiler used for the slide puzzle application is IBM C Set/2™. The command used to compile the slide puzzle application is as follows:

ICC /S2 /Sr /Gm SLIDER.C

This step produces a new file called SLIDER.OBJ which is used in the link step. The linker used to build the slide puzzle SLIDER.EXE file comes with the IBM Developer's Toolkit for OS/2 2.0. The command used to link the slide puzzle application is as follows:

LINK386 SLIDER.OBJ /M /NOI /ST:20000 /NOL /PM:PM,SLIDER.EXE;

This step produces a file called SLIDER.EXE. At this point you may think you are done building the application; for some PM applications, you would be done. However, because the slide puzzle application uses objects called resources, there are more steps! Resources, such as icons, menus, bit maps, and help text, are compiled separately and have to be described and merged with the application .EXE file. This is done with a tool called a resource compiler. Compiling resources is discussed in more detail in Chapter 4, Working with Resources, and is also shown here so you can see how to complete the build for the entire slide puzzle application.

The resource compiler used for the slide puzzle resources comes with the IBM Developer's Toolkit for OS/2 2.0. Following is the resource compile command for the slide puzzle application:

RC -r SLIDER

This step produces a file called SLIDER.RES which is used in the last step for building the final slide puzzle executable file. Now that the resources have been compiled, they must be added to the compiled and linked C code. This is done with the same tool that is used to create the SLIDER.RES file. Following is the step used to merge the SLIDER.RES file to the previously produced SLIDER.EXE file:

RC SLIDER.RES

The output from this step is an updated version of the existing SLIDER.EXE file. The SLIDER.EXE file is now finished and ready to execute, but another piece is still needed to make the application complete. This last piece is the application help text.

The help text for the slide puzzle program is not included in the application itself and must be built as a special separate file that can be referenced when needed. This help text is built with a tool called the Information Presentation Facility Compiler that comes as part of the IBM Developer's Toolkit for OS/2 2.0. This tool operates on a source text file. This file contains the desired help text and special tags that describe where and how the help text will be presented. Following is the step used to build the help text for the slide puzzle application:

IPFC SLIDER.IPF

This step produces a file called SLIDER.HLP that should be stored with other help files or in the same directory as the SLIDER.EXE file.

Another tool that IBM provides for the OS/2 2.0 development environment is IBM WorkFrame/2. This application provides you with a programming work bench environment. This environment helps you manage different programming projects and lets you customize different build options for each development project. It also gives you the option to choose a program editor of your choice and provides an automatic way of starting or bringing the program editor to the foreground when needed. Screen 1-5 shows a sample session using IBM WorkFrame/2. By studying Screen 1-5, you can get an idea of some of the features this tool provides.

SPECIAL NOTES ABOUT THIS BOOK

As you have already discovered, a programmer's view of what a window is may be much different than what the typical user sees. As you read this book, you will see the term *application window*. This term refers to what the typical user perceives as a window which includes everything within the application frame window. (Remember the frame window is a control window that is located on the outside edge of the client area.)

Occasionally, this book provides definitions containing multiple parts. A definition always starts by showing the syntax of the item being defined followed by an

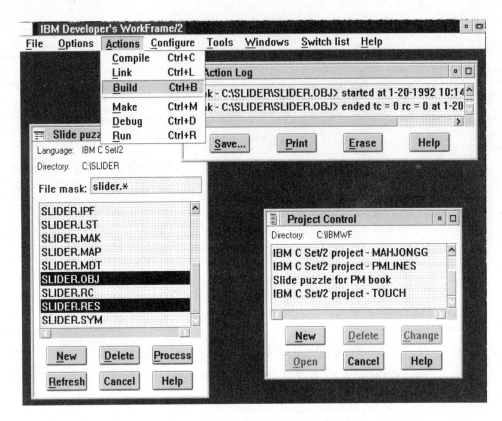

Screen 1-5. IBM WorkFrame/2 Session.

explanation of the variable information. Variable information is always shown in *italics*. Following is an example of a definition:

TERM *var1 var2*
where
      var1 is defined here.
      var2 is defined here.

Listings in this book are excerpts from the source code found on the diskette. Very often several statements are left out of these listings to help maintain focus on the important points about a particular topic. Therefore, even within a routine, several lines of source code may be missing or variables that are used may not have declarations shown. Even though these listings are often a small subset of the total lines of code for a routine, they are still designed to show continuity on a routine basis. If you want to see an entire routine instead of the excerpt, refer to Appendix A.

Finally, the first time a PM or OS/2 function is mentioned in this book it is *italicized* to help bring it to your attention. As functions are introduced, a brief explanation about what the function does and how it is used by the slide puzzle is given. But remember, this book is not a replacement for the technical reference material that comes with the OS/2 Toolkit. For a complete explanation of all the parameters for a function and a total list of OS/2 and Presentation Manager functions, refer to the IBM technical reference material.

2

Working With Messages

A large part of the Presentation Manager programming environment is centered around sending and receiving messages. Chapter 1, Overview, describes the basic structure of a message in the PM environment and gives a high-level description of how a program operates on these messages. However, before Presentation Manager can transmit messages to your application, you must identify your application to the PM environment and set up some structures needed to manage this environment.

To notify Presentation Manager of the existence of your application, use the PM function called *WinInitialize*. This function returns a value called an anchor block handle that you store in a data type called HAB. This handle is assigned to your application thread so Presentation Manager can identify it during communications with it. This handle is needed to request many of the PM functions your application will need.

Once your application has obtained an anchor block handle, it can create a message queue. This queue is used by Presentation Manager as a place to save messages that are sent to your application. To create this message queue, use the PM function called *WinCreateMsgQueue*. Your application must provide a valid anchor block handle as one of the function's parameters and, in return, this function will provide your application with a value called a message queue handle. Save this handle in a data type called HMQ. This message queue handle is used to gain access to messages that will be sent to your application. Once messages are placed in your message queue, your application can pass them to the appropriate window procedure (WinProc). As we've already seen, several window procedures can exist in the PM environment and most of them will probably be predefined window procedures that are part of Presentation Manager, but the client area window procedure is yours to define and code.

Before creating a window to use your application's window procedure, you must define the class name and default style of the window class that your window procedure will control. (The style of the window class controls the appearance and behavior of the window. The different class styles available all start with the prefix CS_ and can be found in the PM technical reference material.) To do this use the PM function called *WinRegisterClass*. This function binds your window procedure address with the class name and lets your application define extra space to be reserved for each window of this class. This extra space can be useful to save information that you'd like to keep for each window of this class created. The WinRegisterClass function only returns an indicator of the success or failure of the function.

Once you have registered your window procedure, you can create a window that will use it. A common way to create an application window is by using the PM function called *WinCreateStdWindow*. There are several parameters passed to this function that control the features and style of the application window. For instance, one of the parameters is a pointer to a word (32-bits) of frame flags that informs Presentation Manager about many of the features you want the application window to possess. Examples of these features are a title bar, scroll bars, a system menu, a size frame, min/max buttons, and so on. Two more parameters for the WinCreateStdWindow function indicate the style of the frame window and the style of the client window. The different styles for these parameters are indicated by predefined keywords that start with the prefix WS_ or FS_ . These keywords can be OR'ed together to indicate, for example, whether the window is to be made visible or not, whether the window should start maximized or not, whether image bits under the window should be saved or not, and so on. These style keywords and their meanings can be found in a PM technical reference manual.

There are three window handles associated with the WinCreateStdWindow function that are fundamental in establishing the window's relationship with other windows. The first window handle is the parent handle that is creating the new application window. If the application window is to be a child of the desktop, this handle is predefined as *HWND_DESKTOP*. The second window handle is created by the WinCreateStdWindow function and is the window handle of your client window. This client window handle is placed at an address that you specify as a parameter to the WinCreateStdWindow function. The last window handle is for the frame window. This window handle is the value that is returned by the WinCreateStdWindow function. You may recall from Chapter 1, Overview, that the frame window is the parent of your client window.

As you may have concluded, the WinCreateStdWindow function actually creates multiple windows for your application. These windows includes the client area window plus standard control windows such as a frame window, a title bar window, min/max control window, and so on. Another PM function called *WinCreateWindow* can be used to create a single window, however, this function is not used by the slide puzzle application.

After you have created an application window, your application's message queue can now start receiving messages. Your application is responsible for taking the messages from this queue and then passing them to the appropriate window procedure. This can be done with two PM functions. The first PM function is called *WinGetMsg*. This function has parameters that will allow it to wait and filter messages in different ways, but the basic way it is used is to wait for a message and return it to your application. After a message is retrieved, a PM function called *WinDispatchMsg* is used to send it to the appropriate window procedure. Generally, a PM application loops receiving messages and dispatches them to the appropriate window procedure until it receives a quit message. Once it receives this quit message, the application releases all the resources that it has acquired and ends.

Figure 2-1 illustrates the basic structure of a PM application's main procedure and shows how the components relate to each other. Listing 2-1 shows a subset of the C source statements that are found in the slide puzzle main procedure. As you can see in Listing 2-1, the window procedure is defined as an external procedure and messages are dispatched to it from the slide puzzle main procedure.

The window procedure is responsible for processing messages that it receives. This is typically done by using a switch statement to process only the messages of interest to the window procedure. If the window procedure receives a message that is of no interest to the application, it can let a default PM routine process it instead. Using the default PM routine is fairly common for most window procedures. For instance, every time the slide puzzle frame is resized, a WM_SIZE message is dispatched to its window procedure; however, because of the way this application is designed, this message is of no use to the window procedure and is

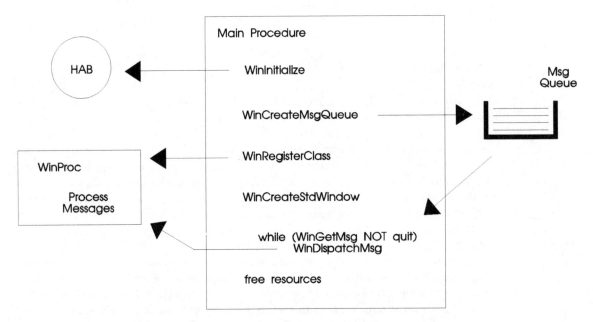

Figure 2-1. Standard PM application main procedure structure.

```
/***************************/
/* Other Global Variables. */
/***************************/
HAB hab;
HWND hwndFrame, hwndClient, hwndMenu;

/*********************************************/
/* Window Procedure Entry Point Definitions. */
/*********************************************/
FNWP ClientWndProc;

/********************/
/* Main Procedure. */
/********************/
int main(int argc, char *argv[])
  {
  ULONG ulFrameFlags=FCF_TASKLIST | FCF_SIZEBORDER |
    FCF_TITLEBAR | FCF_MINMAX |
    FCF_SYSMENU | FCF_MENU | FCF_ICON | FCF_ACCELTABLE;
  HMQ hmq;
  QMSG qmsg;
  hab=WinInitialize(0);
  hmq=WinCreateMsgQueue(hab, 0);
  WinRegisterClass(hab, (PSZ)szClientClass, ClientWndProc,
    CS_SIZEREDRAW, 0);
  hwndFrame=WinCreateStdWindow(HWND_DESKTOP, WS_VISIBLE,
    &ulFrameFlags, (PSZ)szClientClass, 0, 0L, 0,
    ID_SLIDEFRAME, &hwndClient);

  /*************************************/
  /* Get PM messages and dispatch them. */
  /*************************************/
  while(WinGetMsg(hab, &qmsg, 0, 0, 0)){
    WinDispatchMsg(hab, &qmsg);
    }

  /***************************/
  /* Free resources obtained. */
  /***************************/
  WinDestroyWindow(hwndFrame);
  WinDestroyMsgQueue(hmq);
  WinTerminate(hab);
  return 0;
  }
```

Listing 2-1. Main procedure structure.

passed on to a default PM routine for processing. The slide puzzle application allows many of the messages it receives to be processed this way. This is accomplished with a PM function called *WinDefWindowProc*.

Not only can Presentation Manager transmit its predefined messages to your application window, but your application or other applications can also transmit messages to it. These messages can be predefined PM messages or messages of your own design. Your own messages can be whatever you like as long as they have the same structure as a regular PM message and have message IDs above

4096. (The OS/2 Toolkit provides a definition for the value 4096 called WM_USER that you can use to create your own messages.) To transmit a message to a window, a routine only needs to know the handle of the receiving window. The slide puzzle application generates two of its own messages called BUG and ANI-MATE that are detailed in Chapter 8, Working with Time, and Chapter 6, Animation.

Messages can be transmitted with either of two PM functions. The first PM function is called *WinSendMsg*. The parameters to this function are the fields of the PM message. This function acts like a call/return interface to the window procedure that actually processes the message, hence, control is not returned to your application until the message is processed. The second PM function is called *WinPostMsg*. Like the WinSendMsg function, the parameters to this function are the fields of the PM message. The difference between these two functions is that the WinPostMsg function gives control back to the caller immediately after the message is placed on a message queue and does not wait for the message to be processed.

Vertical and horizontal scroll bars present an excellent example of how and why PM applications transmit messages. Though the slide puzzle application does not use scroll bars, they're worth discussing. The scroll bars in this example are owned by a frame window that borders the outside edge of a client window. Because the scroll bar windows are not owned by the client window, their handles must be queried before messages can be sent to them. This is done by using the PM function called *WinWindowFromID*. To use this function, your application must provide the handle of the parent window for the scroll bars and the ID of the scroll bar window being requested. When you create a standard window, the handle of the frame window is returned to your application, and the scroll bar windows are assigned predefined IDs. These IDs are defined as FID_HORZSCROLL and FID_VERTSCROLL. Following are example C statements that return vertical and horizontal scroll bar window handles:

```
hwndVSB=WinWindowFromID(hwndFrame,FID_VERTSCROLL);
hwndHSB=WinWindowFromID(hwndFrame,FID_HORZSCROLL);
```

After obtaining the scroll bar window handles, you can send them messages to set their ranges, set the positions of their sliders, or set the sizes of their sliders. You can also query the ranges of the scroll bars or query the positions of the sliders. Following is an example of sending a message to a vertical scroll bar window:

```
WinSendMsg(WinWindowFromID(hwndFrame,FID_VERTSCROLL),SBM_SETPOS,
  MPFROMSHORT(sVPos),0L);
```

This example assumes that the **hwndFrame** variable contains the application frame window handle and that the **sVPos** variable contains a number within the range of the scroll bar. SBM_SETPOS is the predefined message ID that informs the scroll bar window that this message is to set the slider. The parameters for the WinSendMsg function are the values for mp1 and mp2. Because the mp1 and mp2 parameters can represent multiple subfield types, such as two SHORT variables, the Developer's ToolKit for OS/2 2.0 provides macros to help you build them. *MPFROMSHORT* as shown in the previous example is one of these macros and builds a 32-bit value from a SHORT. Another example of such a macro is *MPFROM2SHORT(s1,s2)*. This macro builds a 32-bit value from two SHORT values, s1 and s2. For this macro, s1 is the low-order 16 bits and s2 is the high-order 16 bits for the 32-bit value. All messages that you transmit to scroll bar windows start with the prefix SB_. To get a complete list of scroll bar messages and their definitions, look up SB_ in a PM technical reference index.

Not only can you send messages to scroll bar windows, but your application's window procedure can also receive messages from them. Remember, scroll bars are windows that have their own window procedures; hence, when the scroll bar windows receive mouse actions, they transmit messages to your client area window procedure to notify it of these actions. Notification messages from control windows typically arrive as WM_CONTROL or WM_COMMAND messages. The WM_CONTROL message is used by the control window procedure to send a notification. If, however, the control window procedure wants to post a notification to your message queue it uses the WM_COMMAND message. The notification code for the message is imbedded in the message parameters.

Unlike many other control windows, scroll bar windows have their own predefined notification messages named WM_HSCROLL and WM_VSCROLL. The WM_HSCROLL message is sent when a horizontal scroll bar event occurs, while the WM_VSCROLL message is sent when a vertical scroll bar event occurs. Because of these scroll bar notification messages, you can appropriately adjust your client area and send messages back to the scroll bar window procedure to make adjustments to the scroll bar control as needed.

Now that you have a feel for how messages flow and how they can be used in the PM environment, look at the window procedure example in Listing 2-2. This listing is only a small subset of the source code found in the slide puzzle application's window procedure, but still shows the window procedure's basic structure.

```
MRESULT EXPENTRY ClientWndProc(HWND hwnd, ULONG msg,
  MPARAM mp1, MPARAM mp2)
  {
  ULONG ulMouse;
  SHORT x, y, i;

  switch(msg){
    /***************************/
    /* Process keyboard items. */
    /***************************/
    case WM_CHAR:
      if((sRandomFlag==1) || (sUndoFlag==1))return 0;
      if(CHARMSG(&msg)->fs & KC_KEYUP)
        return(MRESULT)FALSE;
      if(CHARMSG(&msg)->fs & KC_VIRTUALKEY){
        switch (CHARMSG(&msg)->vkey){
```

```
          case VK_LEFT:      /* Check for left arrow. */
            x=sGridx+1; y=sGridy;
            Slide(hab, hwnd, x, y);
            return(MRESULT)TRUE;
          case VK_RIGHT:     /* Check for right arrow. */
            if(sGridx>0){
              x=sGridx-1; y=sGridy;
              Slide(hab, hwnd, x, y);
              }
            return(MRESULT)TRUE;
          case VK_DOWN:      /* Check for down arrow. */
            y=sGridy+1; x=sGridx;
            Slide(hab, hwnd, x, y);
            return(MRESULT)TRUE;
          case VK_UP:        /* Check for up arrow. */
            if(sGridy>0){
              y=sGridy-1; x=sGridx;
              Slide(hab, hwnd, x, y);
              }
            return(MRESULT)TRUE;
          }
        }
      return(MRESULT)FALSE;

  /*********************************/
  /* Process mouse button 1 down. */
  /*********************************/
  case WM_BUTTON1DOWN:
    if((sRandomFlag==1) || (sUndoFlag==1))return 0;
    x=MOUSEMSG(&msg)->x; /* Convert to grid coordinate. */
    y=MOUSEMSG(&msg)->y;
    x=x/lcxMinMax;
    y=y/lcyMinMax;

    /**************************************/
    /* Check for mouse pointer in bounds. */
    /**************************************/
    if((x<puzzle.sGrid) && (y<puzzle.sGrid)){

      /***************************************************/
      /* Check for in pointer in valid row or column. */
      /***************************************************/
      if((y==sGridy) || (x==sGridx))
        Slide(hab, hwnd, x, y);
      else DosBeep(523, 100);
      }
    return(MRESULT)TRUE;

  /*********************************/
  /* Process mouse move messages. */
  /*********************************/
  case WM_MOUSEMOVE:
```

```
x=MOUSEMSG(&msg)->x;
y=MOUSEMSG(&msg)->y;
x=x/lcxMinMax;
y=y/lcyMinMax;

/************************************************/
/* Set correct pointer icon based on position. */
/************************************************/
if((y==sGridy) || (x==sGridx)){
  if((y<sGridy) && (x==sGridx))
    WinSetPointer(HWND_DESKTOP, hIptr1);
  if((y>sGridy) && (x==sGridx))
    WinSetPointer(HWND_DESKTOP, hIptr3);
  if((x<sGridx) && (y==sGridy))
    WinSetPointer(HWND_DESKTOP, hIptr2);
  if((x>sGridx) && (y==sGridy))
    WinSetPointer(HWND_DESKTOP, hIptr4);
  if((x==sGridx) && (y==sGridy))
    WinSetPointer(HWND_DESKTOP, hIptr5);
  }
else
  WinSetPointer(HWND_DESKTOP, hIptr5);
return(MRESULT)TRUE;
}

/****************************************************/
/* Let default routine process message and return. */
/****************************************************/
return WinDefWindowProc(hwnd, msg, mp1, mp2);
}
```

Listing 2-2. Window procedure structure.

Listing 2-2 only shows three of the commands that are processed by the slide puzzle application. These three commands deal with keyboard input, the pressing of mouse button 1, and mouse movement. To become more familiar with what a message can contain, let's look closer at how the *WM_CHAR* message or keyboard input is processed for the slide puzzle.

The WM_CHAR message is sent to the window procedure whenever the client area window has input focus and keyboard activity occurs. The first thing the WM_CHAR case statement does is start testing information received from the message parameter fields. As you study Listing 2-2 and the entire completed slide puzzle application, you will discover **fs** and **KC_KEYUP** are not defined by the slide puzzle source code. These items are defined in the IBM Developer's Toolkit for OS/2 and assist application writers in parsing messages and testing field information. In fact, as you study more PM code, you'll notice that the OS/2 Toolkit provides many macros and definitions to help you work in this environment. To understand how these definitions relate to keyboard processing, you must know what information is available in the message parameter fields. Figure 2-2 illustrates how information is organized in these two parameters.

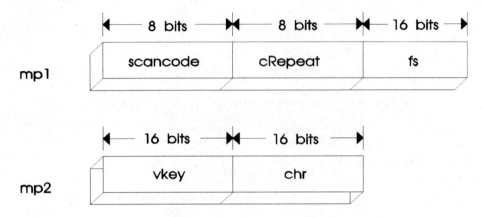

Figure 2-2. WM_CHAR message parameters.

As you can see, a lot of information is passed with every WM_CHAR message. Following is a list of definitions for the information that comes with the WM_CHAR message:

> **scancode** is the 8-bit hardware code that indicates which physical key was pressed or released. Because of the differences in keyboards, it may be wise to avoid using this field if possible.
>
> **cRepeat** is an 8-bit count field that indicates the number of times to repeat the key code.
>
> **fs** is 16 bits of flags that indicate more about the state of the keyboard. Following is a list each flag and its meaning when the described bit is on:
> - **KC_CHAR** is bit 0 and indicates that a valid ASCII character code exists.
> - **KC_VIRTUALKEY** is bit 1 and indicates that a valid virtual key code exists. A virtual key is a key that doesn't have an ASCII codepoint associated with it (such as a function key).
> - **KC_SCANCODE** is bit 2 and indicates that a valid hardware scan code exists.
> - **KC_SHIFT** is bit 3 and indicates the shift key is down.
> - **KC_CTRL** is bit 4 and indicates the ctrl key is down.
> - **KC_ALT** is bit 5 and indicates the alt key is down.
> - **KC_KEYUP** is bit 6 and indicates a key is being released.
> - **KC_PREVDOWN** is bit 7 and indicates the key was previously down.
> - **KC_LONEKEY** is bit 8 and indicates that the only key pressed is being released.
> - **KC_DEADKEY** is bit 9 and indicates the key is a dead key.
> - **KC_COMPOSITE** is bit 10 and indicates the key is composed with a diacritic key sequence.
> - **KC_INVALIDCOMP** is bit 11 and indicates the key is an invalid composite.

- **KC_TOGGLE** is bit 12 and indicates a toggle state.
- **KC_INVALIDCHAR** is bit 13 and indicates the key is invalid.

vkey is a 16-bit code that indicates a virtual key.

chr is a 16-bit code that indicates a character.

For the slide puzzle application, we process only four virtual keys when they are pressed. The way the slide puzzle finds that a key is pressed is by first testing to see if the WM_CHAR message was caused by the release of a key (the KC_KEYUP flag set to TRUE). If the key is being released, then the message is not processes and FALSE is returned. If this message is not caused by a release, the WM_CHAR routine checks for the existence of a valid virtual key. If a valid virtual key exists, the routine tests to see if the message contains one of the arrow keys that, if possible, will cause a puzzle piece to slide in the direction of the arrow. The current location of the blank puzzle piece is tracked with the global variables named **sGridx** and **sGridy**; thus to cause a move, these global variables, along with some simple addition or subtraction, are used to set parameters for the slide function. The slide function (not shown in this listing) provides simple parameter checking, puzzle piece movement, and updates the global variables. The slide function will be discussed in detail in Chapter 6, Animation. If the WM_CHAR message does not contain information about one of the arrow keys, the routine ignores the message and returns a FALSE indicator.

Other applications, such as text editors, would provide much more processing of WM_CHAR messages and draw text in the client area. Even though the slide puzzle application does not do this, you'll see in Chapter 3, Drawing in the Client Area, how to deal with fonts and draw characters in the client area.

Listing 2-2 also shows how the slide puzzle application processes the *WM_BUTTON1DOWN* or mouse button 1 down message. This message is sent to the window procedure whenever the mouse pointer is over our application's client area and mouse button 1 is pressed. There are a series of other mouse messages, such as WM_BUTTON1UP, WM_BUTTON1DBCLK, WM_BUTTON2DOWN, that the slide puzzle could receive but would ignore by passing them on to Presentation Manager for processing.

The items extracted with the PM macro, MOUSEMSG, are the x and y coordinates of the mouse pointer when the button was pressed. Both these coordinates come from the mp1 parameter field. Bits 0-15 of mp1 are the x coordinate and bits 16-31 of mp1 are the y coordinate. These coordinates are relative to the bottom left corner of the application window and are in units called pels. (You will learn what pels are shortly!) The slide puzzle application converts these coordinates to a grid location by dividing them by the number of pels per puzzle piece (which also has an x and y dimension). These dimensions are calculated when the puzzle is first started and saved in the global variables named **lcxMinMax** and **lcyMinMax**. (Chapter 3, Drawing in the Client Area, contains more information about coordinate systems and drawing units.) Once a grid location is determined, a check is made to insure the mouse pointer is in bounds. If it is, the routine then checks for a valid move. For our application, a valid move is when either the x or y grid coordinate that was selected is the same as that of the current blank piece; thus, only horizontal and vertical moves are allowed. When a valid move occurs, it is executed by the slide function. If the move is detected as invalid, a beep is produced and no pieces are moved.

The last message shown in Listing 2-2 is the *WM_MOUSEMOVE* or mouse move message. This message is sent to the window procedure whenever the mouse pointer moves over the application's client area. This message contains the same information as the WM_BUTTON1DOWN message. Also, like the routine that processes the WM_BUTTON1DOWN message, the first thing this routine does is resolve the grid location of the mouse pointer. This routine then chooses a mouse pointer based on the relative position of this grid location in relationship to the blank piece. By doing this, the mouse pointer changes to indicate the direction of a valid move. If a valid move cannot be made, an X pointer is displayed. In Chapter 4, Working with Resources, we will show you how to build and define a pointer for a PM application.

While you are processing a PM message, no other PM messages appear to be moving in the system. Most PM applications display the system wait pointer when they take a long time to process a message. (In previous releases of OS/2 the system wait pointer was an hour-glass icon, but in OS/2 2.0 it's a clock icon.) A better solution to this problem is to keep your message processing routine as short as possible and defer long activities to another thread of execution. Because you are using OS/2, this isn't that difficult to do. Many applications that do complex drawing use this multithreaded technique so processing of PM messages continues while they are drawing. Since the slide puzzle application is multithreaded, this concept is described in Chapter 8, Working with Time.

3

Drawing in the Client Area

Graphic devices produce images in one of two ways. The first way, called bit-mapped or raster graphics has a large array of dots that can be turned on and off as required. These dots are called picture elements but are commonly referred to as pixels or pels. Pels are very close together and, depending on the device, can be associated with different shades or colors. When the pels in this array are turned to the correct on or off state, they form images. Most PC monitors and printers are raster devices. The second way, called vector graphics, produces images by using draw commands; therefore, pictures or diagrams are produced by instructing the device to draw lines or curves within a specified drawing space. For example, a draw command might specify to draw a line between two given points. For many vector devices, the line may also be associated with attributes such as style and color. Pen plotters and oscilloscopes are examples of vector devices.

As you work with the Presentation Manager API, you will notice that it has some functions that perform raster operations and others that perform vector operations. Most likely, the final output device that you use with a PC is a raster device. This does <u>not</u> mean, however, that you can't use the vector functions! Presentation Manager contains logic that can take vector functions and produce raster output from them. In fact, as you work in the PM environment, you will become aware that PM is designed to help you generate device-independent code. Because of this, it is relatively easy to write applications that support a large number of output device types.

DEVICE INDEPENDENCE

By playing with the slide puzzle application on different PC displays, you will notice that it looks pretty much the same on a regular Video Graphics Array (VGA) display as it does on a Super VGA display, even though the device resolutions of these two devices are different. The Super VGA produces a sharper image and may have more colors, but the size of the objects drawn by the slide puzzle are about the same for both device types.

As you perform graphic functions with the Presentation Manager API, these functions are directed toward an object called a presentation space. There are three kinds of presentation spaces available in Presentation Manager. They are called a cached Micro-PS, a Micro-PS, and a Normal-PS. The difference between these presentation space types is the set of graphic functions they support and how quickly you can gain access to them. The Normal-PS consumes the most memory resource but has the most capability. In general, the extra capability provided by the Normal-PS is retained graphics. Retained graphics is the ability of the presentation space to retain drawing commands so a picture can be regenerated automatically. The Micro-PS does not support retained graphics but is smaller in size. The Micro-PS supports all the normal PM drawing commands and can be kept for large periods of time. The slide puzzle application uses the Micro-PS presentation space type. The cached Micro-PS is the same as the Micro-PS, but a pool of these presentation spaces is kept by Presentation Manager for quick access. You should only use a cached Micro-PS for the duration of a single message. Before we look at how to draw with the presentation space, let's see how it relates to other components in the OS/2 environment.

Figure 3-1 shows a conceptual view of the OS/2 PM environment. Your application has access to the regular OS/2 API as well as the Presentation Manager API. Even though you don't directly interface with the presentation space, you operate on it with the PM API and use it like a sheet of paper. A presentation space must have an object called a *device context* associated with it. The device context provides a layer of isolation between the presentation space and the physical device for which its output is targeted. The device context maintains device-dependent information and stores information about the current drawing state of the presentation space. Examples of drawing state information are current color, line style, and shear. The physical device, where output is delivered, is ultimately manipulated by the OS/2 kernel or a *device driver*. (A device driver is a software component that developers can provide to interface with specific hardware adapters.) The structure of this environment not only leads to device independence, but also to an environment that is easy to expand and maintain.

Again, think about the presentation space as a piece of paper on which you perform electronic drawing. When you create a presentation space, you define an object called the *presentation page* which has an X and Y dimension. This piece of paper, or presentation page, maps to the client area of your window, not to the physical device. The presentation page also has a coordinate system that you use to move about the drawing area. Figure 3-2 shows a representation of the presentation page and its coordinate system. Notice that the bottom left of the presen-

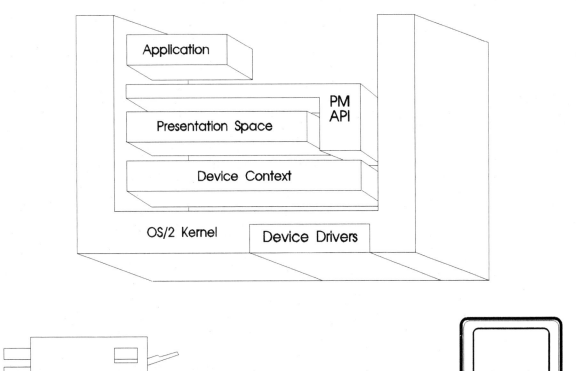

Figure 3-1. Conceptual view of PM environment.

tation page is the origin of the coordinate system. The units for the coordinate system depend on how you create the presentation space. You can create the presentation page to use any of the following metric units:

0.1 mm	(PU_LOMETRIC)
0.01 mm	(PU_HIMETRIC)
0.01 in.	(PU_LOENGLISH)
0.001 in.	(PU_HIENGLISH)
1/440 in.	(PU_TWIPS)

By creating the presentation page in metric units, all your drawing operations are done in the chosen metric units and all aspect ratios are managed. Hence, a one inch line is a one inch line on all device types associated with the presentation space.

You can also create the presentation page in device units which are in pels (PU_PELS) and are device-dependent. If your application manipulates bit-maps, you may choose the PU_PELS units because bit-maps are device-dependent by definition. (The slide puzzle application uses bit-maps extensively.) Even if you

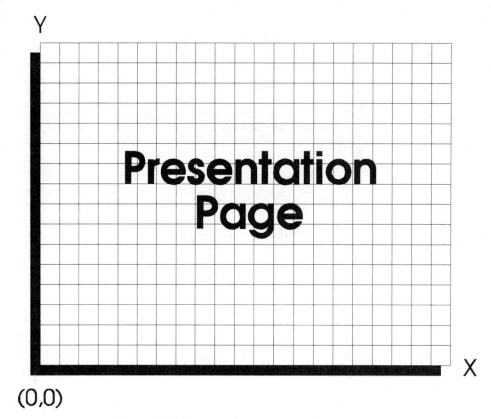

Figure 3-2. Presentation page coordinate system.

choose pels for your presentation page units, many functions are still available to resolve device-dependent information.

To obtain device characteristics, PM provides a function called *DevQueryCaps*. This function returns information about a device you can use to make your application device independent. For instance, this function provides the number of horizontal and vertical pels supported by the device. It also provides the horizontal and vertical resolution of the device in pels per meter. With this type of information, it's easy to convert to other measurement systems and account for things such as aspect ratio. This function also provides information about fonts that is discussed later in this chapter.

Another PM function that returns interesting device-related information is the *WinQuerySysValue* function. This function, however, is specific to the desktop, and can retrieve the width and height of the screen in pels as well. This function also gives you information such as the dimensions of the window borders, scroll bars, title bar, menu item height, maximized client area, and so on. You can use this information to appropriately adjust the contents of your client area.

Finally, part of Presentation Manager called the Graphics Programming Interface (GPI), has the ability to perform advanced drawing functions. Many of these functions can involve transformations of objects. Transformations are things such as rotations, shearing, scaling, translations, and inversions. Furthermore, many of these operations can apply to graphic segments that can be assembled to produce more complex pictures. (A graphic segment represents an object.)

A typical problem caused by producing complex pictures from graphic segments is how to resolve size, location, and distortion of the segments due to device type or presentation space limitations. The solution to this problem involves creating a more abstract presentation space in which graphic segments can be defined. This presentation space is called the *world-coordinate presentation space*. After the graphic segments are defined, they can be used to build composites or pictures in another presentation space where size and location are resolved. This presentation space is called the *model presentation space* and can contain a complete picture. There is one more presentation space called the *presentation-page space* in which multiple model presentation spaces or parts of a single model presentation space can be assembled and scaled. The presentation-page space resolves device-dependent information and is the last step before mapping back to a device presentation space. Hence, a mapping back to device units is performed and considerations for aspect ratio are taken into account. This series of presentation spaces is called the *viewing pipeline.*

All the presentation spaces, except the device space, have a very large coordinate range. This large coordinate range enables each graphics object to be defined with the required precision. Depending on how you define the presentation-page space, the coordinate range can be either -32,768 through 32,767 or -134,217,728 through 134,217,727. For some of the GPI functions, you will need to provide coordinate values based on coordinates from a different presentation space. To convert coordinates from space to space, Presentation Manager provides a function called *GpiConvert.*

As you examine the slide puzzle application, you will notice that it does not produce complex drawings. In fact, for the slide puzzle application, a knowledge of the Micro-PS presentation space is all that is required. The slide puzzle does, however, use some very basic transformations that demonstrate some of the more advanced functions of the GPI. If you become interested in an in-depth knowledge of the OS/2 GPI, you may find the book *OS/2 Presentation Manager GPI* by Graham Winn very useful. This book is also published by Van Nostrand Reinhold and is an excellent reference. Now that we've discussed some PM functions available to produce a device-independent application, let's look at some of the startup code used by the slide puzzle application to resolve device-dependent information. Listing 3-1 shows the main procedure for the slide puzzle application. As you can see, the slide puzzle begins resolving device-dependent information as soon as it creates a standard window. It needs this device information at this time so the slide puzzle can set the frame window's position and size. Applications can let Presentation Manager choose the position and size of the frame window by using a frame flag called FCF_SHELLPOSITION in its frame flags variable. The slide puzzle application, however, needs a certain size frame window. Therefore, the FCF_SHELLPOSITION flag is not used.

To get the needed device-dependent information, the slide puzzle application does a query for the desktop's presentation space handle. This is easy to obtain with a PM function called *WinGetPS* because the handle associated with the desktop window is predefined. Once the desktop's presentation space handle has been obtained, the GpiQueryDevice function can be used to retreive the device context handle. With access to the device context, the DevQueryCaps function queries the device capabilities. This function is used only to retrieve and store the number of pels per meter the screen has even though it can provide a lot of other device information. Once the number of pels per meter in both the vertical and horizontal directions is found, these values are used to calculate the number of pels per inch. This information is saved in the global variables **lcxPelsPerInch** and **lcyPelsPerInch**. The pels per inch information is used later in the startup animation sequence to help size bit-map images. This information is also used, however, to size and locate the application window frame, which is accomplished with the PM function called *WinSetWindowPos*. As you can be see, the window is positioned one half inch up and one half inch to the right and is six inches high and seven inches wide.

Note that if you do <u>not</u> set your own window size or use the FCF_SHELLPOSITION frame flag, Presentation Manager will create your frame window with size zero! Therefore, the window will exist but won't be seen because it has no size.

```
/********************/
/* Main Procedure. */
/********************/
int main(int argc, char *argv[])
   {
   HDC hdcTemp;
   HPS hpsTemp;
   ULONG ulFrameFlags=FCF_TASKLIST | FCF_SIZEBORDER |
      FCF_TITLEBAR | FCF_MINMAX |
      FCF_SYSMENU | FCF_MENU | FCF_ICON | FCF_ACCELTABLE;
   HMQ hmq;
   QMSG qmsg;
   hab=WinInitialize(0);
   hmq=WinCreateMsgQueue(hab, 0);
   WinRegisterClass(hab, (PSZ)szClientClass, ClientWndProc,
      CS_SIZEREDRAW, 0);
   hwndFrame=WinCreateStdWindow(HWND_DESKTOP, WS_VISIBLE,
      &ulFrameFlags, (PSZ)szClientClass, 0, 0L, 0,
      ID_SLIDEFRAME, &hwndClient);

   /*******************************************************/
   /* Resolve the number of pels per inch in both the */
   /* horizontal and vertical directions.          */
   /*******************************************************/
   hpsTemp=WinGetPS(HWND_DESKTOP);
   hdcTemp=GpiQueryDevice(hpsTemp);
   if((hdcTemp!=0L) && (hdcTemp!=HDC_ERROR)){
      DevQueryCaps(hdcTemp, CAPS_VERTICAL_RESOLUTION, 1L,
         &lcyPelsPerMeter);
      DevQueryCaps(hdcTemp, CAPS_HORIZONTAL_RESOLUTION, 1L,
```

```
      &lcxPelsPerMeter);
    lcxPelsPerInch=(lcxPelsPerMeter*254)/10000;
    lcyPelsPerInch=(lcyPelsPerMeter*254)/10000;
    }

/*********************************************/
/* Set window position to be one half inch to right */
/* and one half inch up.  Make the window size       */
/* 7 inches by 6 inches.  Set input focus.           */
/*********************************************/
WinSetWindowPos(hwndFrame, 0L, (SHORT)lcxPelsPerInch/2,
  (SHORT)lcyPelsPerInch/2, (SHORT)lcxPelsPerInch*7,
  (SHORT)lcyPelsPerInch*6, SWP_SIZE | SWP_MOVE);
WinReleasePS(hpsTemp);
WinSetFocus(HWND_DESKTOP, hwndFrame);

/***************************************/
/* Get PM messages and dispatch them. */
/***************************************/
while(WinGetMsg(hab, &qmsg, 0, 0, 0)){
  WinDispatchMsg(hab, &qmsg);
  }

/***************************/
/* Free resources obtained. */
/***************************/
WinDestroyWindow(hwndFrame);
WinDestroyMsgQueue(hmq);
WinTerminate(hab);
return 0;
}
```

Listing 3-1. Setting the window size and location.

Listing 3-2 shows the WM_CREATE message for the slide puzzle application WinProc. This message is the very first message issued to the WinProc after the standard window is created. Because of this, the slide puzzle application uses this opportunity to capture the desktop image. Therefore, the first step performed within the case statement is to open a window device contect and a memory device context and associate them with new presentation spaces. These presentation spaces are Micro-PS presentation spaces and are kept for the life of the application. Next, the desktop dimensions are queried with the WinQuerySysValue function and saved in global variables called **sxPels** and **syPels**. These dimensions are used later by other routines to resolve device-specific information, but are also used by this routine to help resolve the bit-map size of the desktop. Hence, these dimensions are placed in a bit-map header structure for bit-map creation. Other information needed for this bit-map header, such as number of bit-map planes and bits per pel, is obtained with the *GpiQueryDeviceBitmapFormats* function. Once the bit-map header is built, the bit-map is created with the *GpiCreateBitMap* function. In our example, the GpiCreateBitMap function is used so as to leave the bit-map uninitialized.

After the bit-map is created, it is made the current bit-map for our memory presentation space with the *GpiSetBitmap* function. Finally, bits are copied from the desktop presentation page to the memory presentation page with a raster function called *GpiBitBlt*. The GpiBitBlt function operates on the pels in a rectangular space defined by an array of points that gives the lower-left and upper-right coordinates of the involved rectangles. The GpiBitBlt function actually performs many operations besides bit copying and is used frequently by the slide puzzle application. This function will be discussed in much greater detail in Chapter 6, Animation.

```
MRESULT EXPENTRY ClientWndProc(HWND hwnd, ULONG msg,
  MPARAM mp1, MPARAM mp2)
  {
  BITMAPINFOHEADER2 bmp;
  HBITMAP hbmt;
  HDC hdcbm;
  HPS hpsd;
  POINTL aptl[4];
  SIZEL sizl;

  switch(msg){
    /*********************************/
    /* Process window create message. */
    /*********************************/
    case WM_CREATE:
      hdc=WinOpenWindowDC(hwnd);  /* Create window device context. */
      sizl.cx=0;                 /* Create Micro-PS.  Keep as global. */
      sizl.cy=0;
      hps=GpiCreatePS(hab, hdc, &sizl, PU_PELS | GPIT_MICRO |
        GPIA_ASSOC | GPIF_DEFAULT);

      /****************************************************************/
      /* Create memory device context for our screen bit-map. */
      /****************************************************************/
      hdcMemory=DevOpenDC(hab, OD_MEMORY, (PSZ)"*", 0L, 0L, 0L);
      sizl.cx=0;  /* Create presentation space for screen bit-map. */
      sizl.cy=0;
      hpsMemory=GpiCreatePS(hab, hdcMemory, &sizl,
        PU_PELS | GPIF_DEFAULT | GPIT_MICRO | GPIA_ASSOC);

      /*******************************************************/
      /* Get the screen dimension in pels and save it. */
      /*******************************************************/
      sxPels=WinQuerySysValue(HWND_DESKTOP, SV_CXSCREEN);
      syPels=WinQuerySysValue(HWND_DESKTOP, SV_CYSCREEN);

      /*********************************************/
      /* Set up bit-map header for correct size. */
      /*********************************************/
      GpiQueryDeviceBitmapFormats(hpsMemory, 2L, alBmpFormats);
      memset(&bmp, 0, sizeof(bmp));
      bmp.cbFix=sizeof bmp;
```

```
bmp.cx=sxPels;
bmp.cPlanes=(USHORT)alBmpFormats[0];
bmp.cBitCount=(USHORT)alBmpFormats[1];
bmp.cy=syPels;
hbmSrc=GpiCreateBitmap(hpsMemory, &bmp, 0L, NULL, NULL);
GpiSetBitmap(hpsMemory, hbmSrc);
aptl[0].x=0; aptl[0].y=0;
aptl[1].x=bmp.cx; aptl[1].y=bmp.cy;
aptl[2].x=0; aptl[2].y=0;

/**************************************************/
/* Copy the desktop image to our memory device. */
/**************************************************/
hpsd=WinGetScreenPS(HWND_DESKTOP);
GpiBitBlt(hpsMemory, hpsd, 3L, aptl, ROP_SRCCOPY, BBO_AND);

/**************************************************/
/* Calculate a piece size in pels and save it. */
/**************************************************/
lcxMinMax=bmp.cx/puzzle.sGrid;
lcyMinMax=bmp.cy/puzzle.sGrid;

/********************************************/
/* Blank out bottom right piece of puzzle. */
/********************************************/
aptl[0].x=(puzzle.sGrid-1)*lcxMinMax; aptl[0].y=0;
aptl[1].x=aptl[0].x+lcxMinMax; aptl[1].y=lcyMinMax;
GpiBitBlt(hpsMemory, hpsMemory, 2L, aptl, ROP_ZERO, BBO_AND);

/****************************************************/
/* Set blank piece location and release resource. */
/****************************************************/
sGridy=0; sGridx=puzzle.sGrid-1;
WinReleasePS(hpsd);
return(MRESULT)FALSE;
  }

/****************************************************/
/* Let default routine process message and return. */
/****************************************************/
return WinDefWindowProc(hwnd, msg, mp1, mp2);
}
```

Listing 3-2. WM_CREATE message routine.

The bit-map just created and initialized is used as the master image for the slide puzzle. The last thing done with the master image is create the blank puzzle piece. To do this, the number of puzzle pieces must be known. This number is in a global variable called **puzzle.sGrid** which contains the number of puzzle pieces in both the vertical and horizontal directions. With this information, the number of pels per piece is calculated and saved in global variables called **lcxMinMax** and **lcyMinMax**. Finally, the GpiBitBlt function is used again, but in a different way, to turn off all the pels in the piece located in the lower left of the puzzle. The blank puzzle piece coordinates are then saved in the global variables **sGridy** and **sGridx**.

Listing 3-3 shows the slide puzzle program's WM_PAINT message routine. Even though this routine does not resolve any device-dependent information, it does operate on portions of the client area. The WM_PAINT message is sent whenever portions of the client area need to be refreshed due to actions such as resizing or moving windows over the top of our application window. The WM_PAINT message is also sent shortly after window creation to initialize the application client area. For the slide puzzle application, the first WM_PAINT message received is used to transmit our own message to start an animation sequence. To cause our message to be sent only once, the global variable called **FirstTime** is set to TRUE before window creation. Then, right after the first WM_PAINT message starts processing, the FirstTime variable is set to FALSE. To start the animation sequence, the slide puzzle uses the WinSendMsg function to send our own message. This message is defined as ANIMATE. Because the ANIMATE message is sent with the WinSendMsg function, the animation sequence is completed before returning to the caller (WM_PAINT).

```
MRESULT EXPENTRY ClientWndProc(HWND hwnd, ULONG msg,
  MPARAM mp1, MPARAM mp2)
  {
  BOOL fRet=FALSE;
  POINTL aptl[4];
  LONG  lRow, lCol, lTotal, lLcid;
  SIZEL sizl;
  RECTL rclInvalid;

  switch(msg){
    /*************************/
    /* Process paint message. */
    /*************************/
    case WM_PAINT:
      if(FirstTime){   /* This only gets processed once. */
        FirstTime=FALSE;
        WinSendMsg(hwnd, ANIMATE, NULL, NULL);
        }
      else {

        /*****************************************************/
        /* Paint the invalid region with the contents of */
        /* the master bit-map in memory.                  */
        /*****************************************************/
        WinBeginPaint(hwnd, hps, &rclInvalid);
        GpiSetBitmap(hpsMemory, hbmSrc);
        aptl[0].x=rclInvalid.xLeft;   /* Target lower left. */
        aptl[0].y=rclInvalid.yBottom;
        aptl[1].x=rclInvalid.xRight;  /* Target upper right. */
        aptl[1].y=rclInvalid.yTop;
        aptl[2].x=rclInvalid.xLeft;   /* Source lower left. */
        aptl[2].y=rclInvalid.yBottom;
        aptl[3].x=rclInvalid.xRight;  /* Source upper right. */
```

```
        aptl[3].y=rclInvalid.yTop;
        GpiBitBlt(hps, hpsMemory, 4L, aptl, ROP_SRCCOPY, BBO_AND);
        WinEndPaint(hps);
        }
    return(MRESULT)TRUE;
  }


/****************************************************/
/* Let default routine process message and return. */
/***************************************************/
return WinDefWindowProc(hwnd, msg, mp1, mp2);
  }
```

Listing 3-3. WM_PAINT message routine.

Every other time the WM_PAINT message is processed, a PM function called *WinBeginPaint* is used to receive the handle of our client area presentation space. This may seem odd because the presentation space handle is already saved in a global variable and is ready to use. In this case, however, the WinBeginPaint function is <u>not</u> used to get the presentation space handle, but to reset an area called the update region for our client area. If this update region is not reset, the slide puzzle window procedure will keep getting WM_PAINT messages forever. After all, the update region is the reason the WM_PAINT message is sent and the WinBeginPaint function is the means by which the update region is reset to NULL. By using our already defined presentation space handle as an input parameter, we will just get our own handle back. Note, however, that the WinBeginPaint function also provides a convenient way to allocate a cached Micro-PS!

The update region is actually a set of rectangles that represent the areas in the presentation page that have been invalidated. From this set of rectangles, the smallest possible rectangle that can include the set of rectangles is generated and passed as a parameter to the WM_PAINT message processing routine. Therefore, when the WM_PAINT message is processed, the slide puzzle application uses the rectangle passed with the message to update the invalid area in the client area from the master puzzle bit-map image.

WORKING WITH TEXT

Presentation Manager supports both raster fonts and outline fonts. As the name implies, raster fonts are produced by setting pels to a predefined pattern to form different characters. This method of font generation is fast, but is limited in what you can do to manipulate the font. For instance, transformations to provide scaling and rotations are not provided with raster fonts. Outline fonts, on the other hand, are produced with vector functions and can be scaled, rotated, sheared, inverted, and so on. However, because these fonts are drawn and can have transformations applied to them, they may require considerable processing power to be produced. In some situations, the processing required to produce the outline font is noticeable in draw performance.

The slide puzzle doesn't generate much text; in fact, the puzzle draws less than 15 words! However, because of the way these few words are drawn, a lot of information about how to deal with fonts and text is given. But before we start drawing text, more information about fonts and text functions is appropriate.

Fonts are identified by facename and style. Some very common font facenames are Times New Roman™, Courier™, and Helvetica™. Examples of styles that might apply to these font facenames are **bold** and *italic*.The size of these fonts is indicated with a unit of measure called a point. A point is a measure of height for a font and is 1/72 of an inch. Typical font sizes for standard text are 10-point or 12-point. Presentation Manager has a function called *GpiQueryFonts* that lets you query the fonts known by Presentation Manager in a variety of ways. For instance, you can locate all the fonts known by Presentation Manager or you can locate a font by its facename.

Fonts also have attributes that determine their width. Some fonts produce characters that are all the same width. This type of font is called a monospaced or fixed font. Courier is an example of a monospaced font. For many fonts, however, the width of the different characters varies. These fonts are called proportional fonts. Helvetica is an example of a proportional font. Horizontal spacing of text is a bit more challenging when using proportional fonts; but, as you'll soon see, Presentation Manager provides functions and structures to help determine the size of character strings and position them.

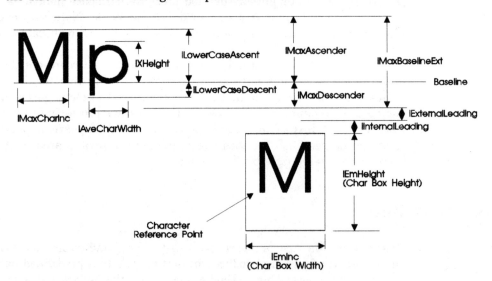

Figure 3-3. Font metrics.

The more you examine all the metrics associated with a font, the more you will become aware of the amount of variable information used to generate a character. Figure 3-3 shows some of the basic font metrics provided by the PM function called *GpiQueryFontMetrics*. But note that there is still much more information about a font that this function provides!

Some fonts also have the ability to be *kerned*. Kerning has to do with the horizontal placement of adjacent characters. Kerning creates the effect of overlapping or sharing of space between certain pairs of characters; but in the process of sharing this space, the characters never touch! For instance, when the characters "AV" are next to each other, the top left of the character "V" is located over the bottom right of the character "A". This is illustrated in greater detail by Figure 3-4. Kerning is useful when applied to text strings and is demonstrated by our slide puzzle application.

Not all fonts support kerning. This is, however, easy to detect because the GpiQueryFontMetrics function returns an indicator that show whether or not a font supports kerning. Note that kerning is applied to pairs of characters and varies depending on which two characters are next to each other; hence, each pair of characters in a string must be dynamically adjusted for kerning. These pairs are called kerning pairs. If you are using a font that can be kerned, Presentation Manager provides a structure that indicates the amount of horizontal adjustment you need to apply.

With this brief background on fonts, it's time to look at some of the functions offered by Presentation Manager that let you move within the presentation page and manipulate text. As mentioned earlier, one of the very first functions to use if you want to perform font selection is GpiQueryFonts. This PM function can be used to find information about available fonts. With this information, you can force the selection of the desired font.

Listing 3-4 shows an example of how to use the GpiQueryFonts function. This function, FindFont, is used by the slide puzzle application to locate an outline font. This function only looks for outline fonts; if you are interested in raster fonts, update this function to test the font metrics to find the desired point size. Because outline fonts can be scaled, our routine doesn't test size information.

Figure 3-4. Kerned Fonts.

```
/****************************/
/* Find outline font by name. */
/****************************/
BOOL FAR FindFont(HPS hps, LONG *lLcid, CHAR *szFontName)
  {
  PFONTMETRICS afmMetrics=NULL;
  LONG lNumFonts, lReqFonts, i, lRemFonts=GPI_ALTERROR;
  BOOL fRet=FALSE;
  HDC hdc=0L;
  USHORT usCodepage=GPI_ERROR;
FATTRS fatAttrs;

  /*************************************************************/
  /* Query number of public fonts known by PM and allocate */
  /* memory in which to read their metrics information.     */
  /*************************************************************/
  lReqFonts=0;
  if(szFontName!=NULL)
    lNumFonts=GpiQueryFonts(hps, QF_PUBLIC, (PSZ)szFontName,
&lReqFonts,
      0L, NULL);
  else lNumFonts=GpiQueryFonts(hps, QF_PUBLIC, NULL, &lReqFonts,
    0L, NULL);

  /*********************************************/
  /* Get memory for font metrics if any exist. */
  /*********************************************/
  if((lNumFonts!=GPI_ALTERROR) && (lNumFonts!=0L))
    afmMetrics=malloc((SHORT)(lNumFonts*sizeof(FONTMETRICS)));

  /*************************************/
  /* Query font information into array. */
  /*************************************/
  if(afmMetrics!=NULL)
    if(szFontName!=NULL)
      lRemFonts=GpiQueryFonts(hps, QF_PUBLIC, (PSZ)szFontName,
        &lNumFonts, (LONG)sizeof(FONTMETRICS), afmMetrics);
    else
      lRemFonts=GpiQueryFonts(hps, QF_PUBLIC, NULL, &lNumFonts,
        (LONG)sizeof(FONTMETRICS), afmMetrics);

  /*****************************************/
  /* Search for outline font and create it. */
  /*****************************************/

  if(lRemFonts!=GPI_ALTERROR){
    for(i=0; i<(INT)lNumFonts; i++){
      if(afmMetrics[i].fsDefn&FM_DEFN_OUTLINE){
        *lLcid=GetSetID(hps);  /* Get a set ID for the font. */

        /*********************************/
        /* Set the attribute of the font. */
        /*********************************/
        if(*lLcid!=GPI_ERROR)usCodepage=GpiQueryCp(hps);
```

```
    fatAttrs.usRecordLength=sizeof(FATTRS);
    fatAttrs.fsSelection=0;
    fatAttrs.lMatch=0L;
    strcpy(fatAttrs.szFacename,  afmMetrics[i].szFacename);
    fatAttrs.idRegistry=afmMetrics[i].idRegistry;
    fatAttrs.usCodePage=usCodepage;
    fatAttrs.lMaxBaselineExt=0L;
    fatAttrs.lAveCharWidth=0L;
    fatAttrs.fsType=0;
    fatAttrs.fsFontUse=(FATTR_FONTUSE_OUTLINE   |
      FATTR_FONTUSE_TRANSFORMABLE);

    /***********************/
    /* Create logical font. */
    /***********************/
    if(usCodepage!=GPI_ERROR){
      fRet=GpiCreateLogFont(hps,   NULL,
      *lLcid,   &fatAttrs)!=GPI_ERROR;
      }
    break  ;
      }
    }
  }
  if(afmMetrics!=NULL) free(afmMetrics); /* Free memory from array.
*/
  return(fRet);
  }
```

Listing 3-4. Find font function.

One of the parameters passed to this find font function is the font facename to be located. If this parameter is NULL, the function operates on the first outline font it finds. Before this function queries all the font information into application memory, it uses the GpiQueryFonts function to return the number of fonts of a particular font facename that Presentation Manager knows about. This is done by setting the length of the metrics to be returned to 0. After finding the number of fonts for a particular facename, the appropriate amount of memory is allocated to hold all the font information and the GpiQueryFonts function is used again to retrieve the font information. Once the font information is retrieved, it is tested to locate an outline font. If an outline font is located, a local set ID is found and the attributes of the font are recorded. Once the set ID and font attribute information have been resolved, the PM function called *GpiCreateLogFont* is used to force font selection.

A local set ID is required for logical font creation. The local set ID is a resource identifier used by the presentation space to locate needed resources. Listing 3-5 shows an example of how to find an available local set ID. As you can see in this function, GetSetID, a PM function called *GpiQueryNumberSetIds* is used to find out how many local set IDs are already allocated to a presentation space. If no local set IDs are currently allocated, then a local set ID of 1 is returned for the caller to use. If some local set IDs do exist, application memory is allocated to read them into and then they are tested. The query of the local set IDs is done with a PM function called *GpiQuerySetIds.* When the first unused local set ID is found, memory is freed and the local set ID is returned to the caller.

```
/*****************************/
/* Get a set ID for our font. */
/*****************************/
LONG FAR GetSetID(HPS hps)
  {
  #define MAXSETID 254L
  INT i;
  LONG lLcid=GPI_ERROR;
  LONG lCount;
  BOOL fRet=FALSE;
  PLONG alLcids=NULL;
  PLONG alTypes;
  PSTR8 aNames;

  /***********************************************/
  /* See if any local set IDs have been used yet. */
  /***********************************************/
  lCount=GpiQueryNumberSetIds(hps);
  if(lCount==0)
    return(1L);

  /*********************************/
  /* Find first unused local set ID. */
  /*********************************/
  if(lCount!=GPI_ALTERROR){
    alLcids=malloc((SHORT)(16*lCount));
    alTypes=(PLONG)(alLcids+lCount);
    aNames=(PSTR8)(alTypes+lCount);
    if(alLcids!=NULL)
      fRet=GpiQuerySetIds(hps, lCount, alTypes, aNames, alLcids);
    if(fRet){
      for(lLcid=1; lLcid<(MAXSETID+1); lLcid++){
        for(i=0; (i<(INT)lCount) && (alLcids[i]!=lLcid); i++);
        if(i==(INT)lCount)break;
        }
      if(lLcid==MAXSETID+1)lLcid=GPI_ERROR;
      }
    free(alLcids);
    }
  return(lLcid);
  }
```

Listing 3-5. Get set ID function.

Again, because we are using outline fonts, we have the flexibility of scaling the font to any size; therefore, another function worth understanding when working with outline fonts is a function to set the font point size. Listing 3-6 shows the function, SetPtSize, used by the slide puzzle application. This function does not actually change the font size; rather, it calculates the width and height information needed to set the font to the desired point size. The font point size is actually set with the PM function called *GpiSetCharBox*.

```
/***********************************/
/* Set point size for outline font. */
/***********************************/
BOOL FAR SetPtSize(HPS hps, LONG lLcid, LONG lPointSize,
  FIXED *width, FIXED *height)
  {
#define POINTSPERINCH 72L
HDC hdc;
BOOL fRet=FALSE;
LONG lYDevResFont;
POINTL aptlPoints[2];
LONG lYSizeInPels;
LONG lYSizeInWC;

  /*******************************************/
  /* Query current font vertical resolution. */
  /*******************************************/
hdc=GpiQueryDevice(hps);
DevQueryCaps(hdc, CAPS_VERTICAL_FONT_RES, 1L, &lYDevResFont);

  /***********************************************************/
  /* Calculate point size and convert to world coordinates. */
  /***********************************************************/
lYSizeInPels=((lYDevResFont*lPointSize)/POINTSPERINCH);
aptlPoints[0].x=0L;  aptlPoints[0].y=0L;
aptlPoints[1].x=0L;  aptlPoints[1].y=lYSizeInPels;
GpiConvert(hps, CVTC_DEVICE, CVTC_WORLD, 2L, aptlPoints) ;
lYSizeInWC=aptlPoints[1].y-aptlPoints[0].y;

  /*********************************************************/
  /* Set the font for the presentation space and make the */
  /* width and height value type fixed.                   */
  /*********************************************************/
 fRet=GpiSetCharSet(hps, lLcid);
 *width=lYSizeInWC*0x10000;
 *height=lYSizeInWC*0x10000;
 return(fRet);
 }
```

Listing 3-6. Set point size function.

As you can see from Listing 3-6, the device capabilities are queried to find a fonts' effective vertical device resolution in pels per inch. Once this resolution is found, the desired point size is converted to effective vertical pels for the device. The vertical height information is then converted from device units to world coordinates with the GpiConvert function. Finally, the font is set for the caller with a PM function called *GpiSetCharSet* and the world coordinate information is converted to a data type of FIXED in the callers address space.

   Notice in the SetPtSize function that the width is set to the same size as the height. This keeps the font in the correct proportion. This function does not set the character box size for the caller because the slide puzzle application also distorts the width of the font. However, a normal PM application would generally set the character box in a function like this on behalf of the caller.

   Once the size has been set, it is possible to get the width of each character. This information is valuable in determining character placement for kerning and in determining string width. PM character string functions can also use this information.

   Listing 3-7 shows a function used by the slide puzzle application to work with character width information. As you can see, this function, SetWidthsTable, gets the entire 256 character width table for a font. It does this with a PM function called *GpiQueryWidthTable*. The SetWidthsTable function also determines if the current font supports kerning. If the font does support kerning, memory is allocated so the PM function called *GpiQueryKerningPairs* can load the kerning pair information. This information is used to make adjustments to the string passed to the SetWidthsTable function. Before adjustments can be made, however, the string's character widths must be saved in an array. Once the array is built, the kerning adjustments can be applied to it as nessesary. This function also provides the caller with the length of the string passed to it based on the adjusted character widths.

```
/************************************************/
/* Set width table and calculate string length. */
/************************************************/
void FAR SetWidthsTable(HPS hps, LONG *alWidths,
   LONG *alWidthTable, CHAR *szStr, LONG *lTotal)
   {
   FONTMETRICS fm;
   PKERNINGPAIRS akpairs=NULL;
   LONG i, j;

   /*********************************************/
   /* Get width table for all 256 codepoints. */
   /*********************************************/
   GpiQueryWidthTable(hps, 0L, 256L, alWidthTable);

   /***********************************************/
   /* Check for kerning font and get pair if needed. */
   /***********************************************/
   GpiQueryFontMetrics(hps, (LONG)sizeof(FONTMETRICS), &fm);
   if(fm.sKerningPairs){
     akpairs=malloc(fm.sKerningPairs*sizeof(KERNINGPAIRS));
     GpiQueryKerningPairs(hps, fm.sKerningPairs, akpairs);
     }

   /*****************************************************/
   /* Set widths for each character in string before kerning. */
   /*****************************************************/
```

```
for(i=0; i<(LONG)strlen(szStr); i++)
  alWidths[i]=alWidthTable[szStr[i]];

/***************************************************/
/* Modify widths array with kerning adjustments. */
/***************************************************/
if(fm.sKerningPairs){
  for(i=0; i<(LONG)strlen(szStr); i++){
    for(j=0; j<fm.sKerningPairs; j++){
      if(szStr[i]==(UCHAR)akpairs[j].sFirstChar  &&
        szStr[i+1]==(UCHAR)akpairs[j].sSecondChar){
        alWidths[i]+=akpairs[j].lKerningAmount;
        break;
        }
      }
    }
  }
if(fm.sKerningPairs)free(akpairs); /* Free kerning values. */

/*********************************/
/* Calculate total string width. */
/*********************************/
*lTotal=0;
for(i=0; i<(LONG)strlen(szStr); i++)
*lTotal=*lTotal+alWidths[i];
return;
}
```

Listing 3-7. Set width table function.

The slide puzzle application uses these font functions as soon as the application starts. In fact, all text processing is done in the animation sequence which is caused when a message called ANIMATE is sent during the first WM_PAINT message. (The ANIMATE message is an application-defined message.) Because the ANIMATE message is sent with the WinSendMsg function, no more messages are processed until the sequence is completed. Hence, the slide puzzle application dominates the desktop until its little show is done.

Figure 3-5 shows the first instance of text being drawn during the animation sequence. As you can see, only one word (SLIDER) is drawn. This one word is produced by selecting a Courier outline font, sizing the font vertically and horizontally, locating and rotating the text 30 degrees, and coloring it red; consequently, a lot of font and text processing information is illustrated by drawing this one word!

Listing 3-8 shows part of the animation message processing code that produces the image shown in Figure 3-5. This code also shows how the blocks are produced with a bit-map and the GpiBitBlt function. Because bit-maps and the GpiBitBlt function are discussed in much greater detail in Chapter 6, Animation, they are not discussed here much.

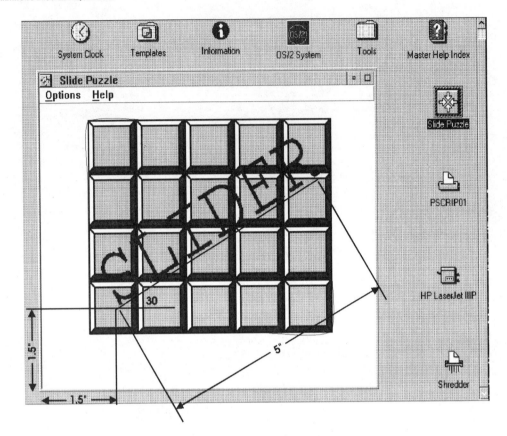

Figure 3-5. SLIDER text.

```
MRESULT EXPENTRY ClientWndProc(HWND hwnd, ULONG msg,
  MPARAM mp1, MPARAM mp2)
  {
  CHAR szProgName[]="SLIDER";
  CHAR szFontName[]="Courier";
  LONG alWidths[80];
  LONG alWidthTable[256];
  SIZEF sizefxCharBox;
  FIXED width, height;
  BOOL fRet=FALSE;
  float fPitch;
  BITMAPINFOHEADER2 bmp;
  HBITMAP hbmt;
  HDC hdcbm;
  HPS hpsd;
  POINTL aptl[4];
  LONG lRow, lCol, lTotal, lLcid;
  SIZEL sizl;
  SHORT x, y, i;
  POINTL shear, ptl;
  MATRIXLF matlfModel;
```

```
switch(msg){
  /*********************************************************/
  /* Process the animate message. This will only occur */
  /* once after the first WM_PAINT message.            */
  /*********************************************************/
  case ANIMATE:
    WinSetPointer(HWND_DESKTOP,
      WinQuerySysPointer(HWND_DESKTOP, SPTR_WAIT, FALSE));
    GpiResetPS(hps, GRES_ALL);
    aptl[0].x=0;          /* Target left. */
    aptl[0].y=0;
    aptl[1].x=sxPels;     /* Target right. */
    aptl[1].y=syPels;
    GpiBitBlt(hps, hps, 2L, aptl, ROP_ONE, BBO_AND);

    /*****************************************************/
    /* Get key bit-map and adjust for an inch square. */
    /*****************************************************/
    hbmt=GpiLoadBitmap(hps, 0, IDB_PIC1,
      (LONG)(lcxPelsPerInch), (LONG)(lcyPelsPerInch));
    for(x=1; x<6; x++){      /* Put 5 keys wide. */
      for(y=1; y<5; y++){    /* Put 4 keys high. */
        ptl.x=x*lcxPelsPerInch;
        ptl.y=y*lcyPelsPerInch;
        WinDrawBitmap(hps, hbmt, NULL, &ptl, CLR_NEUTRAL,
          CLR_BACKGROUND,  DBM_NORMAL);
        }
      }

    /**********************************************/
    /* Find font by name, else any outline font. */
    /**********************************************/
    if(!FindFont(hps, &lLcid, szFontName))
      FindFont(hps, &lLcid, NULL);
    lPointSize=80; /* Set font size to 80 points. */
    fRet=SetPtSize(hps, lLcid, lPointSize, &width, &height);
    if(fRet){
      sizefxCharBox.cy=height;
      sizefxCharBox.cx=width;
      fRet=GpiSetCharBox(hps, &sizefxCharBox);
      }

    /*********************************************/
    /* Set width table and get width of string. */
    /*********************************************/
    SetWidthsTable(hps, alWidths, alWidthTable,
      szProgName, &lTotal);

    /**********************************************/
    /* Calculate pitch factor based on 5 inch space. */
    /**********************************************/
    fPitch=(float)(5*lcxPelsPerInch)/(float)lTotal;
    sizefxCharBox.cx=width*fPitch; /* Adjust width. */
    fRet=GpiSetCharBox(hps, &sizefxCharBox);
```

```
SetWidthsTable(hps, alWidths, alWidthTable,
  szProgName, &lTotal);

/*************************************************/
/* Rotate 30 degrees and put up SLIDER in red. */
/*************************************************/
ptl.x=(LONG)(((float)lcxPelsPerInch)*1.5);
ptl.y=(LONG)(((float)lcyPelsPerInch)*1.5);
GpiRotate(hps, &matlfModel, TRANSFORM_REPLACE,
MAKEFIXED(30, 0), &ptl);
GpiSetModelTransformMatrix(hps, 9L, &matlfModel,
  TRANSFORM_ADD);
GpiMove(hps, &ptl);
GpiSetColor(hps, CLR_RED);
GpiCharStringPos(hps, NULL, CHS_VECTOR,
  (LONG)strlen(szProgName), (PSZ)szProgName, alWidths);
return(MRESULT)TRUE;
}


/*****************************************************/
/* Let default routine process message and return. */
/*****************************************************/
return WinDefWindowProc(hwnd, msg, mp1, mp2);
}
```

Listing 3-8. SLIDER text.

The ANIMATE routine first clears out the presentation page by using the GpiBitBlt function to set all the bits in the presentation page to one and, thus, forcing the color to white. A bit-map image of a block is then loaded and set to an inch square. This is accomplished with a Presentation Manager function called *GpiLoadBitmap*. After the bit-map is loaded and available to the presentation space, the PM function called *WinDrawBitmap* is used to draw a series of the block bit-maps in the presentation page. The position of a block is determined by passing the bottom left corner coordinate of where the block bit-map is to be located within the presentation page. The result is 20 one inch square blocks that form a 5 by 4 pattern starting one inch up and one inch right in the presentation page.

After the blocks are drawn, the animation sequence uses the FindFont function to locate an outline font. This function attempts to find a facename of Courier; but, if this fails, it finds and uses the first outline font that Presentation Manager can locate. Once an outline font has been established, the animation sequence determines the appropriate character box height and width so it is an 80-point font. This point sizing is done with the SetPtSize function. The PM function called *GpiSetCharBox* is then used to set the font size. Once this is done, a width array for the character string, SLIDER, is set by using the SetWidthsTable function; however, instead of drawing text based on this width information, the animation sequence uses the total width of the string to calculate a pitch factor to apply to the character box width. This calculation is based on the character string, SLIDER, fitting in an area that is five inches wide. Once calculated, this factor is used to adjust only the width of the character box. This will distort the font, but enable the string to fit in the dimension of the space desired.

Note that Presentation Manager provides a function called *GpiQueryTextBox* to help you determine the area used by a string. This function, however, also has limitations based on font type and character mode.

Now that the font size is set to the desired height and width, the animation sequence instructs Presentation Manager to rotate subsequent drawing functions 30 degrees. It does this with two PM functions called *GpiRotate* and *GpiSetModelTransformMatrix*. The first function, GpiRotate, builds the appropriate transformation matrix for a 30 degree rotation. The second function, GpiSetModelTransformMatrix, applies the transformation matrix to the presentation space. Note that rotation occurs around a given point in a presentation page. For the character string, SLIDER, the point of rotation is 1.5 inches up and to the right of the presentation page's origin. This rotation point is also the point where the current drawing position is set; hence, when text is drawn, it starts from this point. This is done with the PM function called *GpiMove*.

Right before the text is drawn, the color attribute is set to red by a PM function called *GpiSetColor*. This causes the text drawn to be red. Finally, the PM function called *GpiCharacterStringPos* draws the character string, SLIDER, in the presentation page. This function is set up to draw text with a supplied array of character widths; therefore, if the font used was kerned, this function would draw the adjusted text based on the supplied width table. Courier, however, is not a font that supports kerning!

The GpiCharacterStringPos function can be set up to do other interesting things with your text. For instance, this function can clip text to the size of a supplied rectangle. Besides taking time to understand what else the GpiCharacterStringPos function offers, you might also look at the PM functions called *GpiCharString* and *GpiCharStringAt*. These functions are very useful for more typical text processing routines.

After the word SLIDER is drawn on top of the blocks, the slide puzzle pauses for a few moments and then moves the blocks out of the presentation page one at a time. More text is then drawn in the presentation page in an animated fashion. Screen 3-1 shows what this new text looks like. It is centered in the presentation page, drawn with a new font that is kerned, has different sizes, and is sheared. Listing 3-9 shows how this is implemented in the animation sequence. Remember, these listings show only a subset of the source code found in the actual slide puzzle; thus, even though you've already seen part of the animation sequence, this listing shows a different part of the same routine.

Part of the process that causes the text to be animated is copying it from a memory presentation page to the screen presentation page. Consequently, the text produced by the code shown in Listing 3-9 is drawn in a memory presentation page. How this memory presentation page is used to cause simple animation is

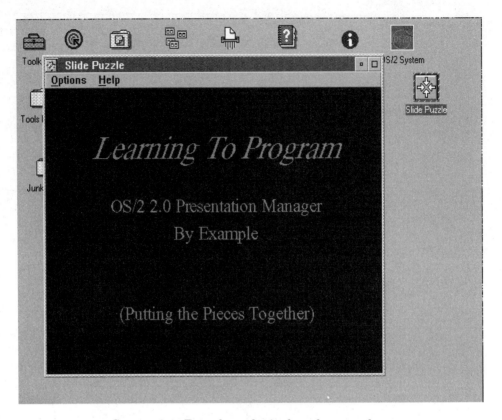

Screen 3-1. Text sheared, sized, and centered.

discussed in Chapter 6, Animation. Because the text must be drawn in a memory presentation page, both presentation pages must first be cleared out and made black by setting all their bits to 0. After a memory presentation space has been established, the animation routine tries to locate an outline font with a facename of Times New Roman. If this fails, it finds and uses the first outline font that Presentation Manager can locate. This outline font is then sized to a 30-point font.

```
MRESULT EXPENTRY ClientWndProc(HWND hwnd, ULONG msg,
  MPARAM mp1, MPARAM mp2)
  {
  CHAR szStr1[]="Learning To Program";
  CHAR szStr2[]="OS/2 2.0 Presentation Manager";
  CHAR szStr3[]="By Example";
  CHAR szStr4[]="(Putting the Pieces Together)";
  CHAR szFontName1[]="Times New Roman";
  LONG alWidths[80];
  LONG alWidthTable[256];
  SIZEF sizefxCharBox;
  FIXED width, height;
  BOOL fRet=FALSE;
  float fPitch;
```

```
BITMAPINFOHEADER2 bmp;
HBITMAP hbmt;
HDC hdcbm;
HPS hpsd;
POINTL aptl[4];
LONG lRow, lCol, lTotal, lLcid;
SIZEL sizl;
SHORT x, y, i;
POINTL shear, ptl;
RECTL rclInvalid;

switch(msg){
  /*********************************************************/
  /* Process the animate message. This will only occur */
  /* once after the first WM_PAINT message.           */
  /*********************************************************/
  case ANIMATE:
    GpiResetPS(hpsMemory, GRES_ALL);
    GpiQueryDeviceBitmapFormats(hpsMemory, 2L, alBmpFormats);
    memset(&bmp, 0, sizeof(bmp));
    bmp.cbFix=sizeof bmp;
    bmp.cx=sxPels;
    bmp.cPlanes=(USHORT)alBmpFormats[0];
    bmp.cBitCount=(USHORT)alBmpFormats[1];
    bmp.cy=syPels;
    hbmt=GpiCreateBitmap(hpsMemory, &bmp, 0L, NULL, NULL);
    GpiSetBitmap(hpsMemory, hbmt);

    /*********************************/
    /* Clear out presentation pages. */
    /*********************************/
    aptl[0].x=0;  aptl[0].y=0;
    aptl[1].x=sxPels;  aptl[1].y=syPels;
    aptl[2].x=0;  aptl[2].y=0;
    GpiBitBlt(hps, hps, 2L, aptl, ROP_ZERO, BBO_AND);
    GpiBitBlt(hpsMemory, hpsMemory, 2L, aptl, ROP_ZERO, BBO_AND);

    /*********************************************************/
    /* Look for font by name else find any outline font. */
    /*********************************************************/
    if(!FindFont(hpsMemory, &lLcid, szFontName1))
      FindFont(hpsMemory, &lLcid, NULL);
    lPointSize=30;  /* Set font to 30 points. */
    fRet=SetPtSize(hpsMemory, lLcid, lPointSize, &width, &height);
    if(fRet){
      sizefxCharBox.cy=height;
      sizefxCharBox.cx=width;
      }
    fRet=GpiSetCharBox(hpsMemory, &sizefxCharBox);

    /*********************************************************/
    /* Set color and shear for memory presentation space. */
    /* Then put all text in this presentation page.       */
    /*********************************************************/
    GpiSetColor(hpsMemory, CLR_CYAN);
```

```
shear.x=10;  shear.y=25;
GpiSetCharShear(hpsMemory,  &shear);
SetWidthsTable(hpsMemory,  alWidths,
 alWidthStr1,  szStr1,  &lTotal);
ptl.x=((7*lcxPelsPerInch)-lTotal)/2; /* Center text 4 */
ptl.y=lcyPelsPerInch*4;              /* inches from bottom */
GpiMove(hpsMemory,  &ptl);
GpiCharStringPos(hpsMemory,  NULL,  CHS_VECTOR,
 (LONG)strlen(szStr1),  (PSZ)szStr1,  alWidths);

/*****************************************************/
/* Change point size of font and get rid of shear. */
/*****************************************************/
lPointSize=18;
fRet=SetPtSize(hpsMemory,  lLcid,  lPointSize,  &width,  &height);
if(fRet){
  sizefxCharBox.cy=height;
  sizefxCharBox.cx=width;
  }
fRet=GpiSetCharBox(hpsMemory,  &sizefxCharBox);
shear.x=0;  shear.y=1;
GpiSetCharShear(hpsMemory,  &shear);

/************************************************************/
/* Center next 2 lines of text in memory presentation page. */
/************************************************************/
SetWidthsTable(hpsMemory,  alWidths,
 alWidthTable,  szStr2,  &lTotal);
ptl.x=((7*lcxPelsPerInch)-lTotal)/2;   /* Center text */
ptl.y=lcyPelsPerInch*3;              /* 3 inches from bottom */
GpiMove(hpsMemory,  &ptl);
GpiCharStringPos(hpsMemory,  NULL,  CHS_VECTOR,
 (LONG)strlen(szStr2),  (PSZ)szStr2,  alWidths);
SetWidthsTable(hpsMemory,  alWidths,
 alWidthTable,  szStr3,  &lTotal);
ptl.x=((7*lcxPelsPerInch)-lTotal)/2; /* Center text */
ptl.y=lcyPelsPerInch*2.5;  /* 2.5 inches from bottom */
GpiMove(hpsMemory,  &ptl);
GpiCharStringPos(hpsMemory,  NULL,  CHS_VECTOR,
 (LONG)strlen(szStr3),  (PSZ)szStr3,  alWidths);

/**********************************************/
/* Change color and center last           */
/* line of text in memory presentation page. */
/**********************************************/
GpiSetColor(hpsMemory,  CLR_YELLOW);
SetWidthsTable(hpsMemory,  alWidths,
 alWidthTable,  szStr4,  &lTotal);
ptl.x=((7*lcxPelsPerInch)-lTotal)/2;   /* Center text */
ptl.y=lcyPelsPerInch*1;              /* 1 inches from bottom */
GpiMove(hpsMemory,  &ptl);
GpiCharStringPos(hpsMemory,  NULL,  CHS_VECTOR,
 (LONG)strlen(szStr4),  (PSZ)szStr4,  alWidths);
```

```
    WinInvalidateRect(hwnd, NULL, FALSE); /* Cause full paint. */
    return(MRESULT)TRUE;
  }


/*****************************************************/
/* Let default routine process message and return. */
/*****************************************************/
return WinDefWindowProc(hwnd, msg, mp1, mp2);
}
```

Listing 3-9. Centered and sheared text.

After the font size is set, the ANIMATE routine sets the color attribute to cyan and uses a PM function called *GpiSetCharShear* to set the shear for drawing characters. The GpiSetCharShear function is passed a horizontal and vertical value with which to set the angle of the shear. For instance, a value of 1 and 1 would create a 45° shear. In this case, these values are 10 and 25, respectively. Next, the width table and total width for the character string "Learning to Program" are built. With the total width information, an X-coordinate is calculated so the string will be centered in the presentation page. This calculation, and others to follow, assumes the width of the presentation page to be 7 inches. A Y-coordinate of 4 inches is then calculated and the current position is set based on these coordinates. Finally, the first character string is drawn in the memory presentation page. Note that this does not cause the text to be displayed because it is not being drawn in the display presentation page!

After the first string of text is drawn, the font size is changed to 18-point and the shear is removed. The next 2 lines of text are then centered and drawn; however, the second line of text is located 3 inches from the bottom and the third line of text is located 2.5 inches from the bottom. Finally, the last line of text is drawn in yellow, centered, and located 1 inch from the bottom of the memory presentation page.

Even though these last 4 lines of text are not drawn in the display presentation page and do not show up on the display, the font and text operations work as if they were drawn in a display presentation page. The rest of the ANIMATE message routine is shown in Chapter 6, Animation, so you can see how the text is placed in the display presentation page.

Presentation Manager also offers a set of functions that affect the cursor. (The slide puzzle application does not use these functions because a cursor is not needed.) Presentation Manager gives you a choice of cursor styles that you can create for your application. When your client area receives input focus, you should create the appropriate cursor and locate it in your presentation page by using the PM function called *WinCreateCursor*. Your window procedure will be informed when it is losing or receiving input focus by receiving a WM_FOCUSCHANGE message. To get the cursor to appear, however, use the PM function called *WinShowCursor*. When the application loses input focus, it should use the PM function called *WinDestroyCursor* to destroy the cursor.

DRAWING LINES

Presentation Manager has a set of functions that let you draw lines and curves. With these functions you can, for example, draw simple straight lines or draw more complex curves such as splines or arcs. The slide puzzle program only draws straight lines with a PM function called *GpiLine*, but as you look at other line and curve functions, you will notice that they are fairly descriptive and easy to use. Examples of some of these other PM functions are *GpiPolyLine*, *GpiPolyFillet*, *GpiPolyFilletSharp*, *GpiPolySpline*, *GpiFullArc*, *GpiPartialArc*, *GpiPointArc*, and *GpiBox*.

Besides line drawing functions, Presentation Manager also provides different line types and modes. For instance, a PM function called *GpiSetLineType* lets you choose from line types such as solid, dotted, dashed, and so on. The PM function called *GpiSetMix* lets you define how the lines are drawn; for example, you can turn all bits in the line on or off, invert bits, or leave the bits alone (invisible).

Even though the slide puzzle only draws a few simply placed lines, some thought and planning was still needed to get the desired effect. For instance, to insure that the lines are always visible when the slide puzzle grid is active, they must be drawn in a way that is not sensitive to the image; therefore, using a mix that inverts the bits in the line is better than a black or white line. The grid state can be changed at any time; thus, restoring the state of the bits is important. Simple bit inverting always accomplishes this.

Besides choosing the right mix for drawing the slide puzzle, choosing the right line type is also important. As the slide puzzle pieces are moved and the grid state changes, it is difficult to manage which bits in the line need to be changed. Unless, however, all bits are affected! For this reason the slide puzzle uses a solid line instead of dotted or dashed lines. Screen 3-2 shows an example of the grid produced by the slide puzzle.

Listing 3-10 shows part of a routine that produces the grid for the slide puzzle. As you can see, the grid operation is performed on the master memory bit-map for the slide puzzle image. After the bit-map is set in a memory presentation page, the bit inversion mode is set with the GpiSetMix function. Once the mix is set, a series of lines are calculated for both the horizontal and vertical directions based on the pel dimension of the display and the number of pels per puzzle piece. The actual line is generated on this bit-map with the GpiLine function. Because the grid state is always toggled and the bit inversion mode produces a toggle effect, the actual grid state doesn't have to be tracked to produce the correct state.

```
/********************************************/
/* Process grid state pull-down option. */
/********************************************/
case IDM_GRIDSTATE:
   /********************************/
   /* Get the master memory bit-map. */
   /********************************/
   GpiResetPS(hpsMemory,  GRES_ALL);
   GpiQueryBitmapParameters(hbmSrc,  &bmpSrc);
   GpiSetBitmap(hpsMemory,  hbmSrc);
```

```
/*************************************************/
/* Set the mix to invert all pixels drawn and */
/* then draw grid lines.                       */
/*************************************************/
GpiSetMix(hpsMemory,  FM_INVERT);
for(lRow=0;  lRow<=syPels/lcyMinMax;  lRow++){
  ptl.x=0;   ptl.y=lRow*lcyMinMax;
  GpiMove(hpsMemory,  &ptl);
  ptl.x=sxPels;
  GpiLine(hpsMemory,  &ptl);
  }
for(lCol=0;  lCol<=sxPels/lcxMinMax;  lCol++){
  ptl.y=0;   ptl.x=lCol*lcxMinMax;
  GpiMove(hpsMemory,  &ptl);
  ptl.y=syPels;
  GpiLine(hpsMemory,  &ptl);
  }
WinInvalidateRect(hwnd,  NULL,  FALSE);
return(MRESULT)TRUE;
```

Listing 3-10. Drawing the grid.

Screen 3-2. Grid lines.

4

Working With Resources

Presentation Manager is designed to let you describe many of the objects you want to use in your application outside of the actual compiled program. These objects, such as bit-maps, icons, mouse pointer icons, text strings, dialog boxes, menus, accelerator keys, and so on are called *resources*.

Presentation Manager has a large list of predefined resources types that you can describe, compile, and make available to a program. Furthermore, you can define your own resource types as well. (IDs with a value from 1 to 255 are reserved for predefined resource types.) By providing external resource capability, Presentation Manager lets you develop many of the items your program manipulates without having to change and rebuild the entire program. This allows other people to personalize your application without having access to your application source code or all the tools required to rebuild the entire program. Other people can, therefore, define things like menu text or icons for your program.

Resources are described in a special ASCII source file called a *resource script*. This file contains keywords that identify the different types of resource objects, and assigns unique identifiers with each object type. It also contains information that describes the stucture of each object. By convention the resource script has a file extension of **.RC**. The resource script for the slide puzzle application is in the file called SLIDER.RC.

Once this file is created and contains the desired object descriptions, it can be compiled and converted to a binary format with a tool called a *resource compiler*. This tool comes with the IBM Developer's Toolkit for OS/2 2.0. Once the resource script is compiled, it can be merged with the compiled application or used to create a *dynamic link library* (DLL). As the name implies, a DLL is an object that you can dynamically link to during the execution of your program. DLLs are an extremely powerful feature of OS/2 and enable useful ways to package and share object level software in the OS/2 environment.

In relationship to the slide puzzle application, only predefined resource types are used and these resources are merged with the application. Even though DLLs and many resource types aren't discussed in this book, you will find that they are not difficult to understand once you learn how the slide puzzle uses resources.

To compile the slide puzzle resource script with the resource compiler, enter the following command:

RC -R SLIDER

This command assumes the .RC extension on the input file and creates a new binary file with a **.RES** extension. Therefore, SLIDER.RES is the file that can be merged with the slide puzzle SLIDER.EXE file. To merge the SLIDER.RES file to the SLIDER.EXE file, use the same resource compiler tool but enter the following command:

RC SLIDER.RES

If the .RES file and the .EXE files were to have different names, the command to merge the two files would be:

RC *RESOURCE*.RES *PROGRAM*.EXE
where
 RESOURCE is the name of the binary resource file.
 PROGRAM is the name of the program object file.

Both the compile and merge steps can be performed in a single step by entering the following command:

RC SLIDER

This command assumes the .RC extension on the input file and the existence of the SLIDER.EXE file. If the .EXE file has a different name than the .RES file, use the following command syntax:

RC *RESOURCE PROGRAM*.EXE
where
 RESOURCE is the name of the resource file.
 PROGRAM is the name of the program object file.

Figure 4-1 illustrates the steps of the development and build process for a typical Presentation Manager application. As you can see, .H files are usually used in both the resource compile and the C program compile steps and are usually the very same files. They are shared because the resource types and unique IDs are defined in these files; hence, the resource script uses the .H files for resource identification and assignments, while the C program uses these definitions for references.

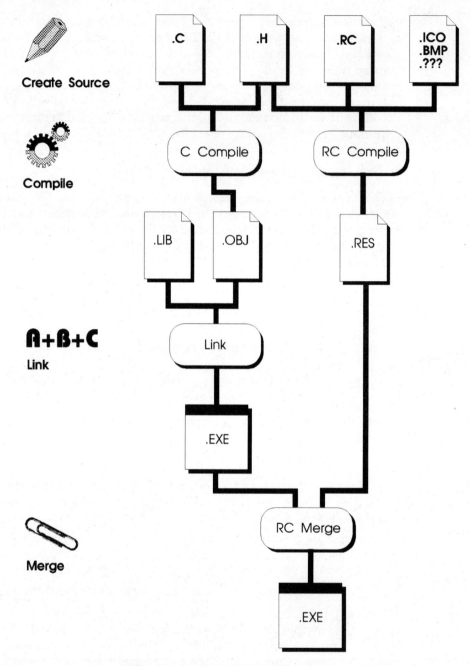

Figure 4-1. Typical PM build process.

The following sections of this chapter show how the slide puzzle application uses resources. They show both the statements used in the resource script, as well as how these resources are referenced by the slide puzzle application. These sections also discuss some of the tools used to generate resources.

USING POINTERS

The slide puzzle application not only uses pointers defined by Presentation Manager, but also five pointers designed just for its use. Four of these pointers are arrows that point up, down, left, and right. The last pointer is the symbol *X*. One of these custom pointers appears whenever the mouse pointer is in the client area of the slide puzzle application window and indicates the direction of a valid puzzle move. This, of course, is determined by the current position of the blank puzzle piece. If the mouse pointer is in an area where a valid move can not be made, the *X* pointer icon is displayed.

To create a pointer image, use the icon editor that comes with OS/2 2.0. This tool is located in the Productivity folder. With the icon editor, you can either create or edit pointers, icons, or bit-maps. Screen 4-1 shows an example of an icon editor session. This particular example shows the up arrow pointer used by the slide puzzle. As you can be see, the icon editor lets you select different colors from a child window containing a palette. After you select a color from the palette, you can apply it to individual pels in the icon edit area. If you are creating or editing a pointer, you can also specify a *hot spot*. The hot spot is the location within the pointer icon that corresponds to the coordinates passed with the mouse move message; so, for instance, the tip of an arrow icon is a good place for the hot spot definition. Once you're done with the edit session, you can save the pointer icon in a file with a name of your choice.

Once you have created a pointer, you can define it in the resource script file so it can be compiled with all the other resources. To do this, use a single-line statement with the following syntax:

> *RESOURCETYPE NAMEID LOADOPTION MEMOPTION FILENAME*
> where
>> *RESOURCETYPE* is the keyword or ID of the resource to be loaded. This field is **required**.
>> *NAMEID* is a unique name or integer that identifies the resource. This field is **required**.
>> *LOADOPTION* is an **optional** field that describes when the resource is loaded for the application. The default is LOADONCALL.
>> *MEMOPTION* is an **optional** field that describes how the resource is to be managed in memory. For pointers and icons, this field has a default of MOVEABLE and DISCARDABLE.
>> *FILENAME* is an ASCII string that specifies where the file containing the resource is found. This field is **required**.

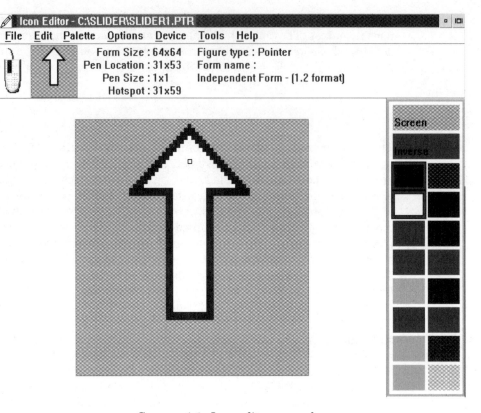

Screen 4-1. Icon editor example.

Listing 4-1 shows the statements used in the slide puzzle resource script to define the pointers used by the slide puzzle application.

```
#include <os2.h>
#include "slider.h"
POINTER IDI_MP1    slider1.ptr
POINTER IDI_MP2    slider2.ptr
POINTER IDI_MP3    slider3.ptr
POINTER IDI_MP4    slider4.ptr
POINTER IDI_MP5    slider5.ptr
```

Listing 4-1. Pointer resource entries.

As you can see in Listing 4-1, only the three required fields are used to define the pointers for the slide puzzle. The first field contains the keyword POINTER. Because this is a predefined resource type, its definition can be found in the OS2.H file. The second field contains a unique identifier for the POINTER type object. This identifier is also used by the application program to reference the pointer. Because both the application source code and the resource script need access to this ID, its definition can be found in the SLIDER.H file. The third and last field is the file name and extension that contains the pointer. This file was produced with the icon editor.

Listing 4-1 shows that five different pointers have been created and defined. SLIDER1.PTR contains the arrow up pointer, SLIDER2.PTR contains the arrow right pointer, SLIDER3.PTR contains the arrow down pointer, SLIDER4.PTR contains the arrow left pointer, and SLIDER5.PTR contains the *X* pointer. Once the resource script has been compiled and merged with the application .EXE file, all these pointers can be accessed.

Before an application can access a custom pointer, it must load the pointer and get a handle with which to reference it. This is done with a PM function called *WinLoadPointer*. The handle for a pointer is stored in a data type called HPOINTER. After the handle for the pointer is obtained, the application can draw the pointer in the presentation page using a PM function called *WinDrawPointer*. Once the application is done with a pointer or before it terminates, it should free the pointer resource with a PM function called *WinDestroyPointer*. Listing 4-2 shows how the slide puzzle application references and uses these pointers.

```
HPOINTER hIptr1, hIptr2, hIptr3, hIptr4, hIptr5;

/******************/
/* Main Procedure. */
/******************/
int main(int argc, char *argv[])
  {
  ULONG ulFrameFlags=FCF_TASKLIST | FCF_SIZEBORDER |
    FCF_TITLEBAR | FCF_MINMAX |
    FCF_SYSMENU | FCF_MENU | FCF_ICON | FCF_ACCELTABLE;
  HMQ hmq;
  QMSG qmsg;
  hab=WinInitialize(0);
  hmq=WinCreateMsgQueue(hab, 0);
  WinRegisterClass(hab, (PSZ)szClientClass, ClientWndProc,
    CS_SIZEREDRAW, 0);
  hwndFrame=WinCreateStdWindow(HWND_DESKTOP, WS_VISIBLE,
    &ulFrameFlags, (PSZ)szClientClass, 0, 0L, 0,
    ID_SLIDEFRAME, &hwndClient);

  /************************************/
  /* Get PM messages and dispatch them. */
  /************************************/
  while(WinGetMsg(hab, &qmsg, 0, 0, 0)){
    WinDispatchMsg(hab, &qmsg);
    }

  /**************************/
  /* Free resources obtained. */
  /**************************/
```

```
                    WinDestroyWindow(hwndFrame);
                    WinDestroyMsgQueue(hmq);
                    WinTerminate(hab);
                    return 0;
                    }

        MRESULT EXPENTRY ClientWndProc(HWND hwnd, ULONG msg,
          MPARAM mp1, MPARAM mp2)
          {
          SHORT x, y, i;

          switch(msg){
            /********************************************************/
            /* Process the animate message.  This will only occur */
            /* once after the first WM_PAINT message.             */
            /********************************************************/
            case ANIMATE:
              WinSetPointer(HWND_DESKTOP,
                WinQuerySysPointer(HWND_DESKTOP, SPTR_WAIT, FALSE));
                    /* ANIMATION LOGIC */

              WinSetPointer(HWND_DESKTOP,
                WinQuerySysPointer(HWND_DESKTOP, SPTR_APPICON, FALSE));
              return(MRESULT)TRUE;


            /*********************************/
            /* Process window create message. */
            /*********************************/
            case WM_CREATE:
              /*****************************************/
              /* Load pointers and save their handles. */
              /*****************************************/
              hIptr1=WinLoadPointer(HWND_DESKTOP, 0, IDI_MP1);  /* Up. */
              hIptr2=WinLoadPointer(HWND_DESKTOP, 0, IDI_MP2);  /* Right. */
              hIptr3=WinLoadPointer(HWND_DESKTOP, 0, IDI_MP3);  /* Down. */
              hIptr4=WinLoadPointer(HWND_DESKTOP, 0, IDI_MP4);  /* Left. */
              hIptr5=WinLoadPointer(HWND_DESKTOP, 0, IDI_MP5);  /* X. */
              return(MRESULT)FALSE;


            /********************************/
            /* Process mouse move messages. */
            /********************************/
            case WM_MOUSEMOVE:
              x=MOUSEMSG(&msg)->x;
              y=MOUSEMSG(&msg)->y;
              x=x/lcxMinMax;
              y=y/lcyMinMax;


              /**************************************************/
              /* Set correct pointer icon based on position. */
              /**************************************************/
              if((y==sGridy) || (x==sGridx)){
                if((y<sGridy) && (x==sGridx))
                  WinSetPointer(HWND_DESKTOP, hIptr1);
```

```
    if((y>sGridy) && (x==sGridx))
      WinSetPointer(HWND_DESKTOP, hIptr3);
    if((x<sGridx) && (y==sGridy))
      WinSetPointer(HWND_DESKTOP, hIptr2);
    if((x>sGridx) && (y==sGridy))
      WinSetPointer(HWND_DESKTOP, hIptr4);
    if((x==sGridx) && (y==sGridy))
      WinSetPointer(HWND_DESKTOP, hIptr5);
    }
  else
    WinSetPointer(HWND_DESKTOP, hIptr5);
  return(MRESULT)TRUE;

/**********************************/
/* Destory resources accumulated.  */
/**********************************/
case WM_DESTROY:
  WinDestroyPointer(hIptr1);
  WinDestroyPointer(hIptr2);
  WinDestroyPointer(hIptr3);
  WinDestroyPointer(hIptr4);
  WinDestroyPointer(hIptr5);
  GpiDestroyPS(hpsMemory);
  DevCloseDC(hdcMemory);
  GpiDestroyPS(hps);
  return(MRESULT)NULL;
  }


/***************************************************/
/* Let default routine process message and return. */
/***************************************************/
return WinDefWindowProc(hwnd, msg, mp1, mp2);
}
```

Listing 4-2. Adding pointer icons.

As you can see in Listing 4-2, the custom pointers are loaded in the
ClientWndProc procedure rather than in the main procedure. The first thing that
the ANIMATE routine in the ClientWndProc procedure does is set a new pointer
by using the *WinSetPointer* function. This pointer is one of the system-defined
pointers. The handle for the desired system pointer is queried with a Presentation
Manager function called *WinQuerySysPointer*. The system pointer being requested
(SPTR_WAIT) is the one that indicates to the user that user input is being
delayed. This pointer is requested because the animate message takes several
seconds to complete and no other messages are processed during this time. Right
before the ANIMATE message routine finishes, another WinSetPointer function
call is used to set the pointer back to a standard application pointer
(SPTR_APPICON).

One of the first messages that Presentation Manager sends to the ClientWndProc
procedure is the WM_CREATE message. Because of this, the custom pointers are

loaded by this routine with the WinLoadPointer function. This function uses the same IDs used in the resource script file. As soon as the pointers are loaded, they can be referenced and used. The routine to use the pointers is in the WM_MOUSEMOVE message routine.

When a WM_MOUSEMOVE message is received, the x and y coordinates of the mouse location are extracted from the message parameters and converted to a puzzle grid location. The converted mouse coordinates are then compared to the coordinates of the blank puzzle piece. Depending on where the converted coordinates are located in relationship to the blank piece, the appropriate pointer is set with the WinSetPointer function.

When the slide puzzle application is terminated, a WM_DESTROY message is sent to the slide puzzle window procedure. At this time, the pointers are destroyed with the WinDestroyPointer function.

ICONS

Creating and defining icons for your application isn't much different than creating and defining pointers. In fact, the two resource types are often interchangeable. In functions that perform direct manipulation, interchanging icons and pointers is very useful. This is because icons can represent the objects you want to manipulate and can easily be moved with the mouse! Even though the slide puzzle application doesn't use icons in a way that provides direct manipulation, it does use an icon to represent the application when it is in a minimized state.

The application icon is created with the same icon editor program is used to generate a pointer. Screen 4-2 shows the icon for the slide puzzle application being edited with the icon editor program. After creating an icon, you can define it in the resource script so it can be compiled with all the other resources and be accessed by the application for which it was designed.

Like the pointer resource, the icon resource is defined in the resource script with a single-line statement. The single-line statement used in the resource script for the slide puzzle icon is as follows:

ICON ID_SLIDEFRAME SLIDER.ICO

This statement uses the keyword ICON to identify the resource as an icon resource type. The unique ID given to the icon is ID_SLIDEFRAME. As you will see later, ID_SLIDEFRAME is also used by other resource types that are associated with the frame window. This isn't a problem because this ID is still unique for each resource type. The ASCII string SLIDER.ICO is the name and extension of the file that contains the slider icon.

If you want Presentation Manager to associate an icon with your application, give the icon file the same name as the program file, and be sure to place the icon file in the same directory as the program. By doing this, Presentation Manager will use the icon defined in the .ICO file to identify your application when it is referenced in a folder or group box from the desktop.

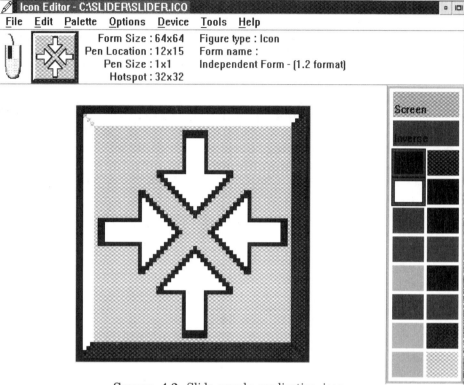

Screen 4-2. Slide puzzle application icon.

To use the icon when your application is minimized, add the FCF_ICON indicator to the frame flags. Then, when you create the standard window with the WinCreateStdWindow function, use the icon ID for the ID parameter. This ID will actually be the frame window ID for your application window. By making all the frame window resources the same ID as the frame, they can be found by the frame window when needed!

Finally, if you want to use a default icon instead of a custom icon, send a message to the frame window informing it to use a default icon. This message would look something like this:

```
WinSendMsg(hwndFrame,WM_SETICON,WinQuerySysPointer
(HWND_DESKTOP,SPTR_APPICON,FALSE),NULL);
```

This message can be sent right after the WinCreateStdWindow function. Remember, if you are using a custom icon, do **not** send this message!

Besides demonstrating how the slide puzzle application implements pointers, Listing 4-2 also shows how the slide puzzle application implements the icon designed for it. As you can see in this listing, the variable named **ulFrameFlags** has the FCF_ICON indicator set and the WinCreateStdWindow uses the icon ID as the second-to-last parameter. Our application icon is done!

Again, creating and defining bit-maps for your application isn't much different than doing so with pointers and icons. Use the icon editor program to create or edit the bit-maps, and use a single-line statement to define them in a resource script. Bit-maps, however, can be much larger than pointers or icons and may have rectangular dimensions other than square. Listing 4-3 shows the entries in the slide puzzle resource script for the bit-maps used by the slide puzzle. These bit-maps are the images of the blocks that the word SLIDER is written on when the application is first started and the grasshopper that randomly runs across the screen. This section shows how the bit-maps are defined and loaded by the slide puzzle application. Chapter 6, Animation, shows how these bit-maps are used to perform the animation effects.

```
#include <os2.h>
#include "slider.h"
BITMAP      IDB_PIC1    slider1.bmp
BITMAP      IDB_PIC2    bug1.bmp
BITMAP      IDB_PIC3    bug1mask.bmp
BITMAP      IDB_PIC4    bug2.bmp
BITMAP      IDB_PIC5    bug2mask.bmp
BITMAP      IDB_PIC6    bug3.bmp
BITMAP      IDB_PIC7    bug3mask.bmp
BITMAP      IDB_PIC8    bug4.bmp
BITMAP      IDB_PIC9    bug4mask.bmp
BITMAP      IDB_PIC10   bug5.bmp
BITMAP      IDB_PIC11   bug5mask.bmp
```

Listing 4-3. Bit-Map resource entries.

As you can see in Listing 4-3, only the three required fields of the single-line statement are used to define the bit-maps. The first field contains the keyword BITMAP. Because this is a predefined resource type, its definition can be found in the OS2.H file. The second field contains a unique identifier for the BITMAP type object. This identifier is also used by the application program to reference the bit-map. Because both the application source code and the resource script need access to this ID, its definition can be found in the SLIDER.H file. The third and last field is the file name and extension that contains the bit-map.

Before an application can use a bit-map, it needs to load it into memory. This is done with the Presentation Manager function called *GpiLoadBitmap*. The GpiLoadBitmap function returns a handle to the bit-map that can be used by the application to access the bit-map. The bit-map handle has a data type called HBITMAP. Once the bit-map is loaded, the application uses the PM function called *WinDrawBitmap* to draw the bit-map in a presentation page. After the application is finished with the bit-map, it should be released from memory with the PM function called *GpiDeleteBitmap*. Listing 4-4 shows how the slide puzzle application accesses one of the bit-maps defined in its resource script. Even though this listing shows only one example from all the bit-maps defined, the other bit-maps are accessed in the same way.

```
MRESULT EXPENTRY ClientWndProc(HWND hwnd, ULONG msg,
  MPARAM mp1, MPARAM mp2)
  {
  HBITMAP hbmt;
  HDC hdcbm;
  HPS hpsd;
  SHORT x, y, i;
  POINTL shear, ptl;

  switch(msg){
    /*********************************************************/
    /* Process the animate message.  This will only occur */
    /* once after the first WM_PAINT message.             */
    /*********************************************************/
    case ANIMATE:
      GpiResetPS(hps, GRES_ALL);
      aptl[0].x=0;              /* Target left. */
      aptl[0].y=0;
      aptl[1].x=sxPels;        /* Target right. */
      aptl[1].y=syPels;
      GpiBitBlt(hps, hps, 2L, aptl, ROP_ONE, BBO_AND);

      /****************************************************/
      /* Get key bit-map and adjust for an inch square. */
      /****************************************************/
      hbmt=GpiLoadBitmap(hps, 0, IDB_PIC1,
        (LONG)(lcxPelsPerInch), (LONG)(lcyPelsPerInch));
      for(x=1; x<6; x++){       /* Put 5 keys wide. */
        for(y=1; y<5; y++){     /* Put 4 keys high. */
          ptl.x=x*lcxPelsPerInch;
          ptl.y=y*lcyPelsPerInch;
          WinDrawBitmap(hps, hbmt, NULL, &ptl, CLR_NEUTRAL,
            CLR_BACKGROUND, DBM_NORMAL);
          }
        }
      GpiDeleteBitmap(hbmt);
      return(MRESULT)TRUE;
    }

  /****************************************************/
  /* Let default routine process message and return. */
  /****************************************************/
  return WinDefWindowProc(hwnd, msg, mp1, mp2);
  }
```

Listing 4-4. Accessing bit-maps.

As you can see in Listing 4-4, the GpiLoadBitmap function requires a presentation space. Depending on the device associated with the presentation space, the bit-map may be loaded into device memory; if not, the bit-map is loaded into regular memory. Because the second parameter of the GpiLoadBitmap function is 0, Presentation Manager looks for the resource in the .EXE file of the application program. The particular bit-map being referenced is the block image on which the word SLIDER is drawn. The last two parameters of the GpiLoadBitmap function specify the width and height of the area the bitmap will fill. For the bit-map in Listing 4-4, this is a one inch square.

After the bit-map is loaded, it is drawn 20 times with the WinDrawBitmap function. This drawing takes place in the display presentation page to form a 5 by 4 matrix of blocks. After the matrix of blocks has been drawn, the bit-map is deleted from memory.

PULL-DOWN MENUS

Pull-down menus are located in the action bar area of the application frame window and provide a convenient way for users to select options or cause actions for the application. Many applications have several pull-down menus to provide different groups of services such as filing, editing, tools, or help information. Of course, the number of pull-down menus, their names, and the number of items in these pull-downs is part of the design of your application. The slide puzzle application only has two pull-down menus called Options and Help. Screen 4-3 shows the Options pull-down menu for the slide puzzle application.

Like pointers, icons, and bit-maps, pull-down menus are also defined as resources in a resource script. Instead of being defined by a single-line statement, however, the menu resource type requires a multiple-line statement. Multiple-line statements found in the resource script are very similar to the structure of those found in the C and Pascal programming languages. This is because the multiple statements for a resource are enclosed by the keywords BEGIN and END or by bracket symbols {}. The resource statement that starts the MENU multiple-line statement is similar to the single-line statements we've already seen. The definition for the MENU resource statement, right up to the point where the keyword BEGIN encloses the other statements for the resource definition, is as follows:

> MENU *NAMEID LOADOPTION MEMOPTION CODEPAGE*
> where
>> *NAMEID* is a unique name or integer used to identify the resource. This field is **required**.
>> *LOADOPTION* is an **optional** field that describes when to load the resource for the application. The default is LOADONCALL.
>> *MEMOPTION* is an **optional** field that describes how the resource is to be managed in memory. For menus this field has a default value of MOVEABLE.
>> *CODEPAGE* is an **optional** field that states the code page of the text.

The MENU resource statement can have different types of statements enclosed between the BEGIN and END keywords, but the slide puzzle application only uses the MENUITEM and SUBMENU statements. The SUBMENU statement is used to define the pull-down menus, while the MENUITEM statement is used to define items within a menu.

The SUBMENU statement is also a multiple-line statement; therefore, it en-

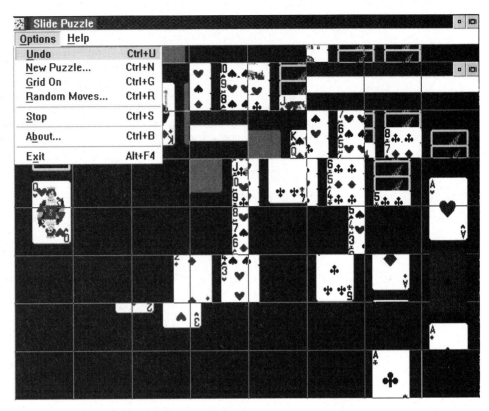

Screen 4-3. Slide puzzle option pull-down menu.

closes other statements with the keywords BEGIN and END. Following is the definition of the SUBMENU statement up to the point where the keyword BEGIN is used to enclose other statements:

SUBMENU *STRING,COMMAND,STYLES,ATTRIBUTES*

where

STRING is an ASCII string enclosed in double quotation marks and is used as the title for the pull-down menu. Within the string, you can use the tilde (~) symbol to precede the character the user may type to select the pull-down menu when the action bar window has input focus. The character marked with the tilde symbol will appear underlined. Make sure each character you mark with the tilde symbol is unique. The *STRING* field is **required**.

COMMAND is the value that is sent with either the WM_COMMAND, WM_HELP, or WM_SYSCOMMAND PM message to identify which menu item is being selected. This is a **required** field.

STYLES is an **optional** field that describes the style of the submenu. The style definitions all start with the MIS_prefix and can be OR'ed together. The default values for this field are MIS_SUBMENU and MIS_TEXT.

ATTRIBUTES is an **optional** field that defines the state of the menu; for instance, a menu can be checked or disabled. The attribute definitions all start with the MIA_ prefix and can be OR'ed together.

The SUBMENU statement can have MENUITEM statements, as well as other SUBMENU statements, within its BEGIN END area. The nesting of SUBMENU statements lets you provide cascading pull-down menus for your application. (The slide puzzle application does not implement cascading pull-down menus.) The MENUITEM statement is a single-line statement that is similar in definition to that of the SUBMENU statement. The MENUITEM statement definition is as follows:

MENUITEM *STRING,COMMAND,STYLES,ATTRIBUTES*
where

STRING is an ASCII string enclosed in double quotation marks and is used as the text for the menu item. Within the string, you can use the tilde (~) symbol to precede the character the user may type to select the menu item from the pull-down menu. The character marked with the tilde symbol will appear underlined. It is important that each character you mark with the tilde symbol is unique within the menu. MENUITEM statements can have two columns of text. You can insert "\a" in the *STRING* to right align the text in the second column. If you insert "\t" instead of "\a", the second column of text is left aligned. The *STRING* field is **required**.

COMMAND is the value that is sent with the WM_COMMAND, WM_HELP, or WM_SYSCOMMAND PM message to identify which menu item is being selected. This is a **required** field.

STYLES is an **optional** field that describes the style of the menu item. The style definitions all start with the MIS_prefix and can be OR'ed together. Examples of styles are MIS_TEXT, which indicates the display object is text; MIS_BITMAP, which indicates the display object is a bit-map; and MIS_SYSCOMMAND, which indicates Presentation Manager should notify your window procedure with a WM_SYSCOMMAND message. The defaults are MIS_TEXT and to notify your window procedure with a WM_COMMAND message.

ATTRIBUTES is an **optional** field that defines the state of the menu item; for instance, a menu item can be checked or disabled. The attribute definitions all start with the MIA_prefix and can be OR'ed together. Examples of attributes are MIA_CHECKED, which places a check mark (✓) next to the item if the state of the attribute is true; and MIA_DISABLE, which disables the item from being selected if the state of the attribute is true. When a menu item is disabled, it appears grayed in the pull-down menu and can not be selected.

Listing 4-5 shows the MENU statement used by the slide puzzle application resource script. As you see in this listing, the MENU statement uses an ID of ID_SLIDEFRAME. You may recall from the section on icons that this is the same ID that was assigned to the application icon. These resources share the same ID because the application wants to associate a set of resources (of different types) to the frame window. To do this, the resources must have the same ID as the frame window for which they were designed. Since the resources used by the frame window are of different types, no ID conflicts exist.

```
#include <os2.h>
#include "slider.h"
MENU ID_SLIDEFRAME
  BEGIN
  SUBMENU "~Options", IDM_OPT
    BEGIN
    MENUITEM "~Undo \tCtrl+U",              IDM_UNDO
    MENUITEM "~New Puzzle... \tCtrl+N",     IDM_NEW
    MENUITEM "~Grid On \tCtrl+G",           IDM_GRIDSTATE
    MENUITEM "~Random Moves... \tCtrl+R",   IDM_MOVES
    MENUITEM SEPARATOR
    MENUITEM "~Stop \tCtrl+S",              IDM_STOP
    MENUITEM SEPARATOR
    MENUITEM "~Product Information... \tCtrl+P", IDM_PRODUCT
    MENUITEM SEPARATOR
    MENUITEM "E~xit \tAlt+F4",              IDM_EXIT
    END
  SUBMENU "~Help", IDM_HELP, MIS_HELP
    BEGIN
    MENUITEM "~Help for help...",  IDM_HELP_FOR_HELP
    MENUITEM "~Extended help...",  SC_HELPEXTENDED,MIS_SYSCOMMAND
    MENUITEM "~Keys help...",      SC_HELPKEYS,MIS_SYSCOMMAND
    MENUITEM "Help ~index...",     SC_HELPINDEX,MIS_SYSCOMMAND
    END
  END
```

Listing 4-5. MENU resource statement.

Listing 4-5 shows that two menus are defined for the slide puzzle. As stated earlier, these menus are titled *Options* and *Help*. Within each SUBMENU statement, you can see the list of menu items defined for each menu. The Options pull-down menu is defined to have a second column that is left aligned. This second column contains a description of the key sequence available to activate items directly from the application without using the pull-down menu. The Options pull-down menu also has MENUITEM statements that don't follow the normal syntax. These MENUITEM statements are with the keyword SEPARATOR. In this special case, a horizontal line is placed across the pull-down menu to separate items. You may also notice that some items end with (...). This is a standard convention indicating to the user that more dialog will follow to complete the item.

To use pull-down menus, you must create the standard window with the frame flag FCF_MENU set. Look at the declaration of the variable called **ulFrameFlags** and you will see that the slide puzzle uses the FCF_MENU flag.

As stated earlier, a PM message will notify your window procedure of item selection. Depending on how an item is defined, your window procedure will receive either a WM_COMMAND, WM_SYSCOMMAND, or WM_HELP message. Listing 4-6 shows the routine used by the slide puzzle to process the WM_COMMAND message. This discussion only applies to the Options pull-down menu; the Help pull-down menu is discussed in Chapter 7, Implementing a Help Interface.

```
MRESULT EXPENTRY ClientWndProc(HWND hwnd, ULONG msg,
   MPARAM mp1, MPARAM mp2)
   {
   HBITMAP hbmt;
   HDC hdcbm;
   HPS hpsd;
   POINTL apt1[4];
   SIZEL sizl;
   SHORT x, y, i;
   POINTL shear, ptl;

   switch(msg){
      /********************************/
      /* Process pull-down menu items. */
      /********************************/
      case WM_COMMAND:
        switch (COMMANDMSG(&msg)->cmd){

           /**********************************/
           /* Process undo pull-down option. */
           /**********************************/
           case IDM_UNDO:
             forward=FALSE;
             WinSendMsg(WinWindowFromID(hwndFrame, FID_MENU),
               MM_SETITEMATTR,
                 MPFROM2SHORT(IDM_MOVES, TRUE),
                 MPFROM2SHORT(MIA_DISABLED, MIA_DISABLED));
             sUndoFlag=1;
             DosPostEventSem(hev);
             return(MRESULT)TRUE;


           /**********************************/
           /* Process stop pull-down option. */
           /**********************************/
           case IDM_STOP:
             if((sUndoFlag==1) || (sRandomFlag==1)){
               StopState=TRUE;
               WinSendMsg(WinWindowFromID(hwndFrame, FID_MENU),
                 MM_SETITEMATTR,
                 MPFROM2SHORT(IDM_UNDO, TRUE),
                 MPFROM2SHORT(MIA_DISABLED, 0));
               WinSendMsg(WinWindowFromID(hwndFrame, FID_MENU),
                 MM_SETITEMATTR,
```

```
                    MPFROM2SHORT(IDM_MOVES, TRUE),
                    MPFROM2SHORT(MIA_DISABLED, 0));
        }
      return(MRESULT)TRUE;

   /******************************************/
   /* Process random move pull-down option. */
   /******************************************/
   case IDM_MOVES:
      if(WinDlgBox(HWND_DESKTOP, hwnd, RandomDlgProc,
         0, IDD_RANDOM, &sMoves)){
         sRandomFlag=1;
         WinSendMsg(WinWindowFromID(hwndFrame, FID_MENU),
           MM_SETITEMATTR,
           MPFROM2SHORT(IDM_UNDO, TRUE),
           MPFROM2SHORT(MIA_DISABLED, MIA_DISABLED));
         DosPostEventSem(hev);
         }
      return(MRESULT)TRUE;

   /******************************************/
   /* Process new puzzle pull-down option. */
   /******************************************/
   case IDM_NEW:
      if(WinDlgBox(HWND_DESKTOP, hwnd, NewPuzzleDlgProc,
         0, IDD_NEWPUZZLE, &puzzle))
         WinStartTimer(hab, hwnd, ID_TIMER, puzzle.sCapTime*1000);
      return(MRESULT)TRUE;

   /***********************************/
   /* Process product pull-down option. */
   /***********************************/
   case IDM_PRODUCT:
      WinDlgBox(HWND_DESKTOP, hwnd, ProductDlgProc,
         0, IDD_PRODUCT, 0);
      return(MRESULT)TRUE;

   /***********************************/
   /* Process exit pull-down option. */
   /***********************************/
   case IDM_EXIT:
      WinPostMsg(hwnd, WM_QUIT, NULL, NULL);
      return(MRESULT)TRUE;

   /******************************************/
   /* Process grid state pull-down option. */
   /******************************************/
   case IDM_GRIDSTATE:
      sGridState=sGridState^1; /* Change grid state flag. */

      /************************************************/
      /* Check or uncheck menu item as appropriate. */
      /************************************************/
      if(!sGridState){
```

```
            WinSendMsg(WinWindowFromID(hwndFrame, FID_MENU),
              MM_SETITEMATTR,
              MPFROM2SHORT(IDM_GRIDSTATE, TRUE),
              MPFROM2SHORT(MIA_CHECKED, 0));
            }
        else {
            WinSendMsg(WinWindowFromID(hwndFrame, FID_MENU),
              MM_SETITEMATTR,
              MPFROM2SHORT(IDM_GRIDSTATE, TRUE),
              MPFROM2SHORT(MIA_CHECKED, MIA_CHECKED));
            }


        /*********************************/
        /* Get the master memory bit-map. */
        /*********************************/
        GpiResetPS(hpsMemory, GRES_ALL);
        GpiQueryBitmapParameters(hbmSrc, &bmpSrc);
        GpiSetBitmap(hpsMemory, hbmSrc);


        /************************************************/
        /* Set the mix to invert all pixels drawn and */
        /* then draw grid lines.                       */
        /************************************************/
        GpiSetMix(hpsMemory, FM_INVERT);
        for(lRow=0; lRow<=syPels/lcyMinMax; lRow++){
          ptl.x=0; ptl.y=lRow*lcyMinMax;
          GpiMove(hpsMemory, &ptl);
          ptl.x=sxPels;
          GpiLine(hpsMemory, &ptl);
          }
        for(lCol=0; lCol<=sxPels/lcxMinMax; lCol++){
          ptl.y=0; ptl.x=lCol*lcxMinMax;
          GpiMove(hpsMemory, &ptl);
          ptl.y=syPels;
          GpiLine(hpsMemory, &ptl);
          }
        WinInvalidateRect(hwnd, NULL, FALSE);
        return(MRESULT)TRUE;

      default:
        return WinDefWindowProc(hwnd, msg, mp1, mp2);
      }
    break;
  }


/*********************************************************/
/* Let default routine process message and return. */
/*********************************************************/
return WinDefWindowProc(hwnd, msg, mp1, mp2);
}
```

Listing 4-6. WM_COMMAND routine.

As you can see in Listing 4-6, the ID of the menu item is extracted from the mp1 message parameter and used to determine which menu item to process. If the item to be processed is the Undo option, a global variable named **forward** is set to FALSE. When this variable is set to FALSE, the slide function will not record moves. After this variable is set, a message is sent to the menu window to disable the Random Moves menu item.

By looking at the WinSendMsg function, you can see that the window handle for the menu is obtained by querying the frame window. This is done with a PM function called *WinWindowFromID* and using the keyword FID_MENU. The MM_SETITEMATTR command informs the menu window to set the attribute of a menu item. (The MM_SETITEMATTR command ID is one of several you can use to manipulate or retrieve menu information. By convention, predefined menu commands all start with the prefix MM_.) The first parameter for the MM_SETITEMATTR command passes two pieces of information: the ID of the menu item for which the command applies and an instruction to search all submenus and dialogs for the item ID if it is not found in the menu. (Dialogs are explained in the next chapter!) The second parameter for the MM_SETITEMATTR also passes two pieces of information: which attributes to be affected by the MM_SETITEMATTR command and whether these attributes are to be turned on or off. The data passed in this second parameter is bit-significant information.

Disabling the menu item causes it to be grayed and disallows the user to select the item. This is done so the user can <u>not</u> choose the Random Moves option while the Undo option is processing. The last two actions performed by this routine are setting the global variable **sUndoFlag** to 1 and posting an event semaphore. These actions tell another thread of execution to process Undo moves. This lets the Undo option perform in the background and allows this routine to finish so other PM messages can be processed. Chapter 8, Working with Time, explains how this other thread of execution is established and operates.

To process the Stop option, the global variable **StopState** is set to TRUE. This tells another thread of execution to stop processing and wait for further instructions. Two messages are then sent to the menu window to enable the Undo and Random Moves options. This is done without regard to the current state of these options.

To process the Random Moves option, a dialog box procedure is invoked to get information from the user about the number of moves to perform. Chapter 5, Message and Dialog Boxes, gives detailed information about how this dialog box procedure works. If the dialog box procedure obtains good information from the user, the Undo menu item is disabled while random moves are occurring. The global variable **sRandomFlag** is then set to 1 and an event semaphore is posted. These actions tell another thread of execution to process random moves, which allows the Random Moves option to perform in the background and this routine to finish so other PM messages can be processed. Chapter 8, Working with Time, explains how this other thread of execution is established and operates.

If the New Puzzle option from the Options pull-down menu is selected, the WM_COMMAND routine passes control to a dialog box procedure. This procedure receives more input from the user about the puzzle grid number and the amount of time to wait before the desktop image is captured. Chapter 5, Message and Dialog Boxes, gives detailed information about how this dialog box procedure works. If good information is returned by the dialog box procedure, a timer is started to time the requested delay. Chapter 8, Working with Time, discusses how this timer is set up and used by this routine. After the timer is set, the WM_COMMAND routine ends.

The Product Information option from the Options pull-down menu does nothing more than pass control to a dialog box procedure. As you'll see in the next chapter on dialog and message boxes, this particular dialog box procedure is extremely simple.

If the user selects the Exit option from the Options pull-down menu, the WM_COMMAND routine posts a WM_QUIT message to the frame window. This message causes the slide puzzle application to terminate.

Finally, if the user selects the Grid On option from the Options pull-down menu, a global variable **sGridState** is toggled to either a 0 or 1 value. If this variable is toggled to 0, a message is sent to the menu window to remove the check mark next to the Grid On menu item. If this variable is toggled to 1, a message is sent to the menu window to place a check mark next to the Grid On menu item. This check mark indicates that the state of the Grid is on. After the check mark is set or reset, the WM_COMMAND routine creates a memory device context and presentation space in which to place the master bit-map of the slide puzzle image. A mix is then set that causes pels to be inverted when lines are drawn in the memory presentation page. Once this mix is set, a series of horizontal and vertical lines comprising the grid are drawn. Because they are drawn by inverting pels, the grid lines appear to be toggled on and off every time this option is taken. After drawing is completed, resources are freed and the entire application client window area is invalidated. Invalidating the client area causes a WM_PAINT message to be sent; hence, the updated master bit-map image is displayed.

ACCELERATOR KEYS

The second column of the Options pull-down menu lists key sequences, as shown in Screen 4-3. These sequences let you choose menu items directly from the application without accessing the pull-down menu. Thus, when the user presses one of these key sequences, a WM_COMMAND, WM_SYSCOMMAND, or WM_HELP message is sent to the window procedure with the appropriate menu item ID.

These key sequences are resources called accelerator keys and are defined in a structure called an accelerator table. The resource statement used to define an accelerator table is a multiple-line statement called ACCELTABLE. The definition for the ACCELTABLE resource statement, up to the point where the keyword BEGIN is used to enclose the other resource definition statements, is as follows:

ACCELTABLE *NAMEID MEMOPTION*
where

NAMEID is a unique name or integer with which to identify the resource. This field is **required**.

MEMOPTION is an **optional** field that describes how the resource is to be managed in memory. For accelerator tables, this field has a default value of MOVEABLE.

The actual key definitions for an accelerator table are enclosed between the keywords BEGIN and END. Following is the definition of the accelerator key statement:

KEY, COMMAND, OPTIONS
where

KEY is the accelerator character code and can be either a constant or a character between double quotes. If you place a caret (^) symbol right before the character code, a CONTROL key sequence is used as part of the key definition. This field is **required**.

COMMAND is the value sent with the WM_COMMAND, WM_SYSCOMMAND or WM_HELP message to identify which menu item is to be processed. This value should be the same as the menu item ID you want to access with the key definition. This field is **required**.

OPTIONS is an **optional** field that specifies more detail about the accelerator key definition. For instance, you could use the keyword ALT to require the Alt key to be pressed as part of the accelerator definition; or you could use the keyword SYSCOMMAND to specify that the accelerator send the WM_SYSCOMMAND message instead of the WM_COMMAND message. Multiple options can be used in a single key definition. Unless otherwise specified, the WM_COMMAND message is sent.

To use accelerator keys, create the standard window with the frame flag FCF_ACCELTABLE or FCF_STANDARD set. In the slide puzzle, the FCF_ACCELTABLE flag is used in the declaration of the variable **ulFrameFlags**.

Listing 4-7 shows the accelerator table definition used by the slide puzzle application. Notice that ID_SLIDEFRAME is used to identify the accelerator table. This is the same resource ID used by the MENU and ICON statements and is the same ID as the application frame window.

```
#include <os2.h>
#include "slider.h"
ACCELTABLE ID_SLIDEFRAME
  BEGIN
  VK_F4,  IDM_EXIT, VIRTUALKEY, ALT
```

```
"^U",   IDM_UNDO
"^N",   IDM_NEW
"^G",   IDM_GRIDSTATE
"^R",   IDM_MOVES
"^S",   IDM_STOP
"^P",   IDM_PRODUCT
"^u",   IDM_UNDO
"^n",   IDM_NEW
"^g",   IDM_GRIDSTATE
"^r",   IDM_MOVES
"^s",   IDM_STOP
"^p",   IDM_PRODUCT
END
```

Listing 4-7. Accelerator table.

The first accelerator key definition shown in Listing 4-7 is for a function key. As you can see, keywords exist for the function key character codes. Because the function keys are considered virtual keys, you must specify them with the VIRTUALKEY keyword as one of the option fields. Listing 4-7 shows that when the Alt and F4 keys are pressed at the same time, the Exit menu item found in the Options pull-down menu is processed.

The rest of the accelerator key definitions shown in Listing 4-7 generate a WM_COMMAND message when the Ctrl key and the appropriate quoted character key are pressed simultaneously. Notice that uppercase and lowercase character codes are both defined for the accelerator keys so the user does not have to be concerned with shift state to access the menu items. Finally, notice that all the command IDs are the same as those defined in the MENU statement. This causes those particular menu items to be processed when the accelerator keys are pressed.

5

Message and Dialog Boxes

As your Presentation Manager application is being used, you may need to notify the user of a situation or supply the user with simple information. For instance, if the user selects an option that can destroy data, you may want to display a warning message informing the user of this situation and giving them an opportunity to reconsider the action.

At other times, your application may need to obtain information from the user in order to provide a service. As you've seen, one simple way of obtaining information from the user is by using pull-down menus. Often, however, the pull-down menu doesn't supply the appropriate level of function to retrieve all the necessary request information. For instance, if the user wants to open a file, your application needs to let the user select a file name from a list or enter a file name. A dialog box retrieves various types of information from the user so your application can service requests. As you may have noticed, dialog boxes are typically presented to gain more information about a pull-down menu item selection.

Message boxes and dialog boxes, like everything else we've seen, are just collections of windows. Notice, however, that their composition is a little different than the standard window. Message boxes and dialog boxes both have frame windows and children windows, but the children windows are control windows. Control windows are objects such as push buttons, radio buttons, entry fields, list boxes, and even simple text. Because control windows are windows, they must have window procedures to control their operation. Thankfully, Presentation Manager supplies all the window procedures for the standard control windows; Thus, the vast majority of the work needed to use the standard control windows is done by Presentation Manager. This doesn't mean that you can't create custom control windows, but you will find that Presentation Manager has a rich set of control windows already available for your use.

Dialog boxes can be either modal or modeless. A modeless dialog box operates independent from its owner or creator. Therefore, once the dialog box is started, the application that created the dialog box regains control and can continue to process other activities. By making a dialog box modeless, it appears to operate as a totally independent object. This feature is very handy in some cases but it can add complexity to your application. This added complexity comes from the asynchronous communication needed to work between your application window and the dialog box; however, because this extra communication is actually just more PM messages, it isn't very difficult to manage. The modal dialog box is more common and easier to implement. This is because when it is created, Presentation Manager doesn't return control to the creator until the dialog box is finished. The modal and modeless dialog boxes are analogous to the WinSendMsg and WinPostMsg functions in how they pass and return control to your application. The slide puzzle application shown in this book only uses modal dialog boxes.

MESSAGE BOXES

Message boxes are a subset of the function available in a dialog box. Since they only pass textual messages requiring minimal user interaction, the message box interface is very simple. A PM function called *WinMessageBox* is used to display a message box. This function has several parameters that let you define how the message box will look and which type of pushbuttons it will possess. Following is the definition of the WinMessageBox function:

WinMessageBox(*Parent,Owner,Text,Title,Window,Style*);
where

Parent is the parent window handle for which the message box is to be created. Typically, you will use the desktop window handle, HWND_DESKTOP, for this parameter. By using the HWND_DESKTOP handle, you can move the message box window around the screen where ever you like.

Owner is the handle of the window that actually owns the message box, such as your application window frame.

Text is the character string for the message to be displayed in the message box.

Title is the character string used in the title bar area of the message box window. This character string should be no more than 40 characters.

Window is an ID for the message box window.

Style determines the controls, operation, and icon used for the message box. This value is set by OR'ing various predefined values together. For instance, to select a pushbutton group that has both the YES and NO pushbuttons, use the predefined value MB_YESNO. To indicate the message is asking a question, OR the predefined value MB_ICONQUESTION with the MB_YESNO value. These predefined message box values all begin with the prefix MB_ and are placed in groups. From each possible group, use only one value for your message box. Following is a list of the predefined message box values and their descriptions by group:

Button Group

MB_OK	OK pushbutton
MB_OKCANCEL	OK and CANCEL pushbuttons
MB_CANCEL	CANCEL pushbutton
MB_ENTER	ENTER pushbutton
MB_ENTERCANCEL	ENTER and CANCEL pushbuttons
MB_RETRYCANCEL	RETRY and CANCEL pushbuttons
MB_ABORTRETRYIGNORE	ABORT, RETRY, and IGNORE pushbuttons
MB_YESNO	YES and NO pushbuttons
MB_YESNOCANCEL	YES, NO, and CANCEL pushbuttons

Help Button

MB_HELP	HELP pushbutton

Color or Icon

MB_NOICON	no icon
MB_ICONHAND	circle with cross icon
MB_ICONQUESTION	question mark icon
MB_ICONEXCLAMATION	exclamation point icon
MB_ICONASTERISK	asterisk icon
MB_INFORMATION	"i" in a square box
MB_QUERY	question mark

Default Action

MB_DEFBUTTON1	first button is the default selection
MB_DEFBUTTON2	second button is the default selection
MB_DEFBUTTON3	third button is the default selection

Modality Indicator

MB_APPLMODAL	message box is application modal
MB_SYSTEMMODAL	message box is system modal

Mobility Indicator

MB_MOVABLE	message box has a title bar and system menu

Presentation Manager also has predefined values for all the message box return values. These predefined return values all start with the prefix MBID_ and describe the pushbutton the user selected in the message box. Following is a list of the predefined return values for a message box and their descriptions:

MBID_ENTER	ENTER pushbutton selected
MBID_OK	OK pushbutton selected
MBID_CANCEL	CANCEL pushbutton selected
MBID_ABORT	ABORT pushbutton selected
MBID_RETRY	RETRY pushbutton selected
MBID_IGNORE	IGNORE pushbutton selected
MBID_YES	YES pushbutton selected
MBID_NO	NO pushbutton selected
MBID_ERROR	error occurred

Screen 5-1 shows an example of a message box displayed by the slide puzzle application. In this example, the message box is displayed because the user entered to large a number; hence, this message is only informational and the user only needs to select the OK pushbutton to proceed.

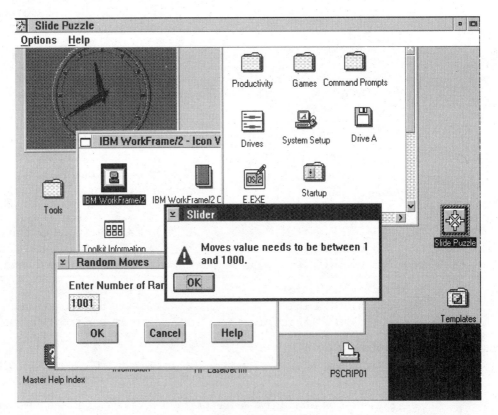

Screen 5-1. Slide puzzle message box.

The single line of code used to produce the message box shown in Screen 5-1 is as follows:

```
WinMessageBox(HWND_DESKTOP, hwnd,
  (PSZ)"Moves value needs to be between 1 and 1000.",
  (PSZ)"Slider",0,
  MB_MOVEABLE | MB_OK | MB_ICONEXCLAMATION);
```

Because the message box shown in Screen 5-1 was created with MB_MOVEABLE, it has a title bar and system menu bar. Having the title bar and system menu bar lets the user move the message box around the desktop, thus allowing the user to see what is underneath. The MB_OK value caused the message box to have only an OK pushbutton; hence, there isn't anything worth testing on return from the WinMessageBox function. Finally, the exclamation point icon is caused by the MB_ICONEXCLAMATION value.

DIALOG BOXES

As stated earlier, a dialog box is composed of a frame window and a collection of control windows. Presentation Manager has a set of predefined control windows and window procedures for each of them. Dialog boxes are discussed in this book **only** in terms of the predefined control window types. When creating a dialog box, you must first define its composition. This is done by creating a dialog box template which is a resource that can be included into your resource script. Most dialog box templates, however, are created outside of the resource script in their own ASCII source file. This ASCII source file has an extension of **.DLG** by convention and is included in the resource script with a statement called *rcinclude*. Therefore, our slide puzzle dialog templates are included into the resource script with the following statement found in the SLIDER.RC source file:

```
rcinclude  dialog.dlg
```

The dialog template is a multiple line resource statement identified with the keyword DLGTEMPLATE. Following is the definition of the DLGTEMPLATE resource statement up to the BEGIN keyword:

> DLGTEMPLATE *resourceid loadoption memoption codepage*
> where
>> *resourceid* is a unique integer used to identify the dialog box resource. This field is **required**.
>> *loadoption* specifies when the resource is loaded. This is an **optional** parameter with a default of LOADONCALL.
>> *memoption* specifies how the resource is to be managed in memory. This is an **optional** parameter with a default of MOVEABLE.

codepage is the code page of the text in the dialog box. This is an **optional** parameter that uses the currently defined code page.

The first statement enclosed between the BEGIN and END keywords for the DLGTEMPLATE resource statement is the DIALOG statement. The DIALOG resource statement is a multiple-line resource statement used to define a dialog box window to be created by your application. Following is the definition of the DIALOG resource statement up to the BEGIN keyword:

DIALOG *title,id,x,y,width,height,style,frameflags*
where

title is a string enclosed in double quotes that will be displayed in the dialog box title bar if one exists.

id is an identifier for the dialog box frame. It is common to use the dialog template resource ID for this ID.

x is the horizontal coordinate in dialog coordinates of the lower left corner of the dialog box. The origin of the coordinate system is usually from the origin of the parent window; however, the box styles FCF_SCREENALIGN and FCF_MOUSEALIGN can change the coordinate system.

y is the vertical coordinate in dialog coordinates of the lower left corner of the dialog box. The origin of the coordinate system is usually from the origin of the parent window; however, the box styles FCF_SCREENALIGN and FCF_MOUSEALIGN can change the coordinate system.

width is the dialog box width in dialog coordinates.

height is the dialog box height in dialog coordinates.

style is any additional window, frame, or class specific style. The default style is WS_SYNCPAINT | WS_CLIPSIBLINGS | WS_SAVEBITS | FS_DLGBORDER.

frameflags is the frame creation flags for the dialog box.

From this definition, you can see that a frame window and some of its children windows are being defined for the dialog box. The term *dialog coordinate* is a unit of measure based on the default character cell size. A unit in the horizontal direction is one-fourth the default character cell width, and a unit in the vertical direction is one-eighth the default character cell height. The last part of the definition needed for the dialog box is for the control windows found within the dialog box frame window. These definitions are enclosed by the BEGIN and END keywords for the DIALOG resource statement. Following is the definition for the resource statement used to define control windows:

controltype text,id,x,y,width,height,style
where

controltype describes the type of control window being defined. Examples of some popular control window types are LTEXT, PUSHBUTTON, ICON, LISTBOX, RADIOBUTTON, and ENTRYFIELD. For a complete list of control window types and their styles, refer to a PM technical reference.

text is a string enclosed in double quotes that will be displayed in the control window. Note that some control window types do not have text associated with them.

id is an unique identifier for the control window.

x is the horizontal coordinate in dialog coordinates of the lower left corner of the control. The coordinate is relative to the origin of the dialog box.

y is the vertical coordinate in dialog coordinates of the lower left corner of the control. The coordinate is relative to the origin of the dialog box.

width is the width of the control in dialog coordinates.

height is the height of the control in dialog coordinates.

style is any additional class specific style.

As you can see from the definition for a control window, several different types of control windows exist and each one of them must be located within the dialog box. Each control window must also have a size associated with it.

As you define control windows, you should understand the style keywords *WS_GROUP* and *WS_TABSTOP*. These two keywords are of particular interest because they define how input focus is passed for the dialog. If you use the WS_TABSTOP style in a control window definition, the control window gains input focus when the tab key is pressed. When there are multiple control window definitions with the WS_TABSTOP style, the order of their definitions determines the order of input focus change. The WS_GROUP style controls the change of input focus when the cursor keys are used. For example, if you keep pressing the Up or Down Arrow keys while in a group of radio buttons, the input focus will keep cycling through that group of buttons. To define a group of control windows, the **first and only the first** control window in the group uses the WS_GROUP style. The next control window in the dialog template that uses the WS_GROUP style terminates the current group and starts a new one.

You can also define control windows by replacing the controltype parameter with the keyword CONTROL and inserting a window class parameter into the definition. With this other definition, you can use all the predefined control windows, as well as provide custom control windows. Since this book only shows predefined control windows, refer to a PM technical reference for a more explicit definition of this method.

Listing 5-1 shows a simple dialog box definition. This definition is the dialog box used by the slide puzzle application when Product Information is requested from the Options pull-down menu. As you can see, creating even a simple dialog box definition with a regular text editor can be a tedious task. The result of this dialog box definition is shown in Screen 5-2.

You can use a regular text editor to create dialog box definitions, but the IBM Developer's Toolkit for OS/2 2.0 has a tool that makes this task much easier. This tool is called the Dialog Editor and can be found in the development tools folder. This tool will allow you to create or change all the dialog boxes for your application and help manage the IDs associated with the different parts of the dialogs.

```
DLGTEMPLATE IDD_PRODUCT LOADONCALL MOVEABLE DISCARDABLE
BEGIN
    DIALOG   "Product Information", IDD_PRODUCT, 10, 9, 295, 98, WS_VISIBLE,
             FCF_SYSMENU | FCF_TITLEBAR
    BEGIN
        ICON         ID_SLIDEFRAME, ID_SLIDEFRAME, 19, 71, 21, 16, WS_GROUP
        LTEXT        "Learning To Program OS/2 2.0", 101, 82, 82, 135, 8
        LTEXT        "Presentation Manager By Example", 102, 73, 74, 152,
                     8
        LTEXT        "(Putting The Pieces Together)", 103, 85, 66, 128, 8
        LTEXT        "(C) Copyright Van Nostrand Reinhold 1992.  All Righ"
                     "ts Reserved.", 104, 9, 31, 278, 8
        PUSHBUTTON   "OK", DID_OK, 128, 9, 40, 14
        LTEXT        " Stephen A. Knight", 106, 103, 49, 86, 8
    END
END
```

Listing 5-1. Product Information dialog template.

To create window controls with the Dialog Editor, select the desired type of control window either from a palette of control windows or from a list. Once you've created a new control window, you can tailor its definition with options found in

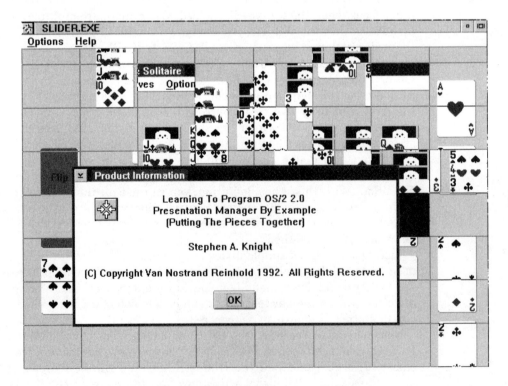

Screen 5-2. Product Information dialog box.

the Dialog Editor's pull-down menus and entry fields found below the Editors action bar.

Once you have defined some control windows, you may want to move or resize them. Like many other graphic editors, the Dialog Editor lets you select one or more objects (or control windows) and manipulate them. For instance, to move a control window, click mouse button 1 on the control window to select it and then use the mouse to drag it around the dialog box. To resize a control window, select the chosen window. Markers will then be displayed on its borders. By dragging a marker with the mouse, you will be resizing the control window in the direction of your mouse movement.

To select a group of control windows with the Dialog Box editor, mark a rectangular area around the group of control windows by pressing and holding mouse button 1, moving the mouse to the opposite corner of the rectangular area, and then releasing the mouse button. Doing this places markers around the borders of the selected control windows. You can now drag all the objects as a single unit. You can also arrange the objects relative to each other with options found in the Arrange pull-down menu.

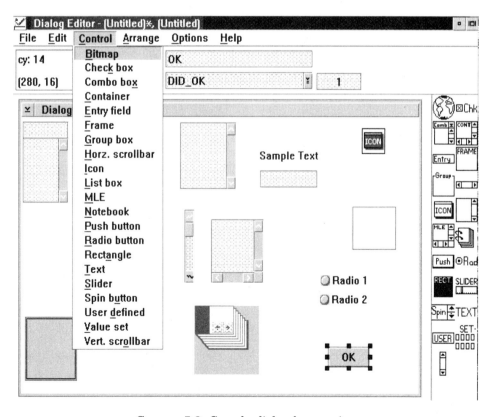

Screen 5-3. Sample dialog box session.

When you decide to save and exit your Dialog Editor session, your edits are placed in an ASCII source file of your choice. By viewing this source file with a regular program editor, you can see that it follows the syntax described in the dialog template definitions.

The Dialog Editor has many features that make working with dialog box definitions a snap! Not all of these features have been discussed here, but hopefully enough have been described to give you an idea of the tool's capability. To get an even better idea of what this tool has to offer, examine Screen 5-3, which shows a sample session using the Dialog Editor. Here you can see the list of potential control window types and the topics that are available from the tool's action bar.

Besides the Product Information dialog box, the slide puzzle application has two more dialog boxes defined for selecting the number of random moves and new puzzle parameters. These dialog box definitions are a little more complex than the Product Information dialog box because they have a number of control windows of different types, styles, and groupings. Listing 5-2 shows the largest dialog definition for the slide puzzle application. This definition is for the New Puzzle pull-down menu option. From this listing, you can see that this dialog has text, two entry fields, and three pushbuttons. You can also see that grouping is used for the entry fields and pushbuttons.

The last thing of interest for the New Puzzle dialog definition is the style of the Help pushbutton. This pushbutton will be used to obtain field level help for the dialog. Field level help provides information about the control window with current input focus. Define the Help pushbutton with the BS_NOPOINTERFOCUS style so that input focus doesn't change when you click on it. Also, because our program uses a PM service called the Information Presentation Facility, our application doesn't need to be directly involved in displaying the help information! To notify this facility that a Help pushbutton has been selected, however, you must use the style BS_HELP. Chapter 7, Providing a Help Interface, describes how the Information Presentation Facility works. Screen 5-4 shows the dialog box presented for the New Puzzle dialog definition.

```
DLGTEMPLATE IDD_NEWPUZZLE LOADONCALL MOVEABLE DISCARDABLE
BEGIN
    DIALOG    "New Puzzle",IDD_NEWPUZZLE,80,64,191,84,WS_VISIBLE,
              FCF_SYSMENU | FCF_TITLEBAR
    BEGIN
        LTEXT             "Enter Time Delay In Seconds.  (1-60)",301,7,71,
                          159,8
        ENTRYFIELD        "12",IDD_TIMEEDIT,10,60,18,8,ES_MARGIN
        LTEXT             "Grid Number.  (4-25)",303,7,41,96,8,NOT
                          WS_GROUP
        ENTRYFIELD        "12",IDD_GRIDEDIT,10,30,18,8,ES_MARGIN
        PUSHBUTTON        "OK",DID_OK,15,6,40,14,WS_GROUP
        PUSHBUTTON        "Cancel",DID_CANCEL,75,6,40,14
        PUSHBUTTON        "Help",ID_HELP,137,6,40,14,BS_HELP |
                          BS_NOPOINTERFOCUS
    END
END
```

Listing 5-2. New Puzzle dialog template.

Once you have created your dialog box definitions and compiled them with the resource compiler, you must add code to your PM application to start them when needed. A PM function called WinDlgBox is used to start dialogs. Like the WinMessageBox function, the *WinDlgBox* function has parameters that identify a parent window handle and an owner window handle; you will usually specify HWND_DESKTOP for the parent so you can move the dialog around the entire screen. Because dialog boxes are resources, there are parameters in the WinDlgBox function that let you identify the resource ID of the dialog box being started and whether this resource is found in the .EXE file or DLL. (The dialog boxes for the slide puzzle application are built as part of the program's .EXE file.) The last couple parameters for the WinDlgBox function define a procedure that you must provide to interface with the dialog box and information to pass to this procedure.

The procedure for your dialog box is called a dialog procedure. Don't get nervous about the dialog procedure. It looks a lot like your client window procedure but, in many ways, is much easier! This is because you don't paint a client area; instead, your dialog procedure communicates with the different types of control windows by sending and receiving messages. As you will see, these control windows are very functional! Before we discuss the definition and content of the dialog procedure, look at Listing 5-3 to see how the slide puzzle application starts its dialogs.

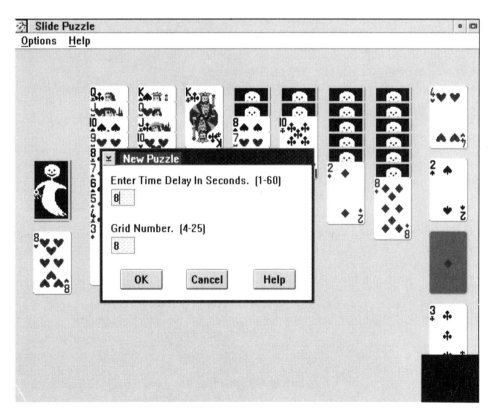

Screen 5-4. New Puzzle dialog box.

```
MRESULT EXPENTRY ClientWndProc(HWND hwnd, ULONG msg,
 MPARAM mp1, MPARAM mp2)
{
switch(msg){
  /********************************/
  /* Process pull-down menu items. */
  /********************************/
  case WM_COMMAND:
    switch (COMMANDMSG(&msg)->cmd){
      /*******************************************/
      /* Process random move pull-down option. */
      /*******************************************/
      case IDM_MOVES:
        if(WinDlgBox(HWND_DESKTOP, hwnd, RandomDlgProc,
          0, IDD_RANDOM, &sMoves)){
          sRandomFlag=1;
          WinSendMsg(WinWindowFromID(hwndFrame, FID_MENU),
           MM_SETITEMATTR,
           MPFROM2SHORT(IDM_UNDO, TRUE),
           MPFROM2SHORT(MIA_DISABLED, MIA_DISABLED));
          }

        return(MRESULT)TRUE;
      /*****************************************/
      /* Process new puzzle pull-down option. */
      /*****************************************/
      case IDM_NEW:
        if(WinDlgBox(HWND_DESKTOP, hwnd, NewPuzzleDlgProc,
          0, IDD_NEWPUZZLE, &puzzle))
          WinStartTimer(hab, hwnd, ID_TIMER, puzzle.sCapTime*1000);
        return(MRESULT)TRUE;


      /***********************************/
      /* Process product pull-down option. */
      /***********************************/
      case IDM_PRODUCT:
        WinDlgBox(HWND_DESKTOP, hwnd, ProductDlgProc,
          0, IDD_PRODUCT, 0);
        return(MRESULT)TRUE;

      default:
        return WinDefWindowProc(hwnd, msg, mp1, mp2);
    } break;
  }


/**********************************************************/
/* Let default routine process message and return. */
/**********************************************************/
return WinDefWindowProc(hwnd, msg, mp1, mp2);
}
```

Listing 5-3. Starting the slide puzzle dialog boxes.

As you can see from Listing 5-3, there are three dialogs for the slide puzzle application that are all started because of menu item selections. When the Random Moves option is selected from the Options pull-down menu, the dialog box defined in the resource script as IDD_RANDOM is started and is associated with a dialog procedure named **RandomDlgProc**. Notice that the address of the variable named **sMoves** is also passed with the WinDlgBox function. The WinDlgBox function lets you pass initialization information to the dialog procedure by passing the address of a variable or structure. For the Random Moves dialog, the slide puzzle application passes the current number of random moves defined for the option; in turn, the dialog procedure initializes the control window structures so you can see the desired information when the dialog box is presented.

The New Puzzle option also shows the concept of passing initialization information to a dialog procedure. The dialog procedure for the New Puzzle option is named **NewPuzzleDlgProc** and the dialog box is defined as IDD_NEWPUZZLE in the resource script. In this case, however, more than one piece of initialization data is passed. This is done by passing the address of a structure named **puzzle** in which a time delay and grid number are defined.

Finally, the Product Information option displays a dialog box defined as IDD_PRODUCT in the resource script. The dialog procedure for this option is named **ProductDlgProc**. In this case, no initialization data is passed; hence, the address of the initialization data is NULL.

In your program, the definition of a dialog procedure is identical to that of your client area window procedure. For the slide puzzle application, the window procedure and dialog procedure definitions are as follows:

```
FNWP ClientWndProc;
FNWP ProductDlgProc;
FNWP RandomDlgProc;
FNWP NewPuzzleDlgProc;
```

The structure of the dialog procedure is similar to that of your client window procedure or WinProc. Just like your window procedure, the dialog procedure receives messages, chooses which messages it needs to process with a switch statement, and passes messages it doesn't need to process to Presentation Manager. The basic difference between these procedures is that instead of using the PM function WinDefWindowProc to pass messages to Presentation Manager, the dialog procedure uses a PM function called *WinDefDlgProc*.

The first message your dialog procedure receives after a dialog box is created is the WM_INITDLG message. The WM_INITDLG message passes a pointer to initialization data in the mp2 message parameter. This pointer is the one supplied as a parameter in the WinDlgBox function for dialog box creation. Typically, initialization data is information used to set information in the control windows. The method used to initialize control windows depends on the control window type. For instance, if the control window you want to initialize is a radio button, use a PM function called *WinSendDlgItem*. This function lets you send a message to a control window. In the case of the radio button, send a BM_SETCHECK message to the appropriate control window ID. The BM_SETCHECK message has parameter information that determines the state of the button control window. If the control window you want to initialize is an entry field, use a PM function called *WinSetDlgItemText*. This function lets you pass a text string to a control window ID.

If no initialization data is passed with the WM_INITDLG message, you can still use this opportunity to provide default values for the dialog procedure's variables or set the initial input focus to a particular control window. Input focus can be set to a specific control window with a PM function called *WinSetFocus*. On return from processing the WM_INITDLG message, however, you need to return a value of 1. If you don't return a value of 1, the default control window for input focus will still be used. (The mp1 parameter for the WM_INITDLG message has the window handle for the default control window for input focus.) If you have no initialization requirements for your dialog box, you may choose not to process the WM_INITDLG message.

Once the dialog box has been initialized, your dialog procedure receives notification messages from the control windows in the same way as your client window procedure does from other windows; hence, control windows send notification information to your dialog procedure by way of the WM_COMMAND or WM_CONTROL messages. To understand what may be sent your dialog procedure, you need to become familiar with the various types of control window notification information. You should also know what messages you may send to the different types of control windows. These different notification and message types can be found in a PM technical reference and are grouped together; for instance, to interface with a list box control window, use should become familiar with the predefined messages that start with the prefix LM_. When you discover the numerous notification and message types you can send or receive from standard control windows, you will understand the tremendous amount of function they provide.

When you are finished interfacing with a dialog box's control windows and want to terminate the dialog, use a PM function called *WinDismissDlg*. Most likely, the dialog will terminate because a pushbutton was pressed. The WinDismissDlg function terminates the dialog, and in the case of a modal dialog, returns control to the window procedure that started it.

Listing 5-4 shows the dialog procedures used by the slide puzzle application. The first dialog procedure shown in this listing is named ProductDlgProc and is used for the Product Information pull-down menu option. This dialog box displays copyright information for this book. Because this dialog box is composed of text, an icon, and a pushbutton, there is no need to initialize the dialog; in fact, all this dialog procedure does is look for the pushbutton notification and then terminate the dialog. The only pushbutton for this dialog box has an ID of DID_OK; hence, the only ID looked for in the WM_COMMAND messages is DID_OK. Notice that all other messages for this dialog are processed by using the WinDefDlgProc function.

The second dialog procedure shown in Listing 5-4 is named RandomDlgProc and is used for the Random Moves pull-down menu option. This dialog box lets the user specify the number of random moves to perform. It is composed of text, an edit box, and some pushbuttons. In this case, the dialog procedure wants to initialize the entry field with a default random move string. This initialization is done during the processing of the WM_INITDLG message. When the WM_INITDLG message is received, this procedure makes a pointer from the mp2 message parameter which references the default value to be placed in the entry field. This value is converted to a character string in a temporary variable named *szTemp* which is then used to initialize the entry field with the WinSetDlgItemText function.

After initialization is complete, the RandomDlgProc dialog procedure waits for notification from either the OK or Cancel pushbutton. These pushbuttons are identified by the window IDs DID_OK and DID_CANCEL. If notification is received from the OK pushbutton, this procedure retrieves text information from the entry field with a PM function called *WinQueryDlgItemText* and converts it to a value. The value is saved in a variable named **sTemp** and is then tested to see if it is in a valid range. If the value is valid, it is copied back to the creator's data area and the dialog is dismissed with a TRUE return value. If the value is invalid, a message box is presented and the dialog continues. If the RandomDlgProc dialog procedure receives notification from the Cancel pushbutton, the dialog is dismissed with a FALSE return value. In this case, no information is copied back to the creator's data area. This leaves the default random moves value in its original state. The FALSE return value indicates to the creator not to process the Random Moves option.

Notice that the entry field window procedure manages all the keyboard input and character drawing. Pretty neat! It even gets better with controls such as list boxes.

```
/*******************************************/
/* Product information dialog procedure. */
/*******************************************/
MRESULT EXPENTRY ProductDlgProc(HWND hwnd, ULONG msg,
  MPARAM mp1, MPARAM mp2){
  switch(msg) {
    case WM_COMMAND:
      switch(COMMANDMSG(&msg)->cmd){
        case DID_OK:
          WinDismissDlg(hwnd, TRUE);
          return(MRESULT)TRUE;
        }
      break;
    }
  return WinDefDlgProc(hwnd, msg, mp1, mp2);
  }


/*********************************/
/* Random moves dialog procedure. */
/*********************************/
```

```
MRESULT EXPENTRY RandomDlgProc(HWND hwnd, ULONG msg,
  MPARAM mp1, MPARAM mp2)
  {
  static SHORT FAR *prandom;
  CHAR szTemp[6];
  SHORT sTemp;
  switch (msg) {
    /***********************/
    /* Initialize dialog. */
    /***********************/
    case WM_INITDLG:
      prandom=PVOIDFROMMP(mp2);
      sprintf(szTemp, "%d\0", *prandom);
      WinSetDlgItemText(hwnd, IDD_MOVEEDIT, (PSZ)szTemp);
      return(MRESULT)OL;

    /**************************/
    /* Process notifications. */
    /**************************/
    case WM_COMMAND:
      switch (COMMANDMSG(&msg)->cmd) {

        /**************************/
        /* Process OK pushbutton. */
        /**************************/
        case DID_OK:
          WinQueryDlgItemText(hwnd, IDD_MOVEEDIT, 5, (PSZ)szTemp);
          sTemp=atoi(szTemp);
          if((sTemp<1) || (sTemp>1000)){
            WinMessageBox(HWND_DESKTOP, hwnd,
            (PSZ)"Moves value needs to be between 1 and 1000.",
            (PSZ)"Random Moves", 0,
            MB_MOVEABLE | MB_OK | MB_ICONEXCLAMATION);
            }
          else {
            *prandom=sTemp;
            WinDismissDlg(hwnd, TRUE);
            }
          return(MRESULT)TRUE;

          /******************************/
          /* Process Cancel pushbutton. */
          /******************************/
          case DID_CANCEL:
            WinDismissDlg(hwnd, FALSE);
            return(MRESULT)TRUE;
          }
        break;
      }
    return WinDefDlgProc(hwnd, msg, mp1, mp2);
    }

/******************************/
/* New puzzle dialog procedure. */
/******************************/
```

```
MRESULT EXPENTRY NewPuzzleDlgProc(HWND hwnd, ULONG msg,
  MPARAM mp1, MPARAM mp2)
  {
  static struct PUZZLEPARMS FAR *pnew;
  CHAR szTemp[5];
  SHORT sTemp;
  switch (msg) {

  /**********************/
  /* Initialize dialog. */
  /**********************/
  case WM_INITDLG:
    pnew=PVOIDFROMMP(mp2);
    sprintf(szTemp, "%d\0", pnew->sCapTime);
    WinSetDlgItemText(hwnd, IDD_TIMEEDIT, (PSZ)szTemp);
    sprintf(szTemp, "%d\0", pnew->sGrid);
    WinSetDlgItemText(hwnd, IDD_GRIDEDIT, (PSZ)szTemp);
    WinSetFocus(HWND_DESKTOP, WinWindowFromID(hwnd, IDD_GRIDEDIT));
    return(MRESULT)1L;

  /*************************/
  /* Process notifications. */
  /*************************/
  case WM_COMMAND:
    switch (COMMANDMSG(&msg)->cmd){

      /************************/
      /* Process OK pushbutton. */
      /************************/
      case DID_OK:
        WinQueryDlgItemText(hwnd, IDD_TIMEEDIT, 5, (PSZ)szTemp);
        sTemp=atoi(szTemp);
        if((sTemp<1) || (sTemp>60)){
          WinMessageBox(HWND_DESKTOP, hwnd,
          (PSZ)"Time value needs to be between 1 and 60.",
          (PSZ)"New Puzzle", 0,
          MB_MOVEABLE | MB_OK | MB_ICONEXCLAMATION);
          return(MRESULT)TRUE;
          }
        pnew->sCapTime=sTemp;
        WinQueryDlgItemText(hwnd, IDD_GRIDEDIT, 5, (PSZ)szTemp);
        sTemp=atoi(szTemp);
        if((sTemp<4) || (sTemp>25)){
          WinMessageBox(HWND_DESKTOP, hwnd,
          (PSZ)"Grid value needs to be between 4 and 25.",
          (PSZ)"New Puzzle", 0,
          MB_MOVEABLE | MB_OK | MB_ICONEXCLAMATION);
          return(MRESULT)TRUE;
          }
        pnew->sGrid=sTemp;
        WinDismissDlg(hwnd, TRUE);
        return(MRESULT)TRUE;

      /*****************************/
      /* Process Cancel pushbutton. */
      /*****************************/
```

```
      case DID_CANCEL:
        WinDismissDlg(hwnd, FALSE);
        return(MRESULT)TRUE;
      }
    break;
  }
  return WinDefDlgProc(hwnd, msg, mp1, mp2);
}
```

Listing 5-4. Slide puzzle dialog procedures.

The third dialog procedure shown in Listing 5-4 is named NewPuzzleDlgProc
and is used for the New Puzzle pull-down menu option. This dialog box lets the
user specify a time delay before a new screen image is captured and a grid
number for the number of puzzle pieces. It is composed of text, two entry fields,
and some pushbuttons. Like the RandomDlgProc dialog procedure, this procedure
also initializes its entry fields with default strings. It does this the same way as
the RandomDlgProc dialog procedure, but the values used for initialization are
taken from a structure instead of a single variable. Another difference in processing the WM_INITDLG message is that this procedure sets the initial input focus
to a particular control window. This control window is the grid number entry field
and is set with the WinSetFocus function. Also, notice that the WM_INITDLG
message routine returns a value of 1. If the return value were to remain 0, the
input focus would not change from the default control window.

The rest of the NewPuzzleDlgProc dialog procedure is similar to that of the
RandomDlgProc dialog procedure. The only difference is that the logic for the
NewPuzzleDlgProc dialog procedure is based on two entry fields instead of one
and the limits for the converted values are different.

WINDOW SUBCLASSING

When working with a control window like an entry field, you'll notice that its
window procedure manages all the keyboard input and paints the window area
as needed. The problem with this is that you may not want the exact function
provided by the window procedure and, thus, may want to modify its behavior.
The behavior of a window is caused by the messages it receives. Therefore, if you
could monitor all the messages sent to a window procedure and modify, filter, or
add messages before the window procedure received them, you could change the
window's behavior. This is exactly what window subclassing lets you do.

With window subclassing, you can subclass a single window or an entire window class. To create a window subclass, you need to provide a subclass procedure
and use a PM function called *WinSubclassWindow* to chain this procedure into
the message path for the window or window class to be modified. The parameters
required by the WinSubclassWindow function are the address of the subclass
procedure and the handle of the window to monitor. The WinSubclassWindow
function returns the address of the original window procedure that is being
monitored. After the WinSubclassWindow function is executed, all messages in-

tended for the original window procedure are sent to the subclass procedure instead. To stop subclassing a window, simply use the WinSubclassWindow function again with the original window's address!

It is the responsibility of the subclass procedure to modify, filter, or pass on the messages to the original window procedure as it sees fit. To filter a message, the subclass procedure performs a regular return statement. To pass a message to the original procedure, the subclass procedure executes the following:

```
(*originalProc)(hwnd,msg,mp1,mp2);
```

The slide puzzle program performs window subclassing on the entry fields for its dialog boxes. It does this because the user should only enter digits into these entry fields; therefore, the subclass procedure filters out all keystroke characters that are not digits. By doing this, the user is then less likely to enter bad information into the dialog boxes. Listing 5-5 demonstrates this with one of the slide puzzle dialog boxes.

```
PFNWP pfwnField1;
/***********************************************/
/* Window Procedure Entry Point Definitions. */
/***********************************************/
FNWP RandomDlgProc;
FNWP NumberSubProc1;


/**********************************/
/* Random moves dialog procedure. */
/**********************************/
MRESULT EXPENTRY RandomDlgProc(HWND hwnd, ULONG msg,
  MPARAM mp1, MPARAM mp2)
  {
  static SHORT FAR *prandom;
  CHAR szTemp[6];
  SHORT sTemp;
  switch (msg) {

    /*********************/
    /* Initialize dialog. */
    /*********************/
    case WM_INITDLG:
      prandom=PVOIDFROMMP(mp2);
      pfwnField1=WinSubclassWindow(
        WinWindowFromID(hwnd, IDD_MOVEEDIT), NumberSubProc1);
      sprintf(szTemp, "%d\0", *prandom);
      WinSetDlgItemText(hwnd, IDD_MOVEEDIT, (PSZ)szTemp);
      return(MRESULT)0L;

    /************************/
    /* Process notifications. */
    /************************/
    case WM_COMMAND:
      switch (COMMANDMSG(&msg)->cmd) {
```

```
/*************************/
/* Process OK pushbutton. */
/*************************/
case DID_OK:
  WinQueryDlgItemText(hwnd, IDD_MOVEEDIT, 5, (PSZ)szTemp);
  sTemp=atoi(szTemp);
  if((sTemp<1) || (sTemp>1000)){
    WinMessageBox(HWND_DESKTOP, hwnd,
    (PSZ)"Moves value needs to be between 1 and 1000.",
    (PSZ)"Random Moves", 0,
    MB_MOVEABLE | MB_OK | MB_ICONEXCLAMATION);
    }
  else {
    *prandom=sTemp;
    WinSubclassWindow(
      WinWindowFromID(hwnd, IDD_MOVEEDIT), pfwnField1);
    WinDismissDlg(hwnd, TRUE);
    }
  return(MRESULT)TRUE;


/*****************************/
/* Process Cancel pushbutton. */
/*****************************/
case DID_CANCEL:
  WinSubclassWindow(
    WinWindowFromID(hwnd, IDD_MOVEEDIT), pfwnField1);
  WinDismissDlg(hwnd, FALSE);
  return(MRESULT)TRUE;
  }
  break;
  }
return WinDefDlgProc(hwnd, msg, mp1, mp2);
}


/*****************************/
/* Window subclass procedure. */
/*****************************/
MRESULT EXPENTRY NumberSubProc1(HWND hwnd, ULONG msg,
  MPARAM mp1, MPARAM mp2)
  {
  switch(msg){
    /*****************************/
    /* Filter keyboard messages. */
    /*****************************/
    case WM_CHAR:
      if((CHARMSG(&msg)->fs & KC_KEYUP) ||
        (CHARMSG(&msg)->fs & KC_VIRTUALKEY))
        return ((*pfwnField1) (hwnd, msg, mp1, mp2));
      if(CHARMSG(&msg)->fs & KC_CHAR)
        if(isdigit(CHARMSG(&msg)->chr))
          return ((*pfwnField1) (hwnd, msg, mp1, mp2));
```

```
      return(MRESULT)NULL;
  default:
    return ((*pfwnField1) (hwnd, msg, mp1, mp2));
  }
}
```

Listing 5-5. Window subclassing.

As you can see from Listing 5-5, subclassing is done in the WM_INITDLG message of the RandomDlgProc dialog procedure. This is accomplished by using the WinSubclassWindow function which references a subclass procedure named **NumberSubProc1**. On return from the WinSubclassWindow function, the original window procedure's address is saved in a variable named **pfwnField1**. Right before the dialog box procedure is dismissed, the WinSubclassWindow function is used again to replace the original window address. The rest of the RandomDlgProc dialog procedure shown in Listing 5-5 is the same as seen in the previous section on dialog boxes.

The NumberSubProc1 subclass procedure only looks for keyboard input by looking for WM_CHAR messages. If the message received is not a WM_CHAR message, it is immediately passed on to the original window procedure for processing and the dialog procedure returns. If the message received is a WM_CHAR message, and the key is being released or is a virtual key, it is also passed to the original window procedure. By passing these types of messages on, the function and cursor keys are still processed by the original window procedure. Finally, if the WM_CHAR message contains a character value and this character is a digit, the message is passed on to the original window procedure. If the character is not a digit, the message is filtered by the subclass window procedure by performing a return.

As you become more familiar with the controls you can place in your dialog boxes and adjust their operation, you will see how these controls enhance the usability of your application. Presentation Manager gives you added bonuses in that these controls look and operate in a consistent manner, and the built-in support for the predefined control windows makes their implementation easy!

6

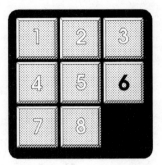

Animation

As you use the slide puzzle application, you will notice several places where motion or special effects occur. For instance, when you start the slide puzzle application, a matrix of blocks with the word SLIDER is drawn. Then, one at a time, each block in this matrix slides out of the application window. This sliding motion is similar to moving pieces in the puzzle. Another effect is the fading in and out of the book title when the application starts. This fading doesn't involve motion, but it does involve bit manipulation that provides an interesting effect. Finally, if you pay attention, you will occasionally notice a grasshopper running across the screen. Since the grasshopper's legs actually move, this effect clearly involves motion.

All the effects used in the slide puzzle application are generated with bit-map manipulation. One very powerful PM function called *GpiBitBlt* provides this manipulation. Because this function operates on areas of pels, it is considered a raster operation; and one of the parameters passed to the GpiBitBlt function specifies exactly which type of raster operation is to be provided. Because the GpiBitBlt function is so powerful and flexible, it is worthwhile to understand the parameters that control this function before we show how it produces the slide puzzle effects.

GPIBITBLT RASTER OPERATIONS

The definition of the GpiBitBlt function call is as follows:
GpiBitBlt(*Target,Source,Count,Points,Rop,Options*)
where
> *Target* is the presentation space on which the raster operation will be applied.

Source is the presentation space that contains source information for the raster operation.

Count is the number of points that are used to specify the rectangular areas for the raster operation. Depending on how this function is used, this value can vary.

Points is an array of *Count* points that defines the rectangular areas. These points are in the order **Tx1,Ty1, Tx2,Ty2,Sx1,Sy1,Sx2,Sy2**. **Tx1,Ty1** specify the bottom left corner of the target rectangle and **Tx2,Ty2** specify the top right corner of the target rectangle. **Sx1,Sy1** specify the bottom left corner of the source rectangle and **Sx2,Sy2** specify the top right corner of the source rectangle.

Rop (Raster Operation) specifies the mixing function used during execution of the function. Mixing involves bit-wise operations on three different bit planes. These bit planes are pattern, source, and destination. This parameter is discussed in greater detail shortly.

Options specifies how to handle eliminated rows or columns if compression is needed. **BBO_OR**, **BBO_AND**, and **BBO_IGNORE** are valid predefined values for this parameter. If the image is white on black, BBO_OR is useful. If the image is black on white, BBO_AND is useful. If the image is color, BBO_IGNORE is useful.

As you can see in the parameters for the GpiBitBlt function, this function can be used to do simple copying, but it can also be used to stretch or compress bitmaps. Furthermore, because this function performs bit-wise logic with up to three different bit-planes, some interesting bit manipulation is possible.

The definition of the bit-wise operations used with the three bit-planes is called the mix. (The mix is the ROP parameter for the GpiBitBlt function.) Setting the correct mix is important in producing the desired output. The way you specify the mix value is by performing logical operations on the following bit patterns *which represent* each of the different bit-planes.

Pattern Bit Plane:	1 1 1 1 0 0 0 0
Source Bit Plane:	1 1 0 0 1 1 0 0
Destination Bit Plane:	1 0 1 0 1 0 1 0

So, for instance, to copy bits from a source bit-plane to a target area without modification, a mix value of hexadecimal 0xCC should be set in the ROP parameter. As you can see from this mix value, it is the bit pattern that represents the source bit-plane. If you want, however, to have all the source bits inverted with the source copy, apply a NOT operation to the bit pattern that represents the source bit-plane; hence, a mix value of hexadecimal 0x33 should be set in the ROP parameter. To copy bits from a source bit-plane to fit within the bounds of a predefined pattern bit-plane, perform an AND operation with the bit patterns that represent the pattern and source bit-planes. In this case, a mix value of hexadecimal 0xC0 should be set in the ROP parameter. In total, there are 256 different mix possibilities available.

TABLE 6-1. RASTER OPERATION IDENTIFIERS

Identifier	ROP Value
ROP_ZERO	0x00
ROP_NOTSRCERASE	0x11
ROP_SRCCOPY	0x33
ROP_SRCERASE	0x44
ROP_DSTINVERT	0x55
ROP_PATINVERT	0x5A
ROP_SRCINVERT	0x66
ROP_SRCAND	0x88
ROP_MERGEPAINT	0xBB
ROP_MERGECOPY	0xC0
ROP_SRCCOPY	0xCC
ROP_SRCPAINT	0xEE
ROP_PATCOPY	0XF0
ROP_PATPAINT	0XFB
ROP_ONE	0xFF

Even though 256 different mix values are possible, only a few are really useful. For these more popular mix values, predefined identifiers are available. Table 6-1 shows a list of these predefined identifiers and their values.

As you can see by the GpiBitBlt function parameters, a pattern bit-map is required for some of the functions mix values. Presentation Manager has a set of predefined patterns available for use. These predefined patterns also have identifiers associated with them. These predefined patterns and their identifiers are shown in Screen 6-1. To make one of these predefined patterns active for a presentation space, use the PM function called *GpiSetPattern*.

Now that we've seen the parameters for the GpiBitBlt function, let's look at how the slide puzzle uses the GpiBitBlt function to produce it's effects.

THE SLIDE EFFECT

As you may have guessed, the slide effect is little more than a series of bit copies. But, besides just copying bits in the correct direction, part of the source bits have to be erased as well. Listing 6-1 shows the code that slides the blocks out of the matrix of 20 blocks when the application first starts.

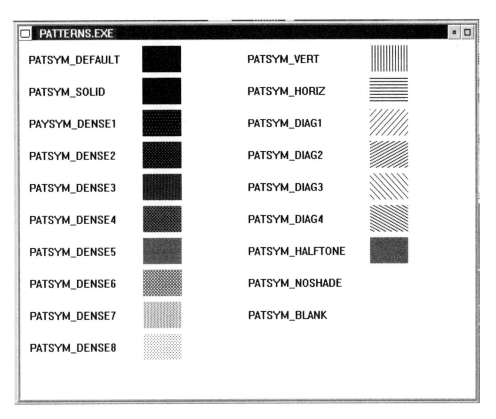

Screen 6-1. Predefined patterns.

```
MRESULT EXPENTRY ClientWndProc(HWND hwnd, ULONG msg,
  MPARAM mp1, MPARAM mp2)
  {
  HBITMAP hbmt;
  HPS hpsd;
  POINTL aptl[4];
  LONG  lRow, lCol, lTotal, lLcid;
  SHORT x, y, i;

  switch(msg){
    /*********************************************************/
    /* Process the animate message.  This will only occur */
    /* once after the first WM_PAINT message.              */
    /*********************************************************/
    case ANIMATE:
      GpiResetPS(hps, GRES_ALL);
```

```
aptl[0].x=0;            /* Target left. */
aptl[0].y=0;
aptl[1].x=sxPels;       /* Target right. */
aptl[1].y=syPels;
GpiBitBlt(hps, hps, 2L, aptl, ROP_ONE, BBO_AND);

/****************************************************/
/* Get key bit-map and adjust for an inch square. */
/****************************************************/
hbmt=GpiLoadBitmap(hps, 0, IDB_PIC1,
  (LONG)(lcxPelsPerInch), (LONG)(lcyPelsPerInch));
for(x=1; x<6; x++){      /* Put 5 keys wide. */
  for(y=1; y<5; y++){    /* Put 4 keys high. */
    ptl.x=x*lcxPelsPerInch;
    ptl.y=y*lcyPelsPerInch;
    WinDrawBitmap(hps, hbmt, NULL, &ptl, CLR_NEUTRAL,
      CLR_BACKGROUND, DBM_NORMAL);
    }
  }


/****************************************************/
/* Slide one inch square out of presentation page. */
/****************************************************/
for(lRow=4; lRow>0; lRow--){
  for(lCol=5; lCol>0; lCol--){
    aptl[0].y=lRow*lcyPelsPerInch;          /* Target bottom */
    aptl[1].y=(lRow+1)*lcyPelsPerInch;      /* Target top */
    aptl[2].y=lRow*lcyPelsPerInch;          /* Source bottom */
    for(x=lCol*lcxPelsPerInch; x<7*lcxPelsPerInch; x=x+SLD_SFT){

      /*****************/
      /* Slide right. */
      /*****************/
      aptl[0].x=x+SLD_SFT;                     /* Target left */
      aptl[1].x=x+SLD_SFT+lcxPelsPerInch;      /* Target right */
      aptl[2].x=x;                             /* Source left */
      GpiBitBlt(hps, hps, 3L, aptl, ROP_SRCCOPY, BBO_AND);

      /****************/
      /* Erase bits. */
      /****************/
      aptl[0].x=x;                             /* Target left */
      aptl[1].x=x+SLD_SFT;                     /* Target right */
      GpiBitBlt(hps, hps, 2L, aptl, ROP_ONE, BBO_AND);
      DosSleep(SLEEPTIME);
      }
    lCol=lCol-1;
    if(lCol>0){
      aptl[0].x=lCol*lcyPelsPerInch;       /* Target left */
      aptl[1].x=(lCol+1)*lcyPelsPerInch;   /* Target right */
      aptl[2].x=lCol*lcyPelsPerInch;       /* Source left */
      for(y=lRow*lcyPelsPerInch; y<6*lcyPelsPerInch; y=y+SLD_SFT){
```

```
/*************/
/* Slide up. */
/*************/
aptl[0].y=y+SLD_SFT;                          /* Target bottom */
aptl[1].y=y+SLD_SFT+1cyPelsPerInch;   /* Target top */
aptl[2].y=y;                                  /* Source bottom */
Gpilt(hps, hps, 3L, aptl, ROP_SRCCOPY, BBO_AND);

/***************/
/* Erase bits. */
/***************/
aptl[0].y=y;                          /* Target bottom */
aptl[1].y=y+SLD_SFT;                  /* Target top */
GpiBitBlt(hps, hps, 2L, aptl, ROP_ONE, BBO_AND);
DosSleep(SLEEPTIME);
}
}
}
}
return(MRESULT)TRUE;
}


/****************************************************/
/* Let default routine process message and return. */
/****************************************************/
return WinDefWindowProc(hwnd, msg, mp1, mp2);
}
```

Listing 6-1. Sliding blocks from matrix.

As you can see in Listing 6-1, the display presentation page is cleared by using the GpiBitBlt function to set all bits to 1. (Setting all bits to 1 will make the presentation page white.) Because the target and source presentation spaces and the rectangular areas to be operated on are the same space, only two points are needed to describe the rectangle. A matrix of blocks is then generated by sizing a bit-map of a single block to be an inch square and drawing 20 images of it in a 5-by-4 pattern. Because each block in this image is calculated and placed, taking it apart with a slide routine is fairly straightforward.

The blocks are slid out of the matrix starting with the block in the top right corner. The blocks are slid in an alternating pattern either to the right or up until all blocks are out of the application window. As you can see, the slide effect is created by copying the block image 15 (SLD_SFT) pels to the right or up, followed by immediately setting the 15 pel offset area to all 1 bits. Notice that only three points are defined for the copy. Because there are only three points defined, the GpiBitBlt function knows that the copy is not to cause a compression or expansion. Finally, a DosSleep function is used to pace the animation, and the copy sequence is started again. This copying and erasing activity continues until the block is out of the application window.

The slide routine just described is similar to the one used to slide pieces in the puzzle; however, because the slide puzzle operates on a memory bit-map, the grid size is variable, and the direction of the slide can be any one of four directions, it is a little more complicated. The slide function used for all puzzle piece movement is shown in Listing 6-2. This listing shows the entire slide function.

```
/*****************************/
/* Slide animation function. */
/*****************************/
void FAR Slide(HAB habs, HWND hwnds, SHORT x, SHORT y)
  {
  POINTL aptl[4], aptlb[4], aptlc[4];
  SIZEL sizl;

  /**************************************/
  /* Record move if this is not an undo. */
  /**************************************/
  if(forward){
    backup[ulUndoIndex].x=sGridx;
    backup[ulUndoIndex].y=sGridy;
    ulUndoIndex++;
    if(ulUndoIndex==SIZEOFUNDO)ulUndoIndex=0;
    }

  /***********************/
  /* Get master bit-map. */
  /***********************/
  GpiQueryBitmapParameters(hbmSrc, &bmpSrc);
  GpiSetBitmap(hpsMemory, hbmSrc);

  /****************************/
  /*  Check for slide to right. */
  /****************************/
  if((y==sGridy) && (x<sGridx)){

    /****************************/
    /* Rectangles for image copy. */
    /****************************/
    aptl[0].y=y*lcyMinMax;                    /* Target bottom. */
    aptl[1].y=aptl[0].y+lcyMinMax;            /* Target top. */
    aptl[2].y=y*lcyMinMax;                    /* Source bottom. */
    aptl[0].x=(x*lcxMinMax)+SLD_SFT;          /* Target left. */
    aptl[1].x=(sGridx*lcxMinMax)+SLD_SFT;     /* Target right. */
    aptl[2].x=x*lcxMinMax;                    /* Source left. */

    /****************************/
    /* Rectangles for blank copy. */
    /****************************/
    aptlb[0].y=y*lcyMinMax;                   /* Target bottom. */
    aptlb[1].y=aptl[0].y+lcyMinMax;           /* Target top. */
    aptlb[0].x=x*lcxMinMax;                   /* Target left. */
```

```
aptlb[1].x=(x*lcxMinMax)+SLD_SFT;  /* Target right. */


/*******************************************/
/* Rectangles for memory to display copy. */
/*******************************************/
aptlc[0].y=y*lcyMinMax;                    /* Target bottom. */
aptlc[1].y=aptl[0].y+lcyMinMax;            /* Target top. */
aptlc[2].y=y*lcyMinMax;                    /* Source bottom. */
aptlc[0].x=x*lcxMinMax;                    /* Target left. */
aptlc[1].x=(sGridx*lcxMinMax)+SLD_SFT; /* Target right. */
aptlc[2].x=x*lcxMinMax;                    /* Source left. */


/********************/
/* Do slide right. */
/********************/
for(sMoveVar=SLD_SFT; sMoveVar<lcxMinMax;
  sMoveVar=sMoveVar+SLD_SFT){
  GpiBitBlt(hpsMemory, hpsMemory, 3L, aptl,  /* Shift image. */
    ROP_SRCCOPY, BBO_AND) ;
  aptl[0].x=aptl[0].x+SLD_SFT;
  aptl[1].x=aptl[1].x+SLD_SFT;
  aptl[2].x=aptl[2].x+SLD_SFT;
  GpiBitBlt(hpsMemory, hpsMemory, 2L, aptlb,  /* Insert blank. */
    ROP_ZERO, BBO_AND);
  aptlb[0].x=aptlb[0].x+SLD_SFT;
  aptlb[1].x=aptlb[1].x+SLD_SFT;


  /****************************************************/
  /* Copy from memory to display presentation page. */
  /****************************************************/
  GpiBitBlt(hps, hpsMemory, 3L, aptlc,
    ROP_SRCCOPY, BBO_AND);
  aptlc[0].x=aptlc[0].x+SLD_SFT;
  aptlc[1].x=aptlc[1].x+SLD_SFT;
  aptlc[2].x=aptlc[2].x+SLD_SFT;
  DosSleep(SLEEPTIME);
  }


/*****************************/
/* Shift remainder of image. */
/*****************************/
aptl[0].x=(x*lcxMinMax)+lcxMinMax;  /* Image rectangle. */
aptl[1].x=(sGridx*lcxMinMax)+lcxMinMax;
aptlb[0].x=(x*lcxMinMax);                  /* Blank rectangle. */
aptlb[1].x=(x*lcxMinMax)+lcxMinMax;
GpiBitBlt(hpsMemory, hpsMemory, 3L, aptl, ROP_SRCCOPY, BBO_AND);
GpiBitBlt(hpsMemory, hpsMemory, 2L, aptlb, ROP_ZERO,BBO_AND);
aptl[0].x=x*lcxMinMax;
aptl[1].x=(sGridx*lcxMinMax)+lcxMinMax;
aptl[2].x=x*lcxMinMax;
GpiBitBlt(hps, hpsMemory, 3L, aptl, ROP_SRCCOPY, BBO_AND);
DosSleep(SLEEPTIME);
}
```

```
/*****************************/
/*  Check for slide to left. */
/*****************************/
if((y==sGridy) && (x>sGridx)){

  /******************************/
  /* Rectangles for image copy. */
  /******************************/
  aptl[0].y=y*lcyMinMax;                              /* Target bottom. */
  aptl[1].y=aptl[0].y+lcyMinMax;                      /* Target top. */
  aptl[2].y=y*lcyMinMax;                              /* Source bottom. */
  aptl[0].x=(sGridx*lcxMinMax)+
    (lcxMinMax-SLD_SFT);                              /* Target left. */
  aptl[1].x=(x*lcxMinMax)+(lcxMinMax-SLD_SFT); /* Target right. */
  aptl[2].x=(sGridx*lcxMinMax)+lcxMinMax;      /* Source left. */

  /******************************/
  /* Rectangles for blank copy. */
  /******************************/
  aptlb[0].y=y*lcyMinMax;                              /* Target bottom. */
  aptlb[1].y=aptl[0].y+lcyMinMax;                      /* Target top. */
  aptlb[0].x=(x*lcxMinMax)+(lcxMinMax-SLD_SFT);  /* Target left. */
  aptlb[1].x=(x*lcxMinMax)+lcxMinMax;                 /* Target right. */

  /*******************************************/
  /* Rectangles for memory to display copy. */
  /*******************************************/
  aptlc[0].y=y*lcyMinMax;                              /* Target bottom. */
  aptlc[1].y=aptl[0].y+lcyMinMax;                      /* Target top. */
  aptlc[2].y=y*lcyMinMax;                              /* Source bottom. */
  aptlc[0].x=(sGridx*lcxMinMax)+(lcxMinMax-SLD_SFT); /* Target left. */
  aptlc[1].x=(x*lcxMinMax)+lcxMinMax;                 /* Target right. */
  aptlc[2].x=(sGridx*lcxMinMax)+(lcxMinMax-SLD_SFT); /* Source left. */

  /******************/
  /* Do slide left. */
  /******************/
  for(sMoveVar=SLD_SFT; sMoveVar<lcxMinMax;
    sMoveVar=sMoveVar+SLD_SFT){
    GpiBitBlt(hpsMemory, hpsMemory, 3L, aptl,   /* Shift image. */
      ROP_SRCCOPY, BBO_AND);
    aptl[0].x=aptl[0].x-SLD_SFT;
    aptl[1].x=aptl[1].x-SLD_SFT;
    aptl[2].x=aptl[2].x-SLD_SFT;
    GpiBitBlt(hpsMemory, hpsMemory, 2L, aptlb,  /* Insert blank. */
      ROP_ZERO, BBO_AND);
    aptlb[0].x=aptlb[0].x-SLD_SFT;
    aptlb[1].x=aptlb[1].x-SLD_SFT;

    /***************************************************/
    /* Copy from memory to display presentation page. */
    /***************************************************/
    GpiBitBlt(hps, hpsMemory, 3L, aptlc,
      ROP_SRCCOPY, BBO_AND);
```

```
      aptlc[0].x=aptlc[0].x-SLD_SFT;
      aptlc[1].x=aptlc[1].x-SLD_SFT;
      aptlc[2].x=aptlc[2].x-SLD_SFT;
      DosSleep(SLEEPTIME);
      }

   /****************************/
   /* Shift remainder of image. */
   /****************************/
   aptl[0].x=sGridx*lcxMinMax;
   aptlb[0].x=x*lcxMinMax;
   aptl[1].x=x*lcxMinMax;
   aptlb[1].x=(x*lcxMinMax)+lcxMinMax;
   GpiBitBlt(hpsMemory, hpsMemory, 3L, aptl, ROP_SRCCOPY, BBO_AND);
   GpiBitBlt(hpsMemory, hpsMemory, 2L, aptlb, ROP_ZERO, BBO_AND);
   aptl[0].x=sGridx*lcxMinMax;
   aptl[1].x=(x*lcxMinMax)+lcxMinMax;
   aptl[2].x=sGridx*lcxMinMax;
   GpiBitBlt(hps, hpsMemory, 3L, aptl, ROP_SRCCOPY, BBO_AND);
   }

/**************************/
/*  Check for slide down. */
/**************************/
if((x==sGridx) && (y>sGridy)){

   /****************************/
   /* Rectangles for image copy. */
   /****************************/
   aptl[0].y=(sGridy*lcyMinMax)+
     (lcyMinMax-SLD_SFT);                           /* Target bottom. */
   aptl[1].y=(y*lcyMinMax)+(lcyMinMax-SLD_SFT); /* Target top. */
   aptl[2].y=(sGridy*lcyMinMax)+lcyMinMax;    /* Source bottom. */
   aptl[0].x=x*lcxMinMax;                      /* Target left. */
   aptl[1].x=(x*lcxMinMax)+lcxMinMax;          /* Target right. */
   aptl[2].x=x*lcxMinMax;                      /* Source left. */

   /****************************/
   /* Rectangles for blank copy. */
   /****************************/
   aptlb[0].y=(y*lcyMinMax)+(lcyMinMax-SLD_SFT); /* Target bottom. */
   aptlb[1].y=(y*lcyMinMax)+lcyMinMax;        /* Target top. */
   aptlb[0].x=x*lcxMinMax;                     /* Target left. */
   aptlb[1].x=(x*lcxMinMax)+lcxMinMax;         /* Target right. */

   /******************************************/
   /* Rectangles for memory to display copy. */
   /******************************************/
   aptlc[0].y=(sGridy*lcyMinMax)+(lcyMinMax-SLD_SFT); /* Target bottom. */
   aptlc[1].y=(y*lcyMinMax)+lcyMinMax;              /* Target top. */
   aptlc[2].y=(sGridy*lcyMinMax)+(lcyMinMax-SLD_SFT); /* Source bottom. */
   aptlc[0].x=x*lcxMinMax;                          /* Target left. */
   aptlc[1].x=(x*lcxMinMax)+lcxMinMax;              /* Target right. */
   aptlc[2].x=x*lcxMinMax;                          /* Source left. */
```

```
/*****************/
/* Do slide down. */
/*****************/
for(sMoveVar=SLD_SFT; sMoveVar<lcyMinMax;
  sMoveVar=sMoveVar+SLD_SFT){
  GpiBitBlt(hpsMemory, hpsMemory, 3L, aptl,    /* Shift image. */
    ROP_SRCCOPY, BBO_AND);
  aptl[0].y=aptl[0].y-SLD_SFT;
  aptl[1].y=aptl[1].y-SLD_SFT;
  aptl[2].y=aptl[2].y-SLD_SFT;
  GpiBitBlt(hpsMemory, hpsMemory, 2L, aptlb,  /* Insert blank. */
    ROP_ZERO, BBO_AND);
  aptlb[0].y=aptlb[0].y-SLD_SFT;
  aptlb[1].y=aptlb[1].y-SLD_SFT;

  /****************************************************/
  /* Copy from memory to display presentation page. */
  /****************************************************/
  GpiBitBlt(hps, hpsMemory, 3L, aptlc,
    ROP_SRCCOPY, BBO_AND) ;
  aptlc[0].y=aptlc[0].y-SLD_SFT;
  aptlc[1].y=aptlc[1].y-SLD_SFT;
  aptlc[2].y=aptlc[2].y-SLD_SFT;
  DosSleep(SLEEPTIME);
  }

/***************************/
/* Shift remainder of image. */
/***************************/
aptl[0].y=sGridy*lcyMinMax;
aptlb[0].y=y*lcyMinMax;
aptl[1].y=y*lcyMinMax;
aptlb[1].y=(y*lcyMinMax)+lcyMinMax;
GpiBitBlt(hpsMemory, hpsMemory, 3L, aptl, ROP_SRCCOPY, BBO_AND);
GpiBitBlt(hpsMemory, hpsMemory, 2L, aptlb, ROP_ZERO, BBO_AND);
aptl[0].y=sGridy*lcyMinMax;
aptl[1].y=(y*lcyMinMax)+lcyMinMax;
aptl[2].y=sGridy*lcyMinMax;
GpiBitBlt(hps, hpsMemory, 3L, aptl, ROP_SRCCOPY, BBO_AND);
}

/***********************/
/*  Check for slide up. */
/***********************/
if((x==sGridx) && (y<sGridy)){

  /***************************/
  /* Rectangles for image copy. */
  /***************************/
  aptl[0].y=(y*lcyMinMax)+SLD_SFT;        /* Target bottom. */
  aptl[1].y=(sGridy*lcyMinMax)+SLD_SFT; /* Target top. */
  aptl[2].y=y*lcyMinMax;                  /* Source bottom. */
  aptl[0].x=x*lcxMinMax;                  /* Target left. */
  aptl[1].x=(x*lcxMinMax)+lcxMinMax;    /* Target right. */
```

```
aptl[2].x=x*lcxMinMax;                      /* Source left. */


/******************************/
/* Rectangles for blank copy. */
/******************************/
aptlb[0].y=y*lcyMinMax;              /* Target bottom. */
aptlb[1].y=(y*lcyMinMax)+SLD_SFT;   /* Target top. */
aptlb[0].x=x*lcxMinMax;              /* Target left. */
aptlb[1].x=(x*lcxMinMax)+lcxMinMax; /* Target right. */


/*******************************************/
/* Rectangles for memory to display copy. */
/*******************************************/
aptlc[0].y=y*lcyMinMax;                       /* Target bottom. */
aptlc[1].y=(sGridy*lcyMinMax)+SLD_SFT; /* Target top. */
aptlc[2].y=y*lcyMinMax;                       /* Source bottom. */
aptlc[0].x=x*lcxMinMax;                       /* Target left. */
aptlc[1].x=(x*lcxMinMax)+lcxMinMax;    /* Target right. */
aptlc[2].x=x*lcxMinMax;                       /* Source left. */


/****************/
/* Do slide up. */
/****************/
for(sMoveVar=SLD_SFT; sMoveVar<lcyMinMax;
  sMoveVar=sMoveVar+SLD_SFT){
  GpiBitBlt(hpsMemory, hpsMemory, 3L, aptl,    /* Shift image. */
    ROP_SRCCOPY, BBO_AND) ;
  aptl[0].y=aptl[0].y+SLD_SFT;
  aptl[1].y=aptl[1].y+SLD_SFT;
  aptl[2].y=aptl[2].y+SLD_SFT;
  GpiBitBlt(hpsMemory, hpsMemory, 2L, aptlb,  /* Insert blank. */
    ROP_ZERO, BBO_AND);
  aptlb[0].y=aptlb[0].y+SLD_SFT;
  aptlb[1].y=aptlb[1].y+SLD_SFT;
  aptlb[2].y=aptlb[2].y+SLD_SFT;


  /*************************************************/
  /* Copy from memory to display presentation page. */
  /*************************************************/
  GpiBitBlt(hps, hpsMemory, 3L, aptlc,
    ROP_SRCCOPY, BBO_AND) ;
  aptlc[0].y=aptlc[0].y+SLD_SFT;
  aptlc[1].y=aptlc[1].y+SLD_SFT;
  aptlc[2].y=aptlc[2].y+SLD_SFT;
  DosSleep(SLEEPTIME);
  }
aptl[0].y=(y*lcyMinMax)+lcyMinMax;
aptlb[0].y=y*lcyMinMax;
aptl[1].y=(sGridy*lcyMinMax)+lcyMinMax;
aptlb[1].y=(y*lcyMinMax)+lcyMinMax;
GpiBitBlt(hpsMemory, hpsMemory, 3L, aptl, ROP_SRCCOPY, BBO_AND);
GpiBitBlt(hpsMemory, hpsMemory, 2L, aptlb, ROP_ZERO, BBO_AND);
aptl[0].y=y*lcyMinMax;
aptl[1].y=(sGridy*lcyMinMax)+lcyMinMax;
```

```
    aptl[2].y=y*lcyMinMax;
    GpiBitBlt(hps, hpsMemory, 3L, aptl, ROP_SRCCOPY, BBO_AND);
    }

    /**************************************************/
    /* Update global variables and release resources. */
    /**************************************************/
    sGridx=x;
    sGridy=y;
    return;
    }
```

Listing 6-2. Slide function.

The slide function shown in Listing 6-2 shows how the slide effect is performed in all four directions. Because the logic is similar for all directions, the function is discussed in a generic way.

The first thing the slide function does is test if the puzzle is in undo mode. It does this by testing the global variable named **forward**. If the slide puzzle is not in undo mode, the slide function records the current location of the blank piece in a global circular buffer named **backup**. This circular buffer is used to undo moves with the Undo option available in the pull-down menu. The slide function then sets the master bit-map image in a memory presentation page and determines the direction of the slide operation.

Once the slide direction is determined, a series of rectangle coordinates are set up for the slide operation. These rectangles include two for copying an image within the master bit-map found in the memory presentation page, a rectangle to erase bits left behided from the bit copy operation, and two more rectangles to copy from the master bit-map to the display presentation page. After the rectangles are set up, the bits of the affected area are copied in the appropriate direction by an offset of 15 (SLD_SFT) pels, and the offset area is set to all 0 bits. (Setting the bits to 0 causes the area to be black.) Note that because pieces can only slide toward the blank or black puzzle piece, we don't have to worry about copying over a part of the image that must be retained.

After each copy of bits within the master bit-map space is done, the affected region is copied to the display presentation page. By operating on the master bit-map in memory presentation page, the master bit-map is kept up to date. This copying of bits continues until a remainder of offset pels to copy is less than 15. Then one last set of copies is done so that the slide operation ends exactly on the intended boundary. The last activity the slide function performs is the updating of the blank puzzle piece location.

THE MOSAIC EFFECT

After the book title fades in and out when the slide puzzle application starts, an image of the puzzle is pieced together by randomly putting small pieces of the puzzle image in the application window. By doing this, a mosaic effect is created.

Screen 6-2. Mosaic effect.

Screen 6-2 shows an example of what a puzzle image could look like while this effect is active. Listing 6-3 shows the code that produces this effect.

As you can see in Listing 6-3, the display presentation space and memory presentation spaces are reset first. Then the master bit-map is set in the memory presentation page and the display presentation page is made black with the GpiBitBlt function. Rectangles a tenth of an inch square are then randomly copied from the visible part of the puzzle to the display presentation page. This is done for eight thousand random squares. Finally, the entire presentation page is invalidated causing the full puzzle image to be filled in with a WM_PAINT message, and the resources are released.

```
MRESULT EXPENTRY ClientWndProc(HWND hwnd, ULONG msg,
  MPARAM mp1, MPARAM mp2)
  {
  BOOL fRet=FALSE;
  POINTL aptl[4];
  LONG  lRow, lCol, lTotal, lLcid;
  SIZEL sizl;
  SHORT x, y, i;
  POINTL shear, ptl;
```

```
        RECTL rclInvalid;

    switch(msg){
      /*******************************************************/
      /* Process the animate message.  This will only occur */
      /* once after the first WM_PAINT message.           */
      /*******************************************************/
      case ANIMATE:
        GpiResetPS(hps, GRES_ALL);
        /**********************************/
        /* Get master bit-map from memory. */
        /**********************************/
        GpiResetPS(hpsMemory, GRES_ALL);
        GpiQueryBitmapParameters(hbmSrc, &bmpSrc);
        GpiSetBitmap(hpsMemory, hbmSrc);


        /****************************************/
        /* Clear out screen presentation page. */
        /****************************************/
        aptl[0].x=0; aptl[0].y=0;
        aptl[1].x=sxPels; aptl[1].y=syPels;
        GpiBitBlt(hps, hps, 2L, aptl, ROP_ZERO, BBO_AND);
        DosSleep(500);   /* Wait .5 seconds. */


        /*************************************************/
        /* Randomly blt in tenth inch squares of master */
        /* bit-map.  Do 8000 squares then stop.       */
        /*************************************************/
        for(i=0; i<8000; i++){
          aptl[0].x=Random_Range(0,
            (7*lcxPelsPerInch)-(lcxPelsPerInch/10), 0, 0);
          aptl[0].y=Random_Range(0,
            (6*lcyPelsPerInch)-(lcyPelsPerInch/10), 0, 0);
          aptl[1].x=aptl[0].x+(lcxPelsPerInch/7);
          aptl[1].y=aptl[0].y+(lcyPelsPerInch/7);
          aptl[2].x=aptl[0].x; aptl[2].y=aptl[0].y;
          GpiBitBlt(hps, hpsMemory, 3L, aptl, ROP_SRCCOPY, BBO_AND);
          }
        WinInvalidateRect(hwnd, NULL, FALSE);  /* Cause full paint. */
        return(MRESULT)TRUE;
      }


    /******************************************************/
    /* Let default routine process message and return. */
    /******************************************************/
    return WinDefWindowProc(hwnd, msg, mp1, mp2);
    }
```

Listing 6-3. Mosaic effect code.

THE FADE IN AND OUT EFFECT

Chapter 2, Drawing in the Client Area, shows how to draw text that can be sized, sheared, and centered. The example shown in Chapter 2, however, was not drawn in the display presentation page, but in a memory device context presentation page. The reason for drawing the text in the memory presentation page was so some GpiBitBlt functions could be applied to it to create a fading effect.

The basic concept for the fading effect is to use a memory presentation page that already contains the text image as the source for a GpiBitBlt function. However, instead of using a regular ROP_SRCCOPY raster operation, a raster operation that uses the standard Presentation Manager pattern bit planes as a mix operand is used. These patterns vary in density, and when they are AND'ed with the source image with a series of GpiBitBlt function calls, they cause the fading effect. Listing 6-4 shows the code that the slide puzzle uses to cause the fading effect.

```
MRESULT EXPENTRY ClientWndProc(HWND hwnd, ULONG msg,
    MPARAM mp1, MPARAM mp2)
    {
    CHAR szStr1[]="Learning To Program";
    CHAR szStr2[]="OS/2 2.0 Presentation Manager";
    CHAR szStr3[]="By Example";
    CHAR szStr4[]="(Putting the Pieces Together)";
    CHAR szFontName1[]="Times New Roman";
    LONG alWidths[80];
    LONG alWidthTable[256];
    SIZEF sizefxCharBox;
    FIXED width, height;
    BOOL fRet=FALSE;
    BITMAPINFOHEADER2 bmp;
    HBITMAP hbmt;
    HDC hdcbm;
    HPS hpsd;
    POINTL aptl[4];
    LONG  lRow, lCol, lTotal, lLcid;
    SIZEL sizl;
    SHORT x, y, i;
    POINTL shear, ptl;
    LONG pattern[]={
        PATSYM_DEFAULT, PATSYM_DENSE1, PATSYM_DENSE2,
        PATSYM_DENSE3, PATSYM_DENSE4, PATSYM_DENSE5,
        PATSYM_DENSE6, PATSYM_DENSE7, PATSYM_DENSE8,
        PATSYM_NOSHADE};

    switch(msg){
```

```
/********************************************************/
/* Process the animate message.  This will only occur */
/* once after the first WM_PAINT message.           */
/********************************************************/
case ANIMATE:
  /********************************************************/
  /* Reset presentation spaces, then get it again and  */
  /* animate with shearing.                           */
  /********************************************************/
  GpiResetPS(hps, GRES_ALL);
  GpiResetPS(hpsMemory, GRES_ALL);
  GpiQueryDeviceBitmapFormats(hpsMemory, 2L, alBmpFormats);
  memset(&bmp, 0, sizeof(bmp));
  bmp.cbFix=sizeof bmp;
  bmp.cx=sxPels;
  bmp.cPlanes=(USHORT)alBmpFormats[0];
  bmp.cBitCount=(USHORT)alBmpFormats[1];
  bmp.cy=syPels;
  hbmt=GpiCreateBitmap(hpsMemory, &bmp, OL, NULL, NULL);
  GpiSetBitmap(hpsMemory, hbmt);


  /*******************************/
  /* Clear out presentation pages. */
  /*******************************/
  aptl[0].x=0; aptl[0].y=0;
  aptl[1].x=sxPels; aptl[1].y=syPels;
  aptl[2].x=0; aptl[2].y=0;
  GpiBitBlt(hps, hps, 2L, aptl, ROP_ZERO, BBO_AND);
  GpiBitBlt(hpsMemory, hpsMemory, 2L, aptl, ROP_ZERO, BBO_AND);


  /********************************************************/
  /* Look for font by name else find any outline font. */
  /********************************************************/
  if(!FindFont(hpsMemory, &lLcid, szFontName1))
    FindFont(hpsMemory, &lLcid, NULL);
  lPointSize=30;  /* Set font to 30 points. */
  fRet=SetPtSize(hpsMemory, lLcid, lPointSize, &width, &height);
  if(fRet){
    sizefxCharBox.cy=height;
    sizefxCharBox.cx=width;
    }
  fRet=GpiSetCharBox(hpsMemory, &sizefxCharBox);


  /********************************************************/
  /* Set color and shear for memory presentation space. */
  /* Then put all text in this presentation page.      */
  /********************************************************/
  GpiSetColor(hpsMemory, CLR_CYAN);
  shear.x=10; shear.y=25;
  GpiSetCharShear(hpsMemory, &shear);
  SetWidthsTable(hpsMemory, alWidths,
    alWidthTable, szStr1, &lTotal);
  ptl.x=((7*lcxPelsPerInch)-lTotal)/2; /* Center text 4 */
  ptl.y=lcyPelsPerInch*4;              /* inches from bottom */
```

```
GpiMove(hpsMemory, &ptl);
GpiCharStringPos(hpsMemory, NULL, CHS_VECTOR,
  (LONG)strlen(szStr1), (PSZ)szStr1, alWidths);

/*****************************************************/
/* Change point size of font and get rid of shear. */
/*****************************************************/
lPointSize=18;
fRet=SetPtSize(hpsMemory, lLcid, lPointSize, &width, &height);
if(fRet){
  sizefxCharBox.cy=height;
  sizefxCharBox.cx=width;
  }
fRet=GpiSetCharBox(hpsMemory, &sizefxCharBox);
shear.x=0; shear.y=1;
GpiSetCharShear(hpsMemory, &shear);


/*************************************************************/
/* Center next 2 lines of text in memory presentation page. */
/*************************************************************/
SetWidthsTable(hpsMemory, alWidths,
  alWidthTable, szStr2, &lTotal);
ptl.x=((7*lcxPelsPerInch)-lTotal)/2;  /* Center text */
ptl.y=lcyPelsPerInch*3;         /* 3 inches from bottom */
GpiMove(hpsMemory, &ptl);
GpiCharStringPos(hpsMemory, NULL, CHS_VECTOR,
  (LONG)strlen(szStr2), (PSZ)szStr2, alWidths);
SetWidthsTable(hpsMemory, alWidths,
  alWidthTable, szStr3, &lTotal);
ptl.x=((7*lcxPelsPerInch)-lTotal)/2;  /* Center text */
ptl.y=lcyPelsPerInch*2.5;  /* 2.5 inches from bottom */
GpiMove(hpsMemory, &ptl);
GpiCharStringPos(hpsMemory, NULL, CHS_VECTOR,
  (LONG)strlen(szStr3), (PSZ)szStr3, alWidths);


/*********************************************/
/* Change color and center last             */
/* line of text in memory presentation page. */
/*********************************************/
GpiSetColor(hpsMemory, CLR_YELLOW);
SetWidthsTable(hpsMemory, alWidths,
  alWidthTable, szStr4, &lTotal);
ptl.x=((7*lcxPelsPerInch)-lTotal)/2;  /* Center text */
ptl.y=lcyPelsPerInch*1;       /* 1 inches from bottom */
GpiMove(hpsMemory, &ptl);
GpiCharStringPos(hpsMemory, NULL, CHS_VECTOR,
  (LONG)strlen(szStr4), (PSZ)szStr4, alWidths);


/*******************************************/
/* Fade in top 3 text lines with Bit Blt. */
/*******************************************/

aptl[0].x=0; aptl[0].y=lcyPelsPerInch*2;
aptl[1].x=lcxPelsPerInch*7; aptl[1].y=lcyPelsPerInch*5;
```

```
         aptl[2].x=0; aptl[2].y=lcyPelsPerInch*2;
         for(x=1; x<10; x++){
           GpiSetPattern(hps, pattern[x]);
           GpiBitBlt(hps, hpsMemory, 3L, aptl, ROP_MERGECOPY, BBO_AND);
           DosSleep(SLEEPTIME);
           }
         DosSleep(2500);  /* Wait 2.5 seconds. */

         /*******************************************/
         /* Fade in last text line with Bit Blt. */
         /*******************************************/
         aptl[0].x=0; aptl[0].y=lcyPelsPerInch*.5;
         aptl[1].x=lcxPelsPerInch*7; aptl[1].y=lcyPelsPerInch*2;
         aptl[2].x=0; aptl[2].y=lcyPelsPerInch*.5;
         for(x=1; x<10; x++){
           GpiSetPattern(hps, pattern[x]);
           GpiBitBlt(hps, hpsMemory, 3L, aptl, ROP_MERGECOPY, BBO_AND);
           DosSleep(SLEEPTIME);
           }
         DosSleep(3000);     /* Wait 3 seconds */

         /***********************************************/
         /* Fade out all text from screen with Bit Blt. */
         /***********************************************/
         aptl[0].x=0; aptl[0].y=lcyPelsPerInch*.5;
         aptl[1].x=lcxPelsPerInch*7; aptl[1].y=lcyPelsPerInch*5;
         aptl[2].x=0; aptl[2].y=lcyPelsPerInch*.5;
         for(x=9; x>1; x--){
           GpiSetPattern(hps, pattern[x]);
           GpiBitBlt(hps, hpsMemory, 3L, aptl, ROP_MERGECOPY, BBO_AND);
           DosSleep(SLEEPTIME);
           }
         GpiDeleteBitmap(hbmt);
         return(MRESULT)TRUE;
       }


  /*******************************************************/
  /* Let default routine process message and return. */
  /*******************************************************/
  return WinDefWindowProc(hwnd, msg, mp1, mp2);
  }
```

Listing 6-4. Fading effect source code.

As you can see in Listing 6-4, the book title is sized, sheared, and centered just as described in Chapter 2. The animation routine then sets up an area that starts 2 inches up from both presentation pages and is 3 inches high and 7 inches wide. This region includes the top three lines of text or title of the book. Once these regions are set up, a loop of ten GpiBitBlt operations takes place. In this loop, the ROP_MERGECOPY raster operation is used which causes the AND'ing of the pattern and source bit planes. A new pattern bit plane is selected on every iteration of the loop. The new pattern bit plane identifiers are retrieved from an array which are ordered from the least dense pattern to the most dense pattern; hence, on the last iteration of the loop, all bits are on. A DosSleep function is used in this loop to pace the fading effect. Once this region has been faded in, a 2.5 second pause occurs. Then the last line, or subtitle of the book is faded in the same way except the region is .5 inches up from the bottom of the presentation pages and is 1.5 inches high and 7 inches wide.

The entire book title and subtitle are left in the display presentation page for three seconds. The entire region is then faded out by using the process just described but the pattern identifier array is indexed in the opposite direction.

THE BUG EFFECT

As you play with the slide puzzle, you will notice that a grasshopper occasionally runs across your display. There are a few items about this effect that make it more interesting than the other effects just described. For instance, the grasshopper is an irregular shape but the area around the bug's shape is preserved. Also, the grasshopper runs across the entire screen instead of being confined to the slide puzzle application window. And finally, the grasshopper's legs appear to move.

To create the effect of motion, a series of bit-maps of the grasshopper were created. In fact, a total of ten bit-maps are used to create five frames for this animation. (Each frame requires two bit-maps.) Each frame is slightly different so the legs look like they are moving when displayed in a rapid progression.

Two bit-maps are required for each frame because of the logic used to put the grasshopper on the screen. When creating the grasshopper bit-maps, the grasshopper body could be composed of any colors except black or white. (You may recall that black is all bits off and white is all bits on.) Then, for each frame or grasshopper image, a bit-map with an entire background of white and another with an entire background of black is produced. With these two bit-maps, the animation logic *cuts a hole* in the screen image for the grasshopper body and then places the body in the hole just cut.

The bit-map with the white background is used to cut the hole in the screen image. This is done by using the ROP_SRCAND raster operation which performs a logical AND of the source bit-map image with the target area. Therefore, because the grasshopper's body is not a solid white color, a black hole with the shape of the grasshopper's body is created. The bit-map with the black background is then used to place the grasshopper's body into the hole just cut. This is done by using the ROP_SRCPAINT raster operation which performs a logical OR of the source bit-map image with the target area. Because the background of the bit-map is all zeros, the target area is preserved; but, because the black hole was cut in the screen image, the grasshopper's body is placed in this area. Figure 6-1 shows the ten bit-map images used to produce the five frames for this animation.

The logic just described is the basic technique used to place an irregular-shaped object in an image. But, making the animation perform well and appear smooth can still be challenging. As the code that produces the grasshopper animation is

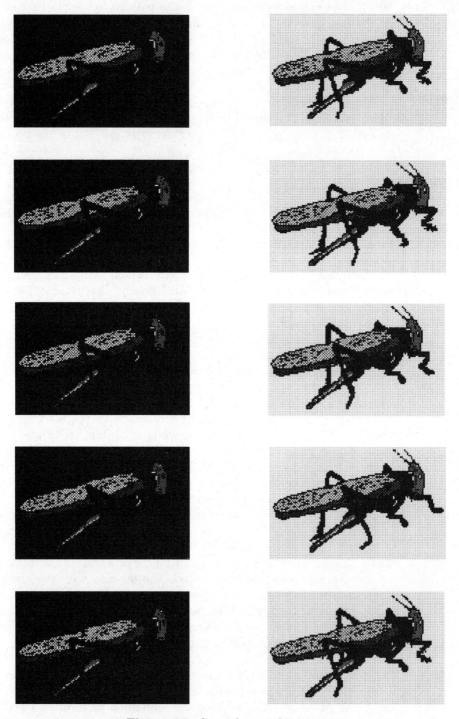

Figure 6-1. Grass hopper bit-maps.

discussed, you will see how some basic performance issues are resolved. As you produce your own animations, however, you may discover better alternatives to manage critical resources for your application. The code used to produce the bug animation is shown in Listing 6-5.

As you can see in Listing 6-5, the bit-map size and number of frames for an animation is controlled with variables. For our grasshopper animation, there are five frames and the bit-map size is 128 pels wide by 80 pels high. The bug animation first creates a presentation space with a memory device context. A presentation page is then made wide enough to hold either the number of frame bit-maps side by side or the width of the master bit-map image, whichever is bigger; and the height of the presentation page is made big enough to hold four times the height of the bit-map image. This presentation page is divided into four rows of equal height. These rows contain the following images:

> **Row 1** contains an image of the bug path, which is used as a backup image of the bug path and is taken from the desktop bit-map image.
> **Row 2** contains an image of the bug path just like Row 1 but this area is used as a work area for *cutting* the bug into the bug path.
> **Row 3** contains a series of the bug bit-maps with a white background.
> **Row 4** contains a series of the bug bit-maps with a black background.

Once the memory presentation page is created with an adequate dimension, the bug bit-maps are loaded and placed into the correct rows and columns of the memory presentation page. The bottom coordinate for the bug path is then generated by using a random number generator routine. The coordinate returned will range from zero to the top of the display presentation page size minus the height of the bug bit-map. With this information, two images of the bug path are copied into the memory presentation page.

```
/*************************/
/* Perform bug animation. */
/*************************/
void FAR Bug(void)
  {
  BITMAPINFOHEADER2 bmp;
  HBITMAP hbmBug, hbmbm1, hbmbmMask1;
  HDC hdcBug;
  HPS hpsBug, hpsDesk;
  POINTL aptl[4];
  SIZEL sizl;
  POINTL ptl;
  LONG frames=5, xsize=128, ysize=80, shift=12, lRow, x, xlag, i;
  INT sBitMapID[]={IDB_PIC2, IDB_PIC3,
                   IDB_PIC4, IDB_PIC5,
                   IDB_PIC6, IDB_PIC7,
                   IDB_PIC8, IDB_PIC9,
                   IDB_PIC10, IDB_PIC11};

  /*******************************************************/
  /* Get memory device context and presentation space. */
  /*******************************************************/
```

```
hdcBug=DevOpenDC(hab, OD_MEMORY, (PSZ)"*", 0L, 0L, 0L);
sizl.cx=0; sizl.cy=0;
hpsBug=GpiCreatePS(hab, hdcBug, &sizl,
  PU_PELS | GPIF_DEFAULT | GPIT_MICRO | GPIA_ASSOC);
GpiQueryDeviceBitmapFormats(hpsBug, 2L, alBmpFormats);
memset(&bmp, 0, sizeof(bmp));
bmp.cbFix=sizeof bmp;
if(sxPels<xsize*frames)bmp.cx=xsize*frames;
else bmp.cx=sxPels;
bmp.cPlanes=(USHORT)alBmpFormats[0];
bmp.cBitCount=(USHORT)alBmpFormats[1];
bmp.cy=ysize*4;
hbmBug=GpiCreateBitmap(hpsBug, &bmp, 0L, NULL, NULL);
GpiSetBitmap(hpsBug, hbmBug);

/**********************************************/
/* Put bit-maps in memory presentation page. */
/**********************************************/
for (x=0; x<5 ; x++){
  hbmbm1=GpiLoadBitmap(hpsBug, 0, sBitMapID[x*2],
    (LONG)xsize, (LONG)ysize);
  hbmbmMask1=GpiLoadBitmap(hpsBug, 0, sBitMapID[(x*2)+1],
    (LONG)xsize, (LONG) ysize);
  ptl.y=ysize*2; ptl.x=xsize*x;
  WinDrawBitmap(hpsBug, hbmbm1, NULL, &ptl, CLR_NEUTRAL,
    CLR_BACKGROUND, DBM_NORMAL);
  ptl.y=ysize*3; ptl.x=xsize*x;
  WinDrawBitmap(hpsBug, hbmbmMask1, NULL, &ptl, CLR_NEUTRAL,
    CLR_BACKGROUND, DBM_NORMAL);
   GpiDeleteBitmap(nbmbm1);
   GpiDeleteBitmap(hbmbmMask1);
   }

/**********************/
/* Copy the bug path. */
/**********************/
lRow=Random_Range(0, syPels-ysize, 0, 0);
aptl[0].x=0; aptl[0].y=0;            /* Target bottom left. */
aptl[1].x=sxPels; aptl[1].y=ysize; /* Target upper right. */
aptl[2].x=0;                        /* Source bottom left. */
aptl[2].y=lRow;
hpsDesk=WinGetScreenPS(HWND_DESKTOP);
GpiBitBlt(hpsBug, hpsDesk, 3L, aptl, ROP_SRCCOPY, BBO_AND);

/************************/
/* Make a bug work area. */
/************************/
aptl[0].x=0; aptl[0].y=ysize;          /* Target bottom left. */
aptl[1].x=sxPels; aptl[1].y=ysize*2; /* Target upper right. */
aptl[2].x=0;                          /* Source bottom left. */
aptl[2].y=lRow;
GpiBitBlt(hpsBug, hpsDesk, 3L, aptl, ROP_SRCCOPY, BBO_AND);

/*****************/
/* Do animation. */
/*****************/
```

```
for (x=0; x<sxPels+shift; i=0){

    /*****************************************************/
    /* Cut hole in bug work area with correct bug mask. */
    /*****************************************************/
    for(i=0; i<frames; i++){
       aptl[0].x=x; aptl[0].y=ysize;          /* Target bottom left. */
       aptl[1].x=xsize+x; aptl[1].y=ysize*2;  /* Target upper right. */
       aptl[2].x=xsize*i; aptl[2].y=ysize*3;  /* Source bottom left. */
       GpiBitBlt(hpsBug, hpsBug, 3L, aptl, ROP_SRCAND, BBO_AND);

       /***********************************/
       /* Copy bug into hole in work area. */
       /***********************************/
       aptl[2].y=ysize*2;                    /* Change source bottom left. */
       GpiBitBlt(hpsBug, hpsBug, 3L, aptl, ROP_SRCPAINT, BBO_AND);

       /*********************************************/
       /* Copy bug frame from work area to screen. */
       /*********************************************/
       if(x==0)xlag=0;
       else xlag=x-shift;
       aptl[0].x=xlag; aptl[0].y=1Row;        /* Target bottom left. */
       aptl[1].x=xsize+x; aptl[1].y=ysize+1Row; /* Target upper right. */
       aptl[2].x=xlag; aptl[2].y=ysize;       /* Source bottom left. */
       GpiBitBlt(hpsDesk, hpsBug, 3L, aptl, ROP_SRCCOPY, BBO_AND);

       /************************************/
       /* Restore work area from save area. */
       /************************************/
       aptl[0].x=x; aptl[0].y=ysize;          /* Target bottom left. */
       aptl[1].x=x+xsize; aptl[1].y=ysize*2;  /* Target upper right. */
       aptl[2].x=x; aptl[2].y=0;              /* Source bottom left. */
       GpiBitBlt(hpsBug, hpsBug, 3L, aptl, ROP_SRCCOPY, BBO_AND);
       DosSleep(SLEEPTIME);
       x=x+shift;
       }
    }
WinReleasePS(hpsDesk);
GpiDestroyPS(hpsBug);
DevCloseDC(hdcBug);
GpiDeleteBitmap(hbmBug);
WinInvalidateRect(HWND_DESKTOP, NULL, TRUE); /* Cause full paint. */
return;
}
```

Listing 6-5. Bug animation code.

With the memory presentation page all set, an inner and outer loop is set up to provide the progression of frames required to produce the bug motion. The inner loop controls the frame sequence and the outer loop makes the frame progression continue until the bit-map exits the right side of the screen presentation page. The process of AND'ing and OR'ing bug bit-maps is then done to place the bug image into the bug path work area. Placing the bug image is accomplished as earlier described. Notice, however, that all activity is done in the memory presentation page instead of the display presentation page so far.

After the bug is cut into the bug path work area, the changed area is copied to the display presentation page. This changed area consists of the area of the previous bug image minus the very first frame for the entire sequence. Finally, the memory presentation page work area is restored from the backup of the bug path, pacing is done, and the loop continues until the sequence is complete.

By processing most of the raster operations in the memory presentation page, performance is improved and flickering of the animation is reduced. Before the bug routine returns, all resources are released and the bug animation is complete.

7

Implementing a Help Interface

As you examine today's most popular software products, you will probably notice that they are rich in function and have user interfaces that are consistent and intuitive. Of course, one of the most attractive aspects of Presentation Manager is that it promotes a consistent user interface across all applications that reside in its environment. However, no matter how much user interface consistency exists between applications, different applications still vary in complexity and provide diverse function. Because of this, customers still need good documentation for the applications they purchase.

One very popular method of providing documentation is through a part of the application itself. This type of interactive documentation is often called a help interface and is usually only a keystroke or mouse-click away. This can be extremely useful and can reduce the dependency on conventional hard-copy documentation. In fact, in many situations, a good interactive help interface can guide the customer to the desired information much faster than conventional hard-copy documentation. Do not assume, however, that if you provide an excellent help interface with your application that you've eliminated the need for good hard-copy documentation! You will probably discover that your customers want both; and if you think about it, you probably would too.

In many operating environments, the application writer must develop the entire help interface. In this case, not only must the developer write the software to present help information, but often the developer writes the help text as well. Furthermore, because the developer implements the help interface as part of the application, the way the help information is accessed and presented to the customer is probably unique. Although unique function is desirable when selling your product, you may not want to focus your resources on developing a unique help interface unless it is absolutely necessary or revolutionary in concept.

Presentation Manager provides a facility that makes the development of a help interface extremely easy and powerful. This facility is called the OS/2 Information Presentation Facility (IPF). Because of how the Information Presentation Facility works, the development of your help text is separate from your application and the ultimate presentation of your help text is done by part of Presentation Manager rather than by your application. Because of this, the presentation of your help text is consistent with all other applications that take advantage of this facility.

You will probably find that the Information Presentation Facility gives you much more function in presenting your help text than you would be willing to develop yourself. For instance, with the Information Presentation Facility, you can do simple text formatting such as producing headers, paragraphs, lists, and highlighted phrases; but, you can also do things like imbed images, provide hyperlinks, and produce indexes. Furthermore, the Information Presentation Facility provides the customer with the ability to perform simple operations on your help text. Examples of these operations are search for a string, copy to file, or print different sections of your help interface. Screen 7-1 shows some of the basic features you can expect by using the Information Presentation Facility.

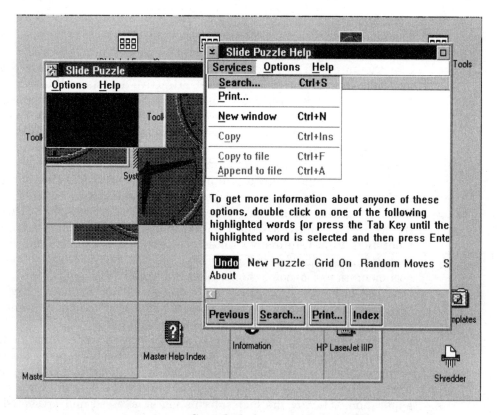

Screen 7-1. Sample help interface window.

To take advantage of the Information Presentation Facility support, you need to do three basic things, as follows:

1. Develop help information to be displayed.
2. Define the links to your help interface.
3. Add the necessary logic to your application code to interface with the Information Presentation Facility support.

DEVELOPING HELP TEXT

To develop the help text using the Information Presentation Facility support, you need is a simple ASCII text editor like the system editor that comes with OS/2 2.0. You also need the Information Presentation Facility compiler that is part of the OS/2 Developer's Toolkit for OS/2 2.0. If you have worked with a markup tag language before, you'll probably find generating help text for the Information Presentation Facility extremely easy.

The basic concept of a markup tag language is to place instructions into the body of the actual text. These instructions, called markup tags, describe how the text is to be formatted and referenced. Markup tags are identified in the body of the text by the occurrence of a leading colon (:) followed by the markup command itself, and ending with a period (.). There are several markup tags that perform a wide variety of functions. For space and simplicity, the markup tag examples shown in this section are made up and are not part of the help text for the slide puzzle application. To see the slide puzzle help text, however, refer to Appendix B or browse the SLIDER.IPF file located on the diskette that comes with this book.

Following is a simple example of help text source that demonstrates how markup tags are imbedded in text. This example causes a new paragraph and highlights a word:

> :p.This is the start of a new :hp2.paragraph:ehp2. The previous occurrence of the word paragraph is highlighted.

The result of the example is as follows:

This is the start of a new **paragraph.** The previous occurrence of the word paragraph is highlighted.

The first markup tag that you must have in your help text source file is **:userdoc.**. This tag informs the Information Presentation Facility Compiler to begin translating the markup tags that follow. The last markup tag you should have in your source file is **:euserdoc.**. This tag signals the end of the help text source. Everything between these two markup tags is help text or markups; however, a couple of special markup tags that start with a period (.) let you develop help text in multiple source files and allow you to place comments in your source file that won't be compiled as help text. These special markup tags are as follows:

.im	Imbed a file.
.*	Comment line.

By using these special markup tags, multiple people can develop help text for your application and add comments to their work; or the help text developer can break the help text source into multiple files for organizational reasons. Whatever the case, only one **:userdoc.** and one **:euserdoc.** markup tag should exist for all the help text; thus, imbedded files should not contain these two markup tags.

The following sections show the common types of markup tags used to generate help text. For a complete list of markup tags, however, refer to OS/2 2.0 technical reference material.

Headings Levels and Index Entries

Heading levels provide a way of organizing and separating different sections of information. Just as books are organized in a hierarchy such as Parts, Chapters, Sections, and Sub-sections, heading levels provide the same type of hierarchy for your help interface. The Information Presentation Facility supports up to six heading levels and are identified with the markup tags **:h1.** through **:h6.**. When you use these heading levels, you must not skip a level that would break the hierarchy. For instance, if you use only three heading levels in your help text, you must use :**h1.** before you can use **:h2.**; and you can not use **:h3.** until you use **:h2.**.

Heading levels are also used to define *panels* of text to the Information Presentation Facility. A panel is basically the start of a section of text that the Information Presentation Facility displays on demand. A panel may actually contain several pages of text that the Information Presentation Facility will let you view. The facility manages large panels of help text with scroll bars. Notice also that the facility automatically redraws your help text as needed when the help text window is re-sized. A panel of information is terminated by the start of new panel via the next **:h1.** markup tag or the end of the help source file.

The Information Presentation Facility locates a panel of text with an ID that is associated with the heading level markup tag. You supply this ID with the keyword parameter *res=*. The ID immediately follows this keyword with a unique value from 1 to 32000. Heading levels **:h4.** through **:h6.** can not have panel IDs associated with them, but do show up within a panel as part of the help text. An example of how to use a heading level follows:

:h1 res=1. Using the Slide Puzzle

The text that immediately follows the heading level markup tag is the title of the panel. This title appears in both the title bar area of the help window and in the client area of the help window unless the keyword *hide* is used. If you use the hide option, the title will <u>not</u> be placed in the client area of the help window. An example of how to use the hide option follows:

:h1 res=1 hide.Using the Slide Puzzle

The Information Presentation Facility also allows you to define an index for your help interface. This index is presented to the user as an alphabetically ordered list box window that can be scrolled. From this list, the user can select an item of interest and the Information Presentation Facility will automatically bring the desired topic to the foreground for viewing. Index entries are defined with the **:i1.** and **:i2.** markup tags. By using these markup tags in the same panel they are to reference, the Information Presentation Facility can find the text that is to be displayed when they are selected in the index.

For simple index entries, use the **:i1.** markup tag. To use this tag, provide the text you want to be displayed for the index entry. Following is an example of how to use this tag:

```
:h1 res=2 hide.The Undo Option
The undo option provides a way for you to undo the last edit operation you
    performed. This is....
:i1.undo
```

This example creates an item in the help index identified with the word undo. When the user selects undo from the index, the panel with ID 2 is presented.

You can also create a two-level index entry by using both the **:i1.** and the **:i2.** markup tags. To do this, use the *id=* keyword parameter with the **:i1.** tag and the *refid=* keyword parameter with the **:i2.** tag. Following is an example of how to use these two tags to create a two-level index item:

```
:i1 id=action.pull-down menus
:i2 refid=action.options
:i2 refid=action.help
```

This example provides the following in the help index:

```
pull-down menus
    options
    help
```

Text Formatting

There are several markup tags that let you control the basic presentation of your help text. One of the most frequently used markup tags is the paragraph markup. To use this markup tag, simply precede the body of a new paragraph with the markup tag command **:p.**. Following is an example of how this markup tag is used:

```
:p.This is the start of a new paragraph.
```

The highlight phrase markup tags control the style of text. There are nine different styles of highlighted phrases available. For each style of highlighted phrase, there is a markup tag to start the highlighting and another to end it; hence, there are nine pairs of highlighting phrase markups. Table 7-1 shows the start markup tag, description, and the end markup tag for each of these pairs.

In Table 7-1, there are three markup tags that change the color of the text. These colors are dependent on the type of display you use.

Table 7-1. HIGHLIGHTING PHRASE MARKUPS

Start Markup	Description	End Markup
:hp1.	*Italic*	:ehp1.
:hp2.	**Bold**	:ehp2.
:hp3.	***Bold Italic***	:ehp3.
:hp4.	Color 1 (Red)	:ehp4.
:hp5.	Underline	:ehp5.
:hp6.	*Underline Italic*	:ehp6.
:hp7.	**Underline Bold**	:ehp7.
:hp8.	Color 2 (Blue)	:ehp8.
:hp9.	Color 3 (Pink)	:ehp9.

If you want to place notes in your help text, there are two different types of markups to assist you. The first type is used if your note is a single paragraph. The markup tag for the single paragraph note is **:note text=' '.**. The *text=* keyword lets you specify a label for the note. This label precedes your note in bold text. If you choose not to use the *text=* option, the default label, **Note:**, is used. Following is an example of the **:note text=' '.** markup tag:

>   :note text='For Example'.This is a note. This note will continue until the
>   start of a new paragraph is found.

The result of the note markup tag just shown is:

For Example: This is a note. This note will continue until the start of a new paragraph is found.

If you have a help text note that is more than a single paragraph, use the **:nt text=' '.** and **:ent.** markup tag pair. The **:nt text=' '.** markup tag signals the start of your note. The *text=* keyword lets you specify a label for the note. This label precedes your note in bold text. If you choose not to use the *text=* option, the default label, **Note:**, is used. You can use the **:p.** markup tag to format multiple paragraphs, but you must use the **:ent.** markup tag to signal the end of the note. Following is an example of how the multiple paragraph note works:

>   :nt.This is the start of the first paragraph for the sample note. This note will
>   only be two paragraphs.
>   :p.This is the start of the second paragraph. Now our note is done.
>   :ent.

The result of the multiple paragraph note just shown is:

Note: This is the start of the first paragraph for the sample note. This note will only be two paragraphs.
This is the start of the second paragraph. Now our note is done.

The Information Presentation Facility also has a couple of markup tag pairs for notices. These markup pairs are **:caution.** and **:ecaution.**, and **:warning.** and **:ewarning.**. These markup pairs are used to inform the user of potential risks or possible error conditions. Both these pairs can also have *text=* option to replace their default labels. An example of these markup tag pairs follows:

> :caution.
> Your PC will blow up if you press enter.
> :ecaution.
> :warning.
> This program contains a bug.
> :ewarning.

The result of the previous markups is:

CAUTION:
Your PC will blow up if you press enter.

Warning: This program contains a bug.

The Information Presentation Facility supports several types of lists. The list types vary in how list items are identified and how formatting is controlled; for instance, one list type places order identifiers in front of all list items, while another type of list provides definitions for list items. Of all the different list types available, the *unordered* and *ordered* lists are the only two shown in this book. From these two types of lists, you can see the basic way lists are created and also see some of their differences. For a complete guide to list types and their controls, refer to an OS/2 2.0 technical reference.

To create a list with a typographical symbol preceding the list items, use the unordered list. The typographical symbols used for unordered lists are the bullet(·) and the dash (-). To start an unordered list, use the **:ul.** markup tag; then, for each item in the unordered list, use the **:li.** markup tag. To terminate the unordered list, use the **:eul.** markup tag. Following is an example of the markup tags used to create an unordered list:

> :ul.
> :li.Cows
> :li.Dogs
> :ul.
> :li.Golden Retriever
> :li.Beagle
> :eul.
> :li.Cats
> :eul.

The result of this unordered list is as follows:

> • Cows
> • Dogs
>   - Golden Retriever
>   - Beagle
> • Cats

The previous unordered list example also illustrates how lists can be nested. As you can see, there is a list inside of a list. *Nesting lists* are supported by several of the list types.

Unordered list items are usually created with blank lines between them. To eliminate the blank lines, start the unordered list with the keyword *compact* (**:ul compact.**).

To list a series of steps, create an ordered list. Items in an ordered list are preceded with an order identifier such as a number. To start an ordered list use the **:ol.** markup tag. Then, for each item in the ordered list, use the **:li.** markup tag. To terminate the ordered list use the **:eol.** markup tag. Following is an example of the markup tags used to create an ordered list:

```
:ol.
:li.Compile your program.
:li.Link your program.
:li.Run your program.
:eol.
```

The result of this unordered list is as follows:

1. Compile your program.
2. Link your program.
3. Run your program.

Like other types of list items, ordered list items are usually created with blank lines between them. To eliminate the blank lines, start the ordered list with the keyword *compact* (**:ol compact.**).

So far you've seen how the Information Presentation Facility does all formatting for your application. Most of the time, this is probably what you want. There may be occasions, however, when you want to disable the formatting capability of the Information Presentation Facility. To do this, use the markup tag pair **:lines.** and **:elines.**. When you place text between these tags, it appears very similar to how it was entered. The reason it may not look exactly the way you entered it is because the Information Presentation Facility uses a proportional font to display your text; hence, horizontal spacing may vary. Following is an example of how to use these markup tags to turn formatting off:

```
:lines.
This is on its own line.
    This text indented and on line 2.
This is the start of line 3.
:elines.
```

The result of this unformatted text is as follows:

```
This is on its own line.
    This text indented and on line 2.
This is the start of line 3.
```

To help illustrate your help interface, use the **:artwork.** markup tag. This tag lets you include bit-mapped images in your help text. The keyword parameter *name="* specifies the name of the bit-map file, and the keyword parameter *align="* lets you specify if the image is to be positioned to the right, left, or center of the current margin. To place an image within a line of text, use the keyword parameter *runin*. As you look at the slide puzzle help text, you'll see a couple of examples of images imbedded in the help interface with this markup tag.

Hypertext

One of the most outstanding features of the help interface is the way it allows users to quickly navigate to needed information. The Information Presentation Facility does this by letting the help text developer provide links between phrases of text within panels to other panel IDs; hence, when a user selects a phrase that has a link associated with it, an associated help panel is displayed. This linking of a phrase of text with another help panel is called hypertext. You can define hypertext in your help interface with the **:link.** and **:elink.** markup tag pair. When you mark a phrase with these tags, it appears highlighted on the help panel so the user can see that it can be selected to receive more information.

When you use the **:link.** tag, you also need to use keyword parameters to define the target information that is to be referenced. If the desired reference is to an entire panel of information, use the *reftype=hd* and *res=* keyword parameters with the **:link.** tag. The *reftype=hd* keyword parameter indicates that the reference is to an entire panel and the *res=* keyword is immediately followed by the ID of the panel to be referenced. Following is an example of how this markup tag pair is used to reference an entire panel:

```
:p.Most of the time, you can use a
:link reftype=hd res=209.
standard window
:elink.
to create windows with client areas your program will manipulate.
```

The result of the previous example is that the phrase, **standard window**, is highlighted in the help interface. If the user selects this phrase when it is displayed, the help interface brings the panel with ID 209 to the foreground.

You can also use the **:link.** markup tag to reference footnote information for a panel. In fact, footnote information only becomes visible to the user if it is selected with this hypertext interface. Footnotes are defined for a panel with the **:fn.** and **:efn.** markup tag pair. The **:fn.** tag uses the keyword parameter *id=* to let you define a reference to the footnote. This reference is contained within the scope of the panel and is specified by name. Following is an example of a footnote that is created with the **:fn.** and **:efn.** tags:

```
:fn id=microchannel.
```

Microchannel is the bus architecture used by IBM in several models of its
PS/2s.
:efn.

To reference the footnote just shown, use the **:link.** markup tag with the *refid=*
and *reftype=fn* keyword parameters. In this case, the *reftype=fn* keyword parameter indicates that a footnote is being referenced and the *refid=* keyword parameter is immediately followed by the ID of the footnote. Following is an example
of how to the **:link.** tag to reference the footnote just shown:

```
:p.The design of
:link refid=microchannel reftype=fn.
microchannel
:elink.
allows for sharing of resources between intelligent hardware adapters.
```

Compiling Help Text

After you have generated help text for your application, you compile the help
source file to produce a binary help file. By convention, a help source file should
have a file extension of .IPF. The Information Presentation Facility Compiler is
used to compile an .IPF file. This compiler comes as part of the OS/2 2.0 Toolkit.
To start the compile, enter the following command:

IPFC *filename*.IPF

where *filename* is the source file name for your application's help text.

As a result of compiling your help text, a file with the same name as your source
file and a file extension of .HLP is created. This is the binary help file and should
be located in your system's help path.

DEFINING LINKS TO HELP FILES

As seen in the previous section, you can define links between phrases in a help
panel and other help panel IDs. This section provides similar information on how
to link help text in context with your application. For instance, when a user is
entering information into an entry field for your application and requests help,
you should present information describing that field. Hence, the Information
Presentation Facility can provide context-sensitive help text.

Links between your application and the help interface are defined in special
tables called help tables. These help tables can be defined dynamically in your
application's memory or as resources in your resource script. The advantage of
defining help tables in application memory is that they can be changed dynamically. But, no matter how help tables are defined, the concept of how they work
is basically the same. For simplicity, this book only shows how the slide puzzle
creates help tables as part of a resource script.

There are two types of help tables that define how the help interface interacts with your application. The first type of table is called the HELPTABLE resource. This resource type is a multiple-line resource statement. The definition of the HELPTABLE statement up to the BEGIN keyword is as follows:

HELPTABLE *TABLE_ID*

Where *TABLE_ID* is an ID you assign to a table so it can be identified by the Information Presentation Facility support.

The sub-statements for the HELPTABLE resource define entries for the HELPTABLE. The statement identifier used for defining HELPTABLE entries is HELPITEM. HELPITEM statements are used to define all the frame windows for which help is to be provided; for example, a definition should be created for your main application frame window with a HELPITEM statement. Besides your main application frame window, you can also provide definitions for all your application's child frame windows and dialog boxes. (After all, a dialog box has a window frame associated with it too and can have all kinds of interesting help information.) The definition for the HELPITEM statement is as follows:

HELPITEM *WindowID, SubTableID, PanelID*
where
> *WindowID* is the ID of the frame window for which help text is to be provided.
> *SubTableID* is the symbolic name for the help subtable structure that applies to the frame window. As you will soon see, this subtable structure lets you define the context-sensitive help text for the frame window.
> *PanelID* is the ID of a panel defined in the .IPF file that will be displayed if the user selects extended help from the Help pull-down menu. This help panel is also used for default help if field level help is not defined. (Field level help is defined via the help subtable structure.)

Listing 7-1 shows the HELPTABLE definition for the slide puzzle application.

```
#include <os2.h>
#include "slider.h"
#include "dialog.h"
/************************/
/* Help Table Definition */
/************************/
HELPTABLE MAIN_HELPTABLE
  BEGIN
  HELPITEM ID_SLIDEFRAME, MENU_SUBTABLE, EXTENDED_HELP_PANEL_ID
  HELPITEM IDD_NEWPUZZLE, DLG_SUBTABLE_PUZZLE, PUZZLE_DLG_PANEL_ID
  HELPITEM IDD_RANDOM, DLG_SUBTABLE_RANDOM, MOVEEDIT_PANEL_ID
  END
```

Listing 7-1. Slide puzzle help table definition.

As you can see in Listing 7-1, there are three different frame windows defined to have help text associated with them. These frame windows are the main application frame window and two dialog boxes. The frame windows are identified by the IDs ID_SLIDEFRAME, IDD_NEWPUZZLE, and IDD_RANDOM. If you look at the resource script, you will find that all these IDs are used to define the different frame resources and dialog boxes.

Each HELPITEM points to a HELPSUBTABLE structure which is also defined in the resource script. The purpose of the HELPSUBTABLE is to define field level help for each frame window; for instance, if a dialog box has an entry field for which you want to provide help text, you can define the field in the HELPSUBTABLE structure. The user accesses this help text by pressing the F1 Key or clicking the Help button in the dialog when the entry field has input focus. This is how the user is given context sensitive help.

The HELPSUBTABLE is also a multiple-line resource statement. The definition of the HELPSUBTABLE statement up to the BEGIN keyword is as follows:

> HELPSUBTABLE *DLG_SUBTABLE_ID*
> where *DLG_SUBTABLE_ID* is the identifier used by the HELPITEM statement in the HELPTABLE structure to point to the HELPSUBTABLE.

The statements enclosed between the BEGIN and END keywords for the HELPSUBTABLE statement are HELPSUBITEM statements. HELPSUBITEM statements are used to define the fields within a frame window for which help text is to be displayed. The definition of the HELPSUBITEM statement is as follows:

> HELPSUBITEM *ID_FIELD, FIELD_PANEL_ID*
> where
> > *ID_FIELD* is the window ID of the field for which help text is to be provided.
> > *FIELD_PANEL_ID* is the help panel ID that will be displayed when help is requested for this field.

Listing 7-2 shows the HELPSUBTABLE definitions for the slide puzzle application.

```
#include <os2.h>
#include "slider.h"
#include "dialog.h"
/*****************************/
/* Help Sub Table Definitions */
/*****************************/
HELPSUBTABLE MENU_SUBTABLE
  BEGIN
  HELPSUBITEM IDM_UNDO,          UNDO_PANEL_ID
  HELPSUBITEM IDM_NEW,           NEW_PANEL_ID
  HELPSUBITEM IDM_GRIDSTATE,     GRIDSTATE_PANEL_ID
  HELPSUBITEM IDM_MOVES,         MOVES_PANEL_ID
  HELPSUBITEM IDM_STOP,          STOP_PANEL_ID
  HELPSUBITEM IDM_PRODUCT,       PRODUCT_PANEL_ID
  HELPSUBITEM IDM_EXIT,          EXIT_PANEL_ID
  END
```

```
HELPSUBTABLE DLG_SUBTABLE_PUZZLE
  BEGIN
  HELPSUBITEM IDD_TIMEEDIT, TIMEEDIT_PANEL_ID
  HELPSUBITEM IDD_GRIDEDIT, GRIDEDIT_PANEL_ID
  END


HELPSUBTABLE DLG_SUBTABLE_RANDOM
  BEGIN
  HELPSUBITEM IDD_MOVEEDIT, MOVEEDIT_PANEL_ID
  END
```

Listing 7-2. Slide puzzle help subtables.

Listing 7-2 shows all three help subtables referenced by the HELPTABLE statement for the slide puzzle. As you can see in the MENU_SUBTABLE subtable, menu items can also have help text associated with them. All the menu items for the Options pull-down menu have help panels defined for them. The user accesses help for a menu item by pressing the F1 key when the menu item is highlighted. The DLG_SUBTABLE_PUZZLE subtable defines the fields for the new puzzle dialog box and the DLG_SUBTABLE_RANDOM subtable defines the field in the random moves dialog box.

When the user requests help for a field or item, the Information Presentation Facility looks for a HELPSUBITEM entry to locate the help panel to display. If a help panel is not defined for a field or item, the Information Presentation Facility looks back at the HELPTABLE, finds the appropriate HELPITEM entry, and displays default help text for the frame window. If the user selects extended help from the Help pull-down menu, the Information Presentation Facility displays the help panel ID given in the HELPITEM statement that refererces the frame window ID (ID_SLIDEFRAME).

Figure 7-1 shows how the help table and help subtables relate to the actual slide puzzle application. Even though this figure only represents one of the dialogs for the slide puzzle, the other subtables work the same way.

INTERFACING WITH THE INFORMATION PRESENTATION FACILITY

To use the services of the Information Presentation Facility, your application must define how the facility is to interface with it. This is done by creating an object called a help instance and then associating this object with the application frame window. Once you are done with the help instance, you need to destroy it. There are three Presentation Manager functions that let you create and deal with the help instance. These PM functions are called *WinCreateHelpInstance*, *WinAssociateHelpInstance*, and *WinDestoryHelpInstance*.

The first function you'll need to use is WinCreateHelpInstance. This function passes the address of a special structure called a help initialization structure. If the WinCreateHelpInstance function is successful, it returns a handle to the help instance. The help initialization structure contains several items that describe information about where the application help text can be found and how the

```
HELPTABLE  MAIN_HELPTABLE
  BEGIN
  HELPITEM  ID_SLIDEFRAME,MENU_SUBTABLE,EXTENDED_HELP_PANEL_ID
  HELPITEM  IDD_NEWPUZZLE,DLG_SUBTABLE_PUZZLE,PUZZLE_DLG_PANEL_ID
  HELPITEM  IDD_RANDOM,DLG_SUBTABLE_RANDOM,MOVEEDIT_DLG_PANEL_ID
  END


HELPSUBTABLE  DLG_SUBTABLE_PUZZLE
  BEGIN
  HELPSUBITEM  IDD_GRIDEDIT,GRIDEDIT_PANEL_ID
  HELPSUBITEM  IDD_TIMEEDIT,TIMEEDIT_PANEL_ID
  END
```

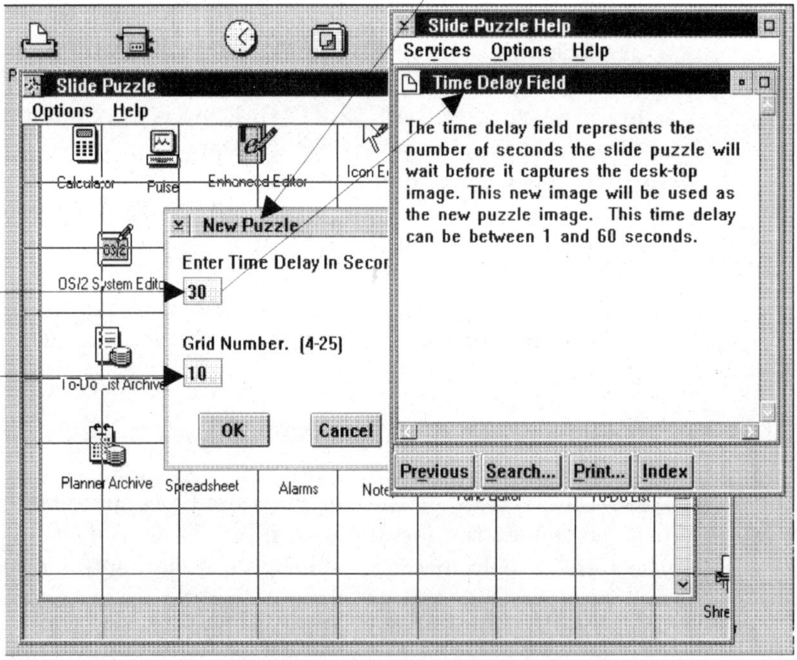

Figure 7-1. Help table flow.

application interfaces with the Information Presentation Facility. Creating the help instance actually allows the Information Presentation Facility to intercept all messages that are placed in your message queue. This allows it to intercept help-related requests and process them on your behalf.

Once the Information Presentation Facility intercepts help requests from your application, it needs to have the help instance associated with a chain of application windows. This is the purpose of the WinAssociateHelpInstance function. The handle of the application window frame and the handle of the appropriate help instance is passed to this function to resolve the association.

After the help instance is associated, your application can use the Information Presentation Help services until it terminates. But, before your application does terminate, you must inform the Information Presentation Facility to eliminate the help instance. This is the purpose of the WinDestroyHelpInstance function. Listing 7-3 shows how the slide puzzle application uses these functions to interface with the Information Presentation Facility.

```c
/*******************************************/
/* Required IPF Structures For Help Text. */
/*******************************************/
HELPINIT hmiHelpData;
HWND hwndHelpInstance;
HWND hwndFrame, hwndClient, hwndMenu;
/********************/
/* Main Procedure. */
/********************/
int main(int argc, char *argv[])
  {
  ULONG ulFrameFlags=FCF_TASKLIST | FCF_SIZEBORDER |
    FCF_TITLEBAR | FCF_MINMAX |
    FCF_SYSMENU | FCF_MENU | FCF_ICON | FCF_ACCELTABLE;
  HMQ hmq;
  QMSG qmsg;
  hab=WinInitialize(0);
  hmq=WinCreateMsgQueue(hab, 0);


  /*******************************/
  /* IPF Initialization Structure. */
  /*******************************/
  hmiHelpData.cb=sizeof(HELPINIT);
  hmiHelpData.ulReturnCode=0;
  hmiHelpData.pszTutorialName=NULL;
  hmiHelpData.phtHelpTable=(PVOID)(0xffff0000 | MAIN_HELPTABLE);
  hmiHelpData.hmodAccelActionBarModule=0;
  hmiHelpData.idAccelTable=0;
  hmiHelpData.idActionBar=0;
  hmiHelpData.pszHelpWindowTitle=(PSZ)"Slide Puzzle Help";
  hmiHelpData.hmodHelpTableModule=0;
  hmiHelpData.fShowPanelId=0;
  hmiHelpData.pszHelpLibraryName=(PSZ)"SLIDER.HLP";


  /**************************/
  /* Create instance of IPF. */
  /**************************/
  hwndHelpInstance=WinCreateHelpInstance(hab, &hmiHelpData);
  if(!hwndHelpInstance)
    WinMessageBox(HWND_DESKTOP, HWND_DESKTOP,
      (PSZ)"Help Not Available", (PSZ)"Help Creation Error",
```

```
        1, MB_OK | MB_APPLMODAL | MB_MOVEABLE);
  else {
    if(hmiHelpData.ulReturnCode){
      WinMessageBox(HWND_DESKTOP, HWND_DESKTOP,
        (PSZ)"Help Terminated Due to Error",
        (PSZ)"Help Creation Error",
        1, MB_OK | MB_APPLMODAL | MB_MOVEABLE);
      WinDestroyHelpInstance(hwndHelpInstance);
      }
    }
WinRegisterClass(hab, (PSZ)szClientClass, ClientWndProc,
  CS_SIZEREDRAW, 0);
hwndFrame=WinCreateStdWindow(HWND_DESKTOP, WS_VISIBLE,
  &ulFrameFlags, (PSZ)szClientClass, 0, 0L, 0,
  ID_SLIDEFRAME, &hwndClient);

/*****************************/
/* Associate instance of IPF. */
/*****************************/
  if(hwndHelpInstance)
    WinAssociateHelpInstance(hwndHelpInstance, hwndFrame);

/***************************************/
/* Get PM messages and dispatch them. */
/***************************************/
while(WinGetMsg(hab, &qmsg, 0, 0, 0)){
  WinDispatchMsg(hab, &qmsg);
  }

/***************************/
/* Free resources obtained. */
/***************************/
if(hwndHelpInstance)WinDestroyHelpInstance(hwndHelpInstance);
WinDestroyWindow(hwndFrame);
WinDestroyMsgQueue(hmq);
WinTerminate(hab);
return 0;
}
```

Listing 7-3. Work with the help instance.

As you can see in Listing 7-3, the slide puzzle application has a HELPINIT structure named **hmiHelpData**. (The OS/2 Developer's Toolkit provides a definition of the HELPINIT structure.) The first thing the application does is initialize the HELPINIT structure. From this structure, you can deduce many of the features and functions the Information Presentation Facility can provide your application. For a complete explanation of all the fields and how to use them, refer to an OS/2 technical reference manual. But, for a basic help interface, you only need to focus on the fields that are about to be discussed.

The **phtHelpTable** field is a pointer to your help table. Because the slide puzzle help table is a resource, you build this pointer by OR'ing the resource ID of the help table with hexadecimal FFFF0000. The **pszHelpWindowTitle** field points to a text string to be displayed in the title bar area of the main help window. The **hmodHelpTableModule** field is used if the help table is part of a DLL. To indicate that your help table is not part of a DLL, this field must be 0. The **fShowPanelID** field indicates to the Information Presentation Facility whether or not to show help panel IDs in the panel bar area. Showing panel IDs may be useful during the development of your help interface. To indicate that you would like to see panel IDs, use the predefined value CMIC_SHOW_PANEL_ID. Finally, the **pszHelpLibraryName** field is a pointer to the text string that identifies the name of your help file. This is the file that you compiled with the Information Presentation Facility compiler and should be located in the help path.

Once the HELPINIT structure is initialized, the WinCreateHelpInstance function is used to create the help instance and the returned handle is saved in a variable named **hwndHelpInstance**. Next, the help handle is tested for null or 0 to see if help is available. If it is not, a message box is displayed and the slide puzzle continues without a help interface. If help is available, the slide puzzle checks for a creation error in the return field of the HELPINIT structure. If there is an error, a message box is displayed and the help instance is destroyed before the slide puzzle continues. (The slide puzzle will continue without a help interface.)

After the help instance is created, the slide puzzle registers and creates its standard window and then associates the help instance with the application frame window. From this point, the slide puzzle application starts processing all messages until a WM_QUIT message is received. It then releases the resources it has obtained and terminates. In particular, the slide puzzle uses the WinDestoryHelpInstance function to release the help instance that it created.

Now that the help instance is created and associated, the Information Presentation Facility can intercept all messages that are sent to your application and take action on the ones that are help-related. Because of this, you may think you are done; and you almost are! But, you still need to define the Help pull-down menu, and there are a few messages that the Information Presentation Facility will send to your window procedure.

Creating a Help pull-down menu is basically the same as any other menu resource. Listing 7-4 shows the menu resource statement used in the slide puzzle resource script:

```
#include <os2.h>
#include "slider.h"
MENU ID_SLIDEFRAME
  BEGIN
  SUBMENU "~Options", IDM_OPT
    BEGIN
    MENUITEM "~Undo \tCtrl+U",            IDM_UNDO
    MENUITEM "~New Puzzle... \tCtrl+N",   IDM_NEW
    MENUITEM "~Grid On \tCtrl+G",         IDM_GRIDSTATE
    MENUITEM "~Random Moves... \tCtrl+R", IDM_MOVES
    MENUITEM SEPARATOR
    MENUITEM "~Stop \tCtrl+S",            IDM_STOP
    MENUITEM SEPARATOR
```

```
      MENUITEM "~Product Information... \tCtrl+P", IDM_PRODUCT
      MENUITEM SEPARATOR
      MENUITEM "E~xit \tAlt+F4",              IDM_EXIT
      END
    SUBMENU "~Help", IDM_HELP, MIS_HELP
      BEGIN
      MENUITEM "~Help for help...", IDM_HELP_FOR_HELP
      MENUITEM "~Extended help...", SC_HELPEXTENDED,MIS_SYSCOMMAND
      MENUITEM "~Keys help...",     SC_HELPKEYS,MIS_SYSCOMMAND
      MENUITEM "Help ~index...",    SC_HELPINDEX,MIS_SYSCOMMAND
      END
    END
```

Listing 7-4. Help pull-down menu definition.

As you can see in Listing 7-4, the Help pull-down menu is defined in the same way as the Options pull-down menu, but uses different menu styles and attributes. The Help submenu identified with the IDM_HELP ID uses the MIS_HELP style. This causes PM to send a WM_HELP message rather than a WM_COMMAND message when the menu is selected. Likewise, several of the menu items for the Help pull-down menu use the style MIS_SYSCOMMAND. This style causes WM_SYSCOMMAND messages to be sent instead of WM_COMMAND messages when these menu items are selected. Remember, the help interface is monitoring all messages to your application, hence, the help interface can quickly interrogate all WM_SYSCOMMAND and WM_HELP messages sent to your application and take the appropriate action when the help messages are found.

All menu-related IDs defined by the slide puzzle application start with the prefix IDM_. You will notice, however, that some IDs start with SC_. These IDs are predefined and used by the Information Presentation Facility to identify different help menu items for the Help menu. Hence, your Extended help menu item must use the ID SC_HELPEXTENDED no matter where the item is located in the Help menu. This applies to the Keys help and Help index menu items as well.

As you have probably already guessed, there is one menu item in the slide puzzle application Help menu that is not directly operated on by the Information Presentation Facility. This menu item is Help for Help and has an ID assigned by our application. Because of this, this menu item generates a WM_COMMAND message when selected. Actually, there are a couple other help interface messages that are sent to your window procedure for you to deal with. Listing 7-5 shows the message routines that the slide puzzle application has for dealing with help messages.

```
MRESULT EXPENTRY ClientWndProc(HWND hwnd, ULONG msg,
  MPARAM mp1, MPARAM mp2)
  {
  switch(msg){
    /*******************************/
    /* Process pull-down menu items. */
    /*******************************/
    case WM_COMMAND:
```

```
              switch (COMMANDMSG(&msg)->cmd){

                /***************************/
                /* Display HELP_FOR_HELP. */
                /***************************/
                case IDM_HELP_FOR_HELP:
                  if(hwndHelpInstance)
                    WinSendMsg(hwndHelpInstance, HM_DISPLAY_HELP, OL, OL);
                  break;

                default:
                  return WinDefWindowProc(hwnd, msg, mp1, mp2);
              }
              break;

            /*******************************/
            /* Process help error message. */
            /*******************************/
            case HM_ERROR:
              if((hwndHelpInstance && (ULONG)mp1)==HMERR_NO_MEMORY){
                WinMessageBox(HWND_DESKTOP, HWND_DESKTOP,
                  (PSZ)"Help Terminated Due to Error",
                  (PSZ)"Help Error",
                  1, MB_OK | MB_APPLMODAL | MB_MOVEABLE);
                WinDestroyHelpInstance(hwndHelpInstance);
              }
              else {
                WinMessageBox(HWND_DESKTOP, HWND_DESKTOP,
                  (PSZ)"Help Error Occurred",
                  (PSZ)"Help Error",
                  1, MB_OK | MB_APPLMODAL | MB_MOVEABLE);
              }
              break;

            /***********************************/
            /* Process query keys help message. */
            /***********************************/
            case HM_QUERY_KEYS_HELP:
              return((MRESULT)KEYS_HELP_PANEL_ID);
              break;
          }

    /****************************************************/
    /* Let default routine process message and return. */
    /****************************************************/
    return WinDefWindowProc(hwnd, msg, mp1, mp2);
  }
```

Listing 7-5. Help message processing.

As you can see in Listing 7-5, the slide puzzle application has a case statement
for the IDM_HELP_FOR_HELP menu item in the WM_COMMAND message
routine. By receiving this message, the WinProc has the opportunity to process
this message as it likes. In this case, however, the slide puzzle application lets the

Information Presentation Facility display its help for help by sending a HM_DISPLAY_HELP message to the help instance. This is a common way of dealing with Help for Help.

The Information Presentation Facility can also send a message to your application if it detects an error while processing. This is done with the HM_ERROR message. The slide puzzle application processes the HM_ERROR message by first testing to see if it was sent because of a lack of memory. If this is the case, a message box is displayed and the help instance is destroyed with the WinDestroyHelpInstance function. If lack of memory is not the cause of the error, a message box with a general help error message is displayed and normal message processing continues.

Lastly, the Information Presentation Facility may send your application the HM_QUERY_KEYS_HELP message which is caused by the user requesting Keys help from the Help pull-down menu. To have your Keys help displayed, return the help panel ID that has the Keys help information. As seen in List 7-5, this is what the slide puzzle application does.

As you can see, the Information Presentation Facility provides a lot of service and flexiblity at a very low software development cost. There is little doubt that this service can increase the usability and richness of your application.

8

Working With Time

As you program in the Presentation Manager environment, there may be occasions when you want or need time-related services. Because OS/2 is designed to be a true multitasking operating system, it has good time management and interprocess communication mechanisms. When working with OS/2 2.0, you will find many functions and features available to deal with time.

If you have been using the slide puzzle application, you have probably noticed places where time-related services are used. For instance, when you capture a new puzzle image from the Options pull-down menu, you enter a time delay for the puzzle to wait before the new desktop image is captured. This option is probably the most obvious example of where time services are used. Also, as we've discussed the slide puzzle code, you've seen several places where the DosSleep function has been used to pace animation sequences. This is another simple example of where time services have been used.

There are, however, other less obvious places where time is managed. One of these places occurs when drawing is performed for the random moves and undo options. This drawing is performed in a different thread of execution than message processing. Thus, the message processing thread is kept short. If this was not done, the slide puzzle program could keep focus much longer than a well designed PM application should and, therefore, not allow other applications to gain input focus. If other applications are not allowed to gain input focus, the user is not allowed to work with them. When user input is delayed for long periods of time, the application should use the wait pointer icon to indicate the situation. However, a good PM application should not keep input focus for long periods of time after the user has requested a change. Remember, playing well with others and keeping the customer happy is the goal!

Another less obvious place where time is managed is in the routine that determines when the grasshopper should run across the screen. As you will soon see, this is also done in a separate thread of execution that interfaces with the main process thread for drawing the animation.

USING THE DOSSLEEP FUNCTION

The DosSleep function causes your thread of execution to be suspended for a certain period of time. When your thread uses this function, OS/2 allows other threads of execution in the system to run. Once the specified time period elapses, OS/2 allows your thread of execution to run again.

The only operand of the DosSleep function is the period of time to sleep or be suspended. This period of time is specified in milliseconds, but the OS/2 timer interrupt rate is 32 times per second. Hence, even though this function appears as though millisecond resolution is possible, it really isn't. Besides the timer interrupt frequency, your application may be one of several competing for processing time from OS/2. For many applications, this sharing of processing time is not noticeable by the user, but there are some situations where it can be. Even though OS/2 has several features to help manage time sharing, your application does not have absolute control over time. Therefore, this time parameter is better thought of as an approximate time with a resolution of about 1/32 of a second. This does not mean that the units of time for this operand are 1/32 of a second, but rather the accuracy of the function is typically within 1/32 of a second of the millisecond value specified. For example, if a value of 1 is specified for the DosSleep function, control will be returned to your thread no sooner than 1/32 of a second but probably within 1/16 of a second. If a value of 1,000 is specified for the DosSleep function, control will be returned to your thread no sooner than 1 full second, but probably within 1.032 seconds.

Because this function is fairly straightforward, and so many examples of this function have already been shown, no code example is given here. If you would like to see an example of this function, refer to Listing 6-4 in Chapter 6, Animation.

USING THE WM_TIMER MESSAGE

For simple time delay notification, Presentation Manager provides a WM_TIMER message that is fairly easy to use. What makes this message so useful is that your application can set the message frequency with a PM function called *WinStartTimer*. Not only can the frequency of the WM_TIMER message be selected, but a timer ID can be associated with the message. Because of this, multiple timers can be started with different frequencies. There is, however, a limited number of OS/2 timers available, so if you want to be a good OS/2 citizen, be conservative in the number of timers you use.

Just like the DosSleep function, the frequency of the WM_TIMER message can not be any greater than the timer interrupt rate of the personal computer. Therefore, the shortest timer interval possible is not a millisecond, but about 32 milliseconds. Timer messages are low priority queued messages; however, only a single instance of a timer message with a specific timer ID is allowed on the message queue.

Once you are done using a timer, you can give it back to OS/2 with a PM function called *WinStopTimer*. This timer is then available to other applications again. With this brief description of the WM_TIMER message, let's look at how the slide puzzle application uses it to provide a simple time delay before capturing a new desktop image.

```
MRESULT EXPENTRY ClientWndProc(HWND hwnd, ULONG msg,
  MPARAM mp1, MPARAM mp2)
  {
  BITMAPINFOHEADER2 bmp;
  HBITMAP hbmt;
  HDC hdcbm;
  HPS hpsd;
  POINTL aptl[4];
  SIZEL sizl;
  SHORT x, y, i;
  POINTL shear, ptl;
  RECTL rclInvalid;

  switch(msg){
    /********************************/
    /* Process pull-down menu items. */
    /********************************/
    case WM_COMMAND:
      switch (COMMANDMSG(&msg)->cmd){

        /*****************************************/
        /* Process new puzzle pull-down option. */
        /*****************************************/
        case IDM_NEW:
          if(WinDlgBox(HWND_DESKTOP, hwnd, NewPuzzleDlgProc,
            0, IDD_NEWPUZZLE, &puzzle))
            WinStartTimer(hab, hwnd, ID_TIMER, puzzle.sCapTime*1000);
          return(MRESULT)TRUE;

        default:
          return WinDefWindowProc(hwnd, msg, mp1, mp2);
      }
      break;

    /********************************/
    /* Process timer create message. */
    /********************************/
    case WM_TIMER:
```

```
/***********************************************************/
/* Only one timer is started so assume that timer caused */
/* this message to occur and delete old bitmap.          */
/***********************************************************/
WinStopTimer(hab, hwnd, ID_TIMER);  /* Stop the time. */
GpiDeleteBitmap(hbmSrc);

/***********************************************************/
/* Reset presentation space for master bit-map image. */
/***********************************************************/
GpiResetPS(hpsMemory, GRES_ALL);
GpiQueryDeviceBitmapFormats(hpsMemory, 2L, alBmpFormats);
memset(&bmp, 0, sizeof(bmp));
bmp.cbFix=sizeof bmp;
bmp.cx=sxPels;
bmp.cPlanes=(USHORT)alBmpFormats[0];
bmp.cBitCount=(USHORT)alBmpFormats[1];
bmp.cy=syPels;
hbmSrc=GpiCreateBitmap(hpsMemory, &bmp, 0L, NULL, NULL);
GpiSetBitmap(hpsMemory, hbmSrc);

/*********************************************************/
/* Copy desktop image into memory presentation page. */
/*********************************************************/
aptl[0].x=0; aptl[0].y=0;             /* Target lower left. */
aptl[1].x=bmp.cx; aptl[1].y=bmp.cy; /* Target upper right. */
aptl[2].x=0; aptl[2].y=0;             /* Source lower left. */
hpsd=WinGetScreenPS(HWND_DESKTOP);
GpiBitBlt(hpsMemory, hpsd, 3L, aptl, ROP_SRCCOPY, BBO_AND);

/***********************************************************/
/* Calculate the number of pels for the width and height */
/* of a puzzle piece.                                    */
/***********************************************************/
lcxMinMax=bmp.cx/puzzle.sGrid;
lcyMinMax=bmp.cy/puzzle.sGrid;

/************************************************************/
/* Create blank puzzle piece in lower right puzzle corner. */
/************************************************************/
aptl[0].x=(puzzle.sGrid-1)*lcxMinMax; aptl[0].y=0;
aptl[1].x=aptl[0].x+lcxMinMax; aptl[1].y=lcyMinMax;
GpiBitBlt(hpsMemory, hpsMemory, 2L, aptl, ROP_ZERO, BBO_AND);

/*************************************************/
/* Turn on the grid if the grid state is set. */
/*************************************************/
if(sGridState) {
  GpiSetMix(hpsMemory, FM_INVERT);
  for(lRow=0; lRow<=syPels/lcyMinMax; lRow++){
    ptl.x=0; ptl.y=lRow*lcyMinMax;
    GpiMove(hpsMemory, &ptl);
    ptl.x=sxPels;
    GpiLine(hpsMemory, &ptl);
    }
```

```
      for(lCol=0; lCol<=sxPels/lcxMinMax; lCol++){
        ptl.y=0; ptl.x=lCol*lcxMinMax;
        GpiMove(hpsMemory, &ptl);
        ptl.y=syPels;
        GpiLine(hpsMemory, &ptl);
        }
      }


    /*****************************************************/
    /* Initialize undo index, buffer, and blank location. */
    /*****************************************************/
    ulUndoIndex=0;
    for(i=0; i<SIZEOFUNDO; i++){
      backup[i].x=30;
      backup[i].y=30;
      }
    forward=TRUE;
    sGridy=0;
    sGridx=puzzle.sGrid-1;


    /*******************************************************/
    /* Release resources and cause beep to let user know a */
    /* screen has been captured.                           */
    /*******************************************************/
    WinReleasePS(hpsd);
    WinInvalidateRect(hwnd, NULL, FALSE);  /* Cause full paint. */
    DosBeep(523, 100);
    return(MRESULT)TRUE;
  }


/***************************************************/
/* Let default routine process message and return. */
/***************************************************/
return WinDefWindowProc(hwnd, msg, mp1, mp2);
}
```

Listing 8-1. WM_TIMER processing code example.

As you can see in Listing 8-1, the slide puzzle program starts a timer after the dialog from the new puzzle option returns successfully. During the processing of the dialog procedure, the variable named **puzzle.sCapTime** is set to a value that represents seconds. This value is limited to 60 and is used by the WinStartTimer function to set the timer interval for the WM_TIMER message. (The variable is multiplied by 1000 to convert from seconds to milliseconds.) After the timer is set, regular processing for the slide puzzle resumes until a WM_TIMER message is received.

Once the WM_TIMER message is received, the WM_TIMER routine assumes that it was caused by the screen capture timer because this is the only timer started by the slide puzzle application. If more than one timer were started, a case statement could be applied against the low order 16 bits of the mp1 message parameter to determine which timer caused the WM_TIMER message. The first action taken by the WM_TIMER routine is to stop the new puzzle timer from occurring again. It does this by using the WinStopTimer function. A memory presentation space is then reset in preparation to hold the master puzzle bit-map image.

When the presentation space is prepared, the current desktop image is copied to the memory presentation page, the grid size is determined, the blank puzzle piece is created, and the grid is turned on if appropriate. Finally, the undo buffer and grid variables are initialized and a beep is generated to inform the user that the capture has been completed. The entire window is then invalidated so the WM_PAINT routine updates the display presentation page.

USING MULTIPLE THREADS OF EXECUTION

OS/2 is designed to manage multiple processes and threads of execution while providing good memory management. Many programs or applications consist of only one process, but they can consist of several processes. Each OS/2 process is isolated through a hardware protection scheme, but there are functions and mechanisms allowing these processes to communicate with each other and share resources. By doing this, OS/2 provides an environment that allows cooperation between programs and increases the security and integrity of the entire work station. For instance, no process can access the memory of another unless given permission from the target process; hence, accidently damaging another process's resources is unlikely. If this is attempted, OS/2 detects which process caused the resource violation and terminates it, while all other processes continue.

A process is a thread of execution all on its own. OS/2, however, allows a process to create other threads of execution within itself. This is done with an OS/2 function called *DosCreateThread*. A thread has its own stack and OS/2 maintains the registers and an instruction pointer for each thread. Therefore, a thread operates as an independent piece of code but shares the resources of the parent process.

Even though a thread of execution performs processing on its own, it is typically created to provide some sort of parallel or background function. Because of this, the thread usually needs to communicate with or be notified by the parent or another thread when it has work to perform. A thread could continuously poll a shared memory location for notification to start work, but, polling is a wasteful use of processing resources. To solve this problem, OS/2 provides a structure called a semaphore that allows signaling between processes or threads and controls when a thread starts processing.

Semaphores are shared resources that can be created, reset, posted, and waited on between threads of execution; hence, a thread of execution can be put in a situation where it must wait for a semaphore to be posted before it can continue processing. This is exactly the type of activity the slide puzzle application performs. An OS/2 function called *DosCreateEventSem* creates a semaphore, an OS/2 function called *DosResetEventSem* resets a semaphore, an OS/2 called *DosPostEventSem* posts a semaphore, and an OS/2 function called *DosWaitEventSem* waits on a semaphore.

When multiple threads of execution in a process are all executing, there may be times when they don't want to compete for resources and want to temporarily stop all other threads in the same process. An OS/2 function called *DosEnterCritSec* solves this situation. This function blocks all the other threads of execution within the same process from executing. This state continues until the thread of execution that requested the DosEnterCritSec function calls the OS/2 function called *DosExitCritSec*. Hence, these OS/2 functions allow threads within a process to have exclusive control over processing.

Listing 8-2 shows how the slide puzzle uses a separate thread of execution to perform background drawing for the Random Moves and Undo options. The name of this background drawing thread is **Background**. This listing also shows how the slide puzzle uses a thread of execution named **Bugtime** to randomly signal the message processing thread to perform the bug animation. As Listing 8-2 is discussed, you will be informed when to look forward or backward at different parts of this listing to see how the different pieces of the application relate to each other.

```c
/*********************/
/* Thread Variables. */
/*********************/
TID tidBack, tidBug;
USHORT usRC;
HEV hev;
ULONG ulPostCt;


/**************************/
/* Other Global Variables. */
/**************************/
HAB hab;
HDC hdc, hdcMemory;
HPS hps, hpsMemory;
BITMAPINFOHEADER bmpSrc;
HBITMAP hbmSrc;
HWND hwndFrame, hwndClient, hwndMenu;
SHORT sGridy, sGridx;
LONG lcxMinMax, lcyMinMax;
SHORT sMoves, sRandomFlag=0, sUndoFlag=0;
ULONG ulUndoIndex;
BOOL forward;
POINTS backup[SIZEOFUNDO];
struct PUZZLEPARMS {
  SHORT sCapTime;
  SHORT sGrid;
  };
struct PUZZLEPARMS puzzle;

SHORT sGridState=0;
BOOL StopState=FALSE, FirstTime=TRUE;
LONG alBmpFormats[2];


/*******************/
/* Main Procedure. */
/*******************/
```

```
int main(int argc, char *argv[])
  {
  HDC hdcTemp;
  HPS hpsTemp;
  ULONG ulFrameFlags=FCF_TASKLIST | FCF_SIZEBORDER |
    FCF_TITLEBAR | FCF_MINMAX |
    FCF_SYSMENU | FCF_MENU | FCF_ICON | FCF_ACCELTABLE;
  HMQ hmq;
  QMSG qmsg;
  hab=WinInitialize(0);
  hmq=WinCreateMsgQueue(hab, 0);
  WinRegisterClass(hab, (PSZ)szClientClass, ClientWndProc,
    CS_SIZEREDRAW, 0);
  hwndFrame=WinCreateStdWindow(HWND_DESKTOP, WS_VISIBLE,
    &ulFrameFlags, (PSZ)szClientClass, 0, 0L, 0,
    ID_SLIDEFRAME, &hwndClient);

  /***************************************/
  /* Get PM messages and dispatch them. */
  /***************************************/
  while(WinGetMsg(hab, &qmsg, 0, 0, 0)){
    DosEnterCritSec();
    WinDispatchMsg(hab, &qmsg);
    DosExitCritSec();
    }

  /***************************/
  /* Free resources obtained. */
  /***************************/
  GpiDeleteBitmap(hbmSrc);
  WinDestroyWindow(hwndFrame);
  WinDestroyMsgQueue(hmq);
  WinTerminate(hab);
  return 0;
  }

MRESULT EXPENTRY ClientWndProc(HWND hwnd, ULONG msg,
  MPARAM mp1, MPARAM mp2)
  {
  BOOL fRet=FALSE;
  BITMAPINFOHEADER2 bmp;
  HBITMAP hbmt;
  HDC hdcbm;
  HPS hpsd;
  POINTL aptl[4];
  SIZEL sizl;
  SHORT x, y, i;
  POINTL shear, ptl;
  RECTL rclInvalid;

  switch(msg){
    /***********************/
    /* Process bug request. */
    /***********************/
```

```
case BUGRUN:
  Bug();
  return(MRESULT)TRUE;


/**********************************/
/* Process window create message. */
/**********************************/
case WM_CREATE:
  /*************************************************************/
  /* Set semaphore before thread is created so it will wait */
  /* right away.  This semaphore is used by the background  */
  /* thread.                                                */
  /*************************************************************/
  DosCreateEventSem(NULL, &hev, 0, 0);


  /*******************/
  /* Create threads. */
  /*******************/
  DosCreateThread(&tidBack, Background, 0UL, 0UL, 4096);
  DosCreateThread(&tidBug, Bugtime, 0UL, 0UL, 4096);


  /*************************/
  /* Initialize undo array. */
  /*************************/
  ulUndoIndex=0;
  for(i=0; i<SIZEOFUNDO; i++){
    backup[i].x=30;
    backup[i].y=30;
    }
  forward=TRUE;
  return(MRESULT)FALSE;


/*********************************/
/* Process pull-down menu items. */
/*********************************/
case WM_COMMAND:
  switch (COMMANDMSG(&msg)->cmd){

    /*********************************/
    /* Process undo pull-down option. */
    /*********************************/
    case IDM_UNDO:
      forward=FALSE;
      WinSendMsg(WinWindowFromID(hwndFrame, FID_MENU),
        MM_SETITEMATTR,
          MPFROM2SHORT(IDM_MOVES, TRUE),
          MPFROM2SHORT(MIA_DISABLED, MIA_DISABLED));
      sUndoFlag=1;
      DosPostEventSem(hev);
      return(MRESULT)TRUE;


    /*********************************/
    /* Process stop pull-down option. */
    /*********************************/
```

```
          case IDM_STOP:
            if((sUndoFlag==1) || (sRandomFlag==1)){
              StopState=TRUE;
              WinSendMsg(WinWindowFromID(hwndFrame, FID_MENU),
                MM_SETITEMATTR,
                MPFROM2SHORT(IDM_UNDO, TRUE),
                MPFROM2SHORT(MIA_DISABLED, 0));
              WinSendMsg(WinWindowFromID(hwndFrame, FID_MENU),
                MM_SETITEMATTR,
                MPFROM2SHORT(IDM_MOVES, TRUE),
                MPFROM2SHORT(MIA_DISABLED, 0));
              }
            return(MRESULT)TRUE;


          /*******************************************/
          /* Process random move pull-down option. */
          /*******************************************/
          case IDM_MOVES:
            if(WinDlgBox(HWND_DESKTOP, hwnd, RandomDlgProc,
              0, IDD_RANDOM, &sMoves)){
              sRandomFlag=1;
              WinSendMsg(WinWindowFromID(hwndFrame, FID_MENU),
                MM_SETITEMATTR,
                MPFROM2SHORT(IDM_UNDO, TRUE),
                MPFROM2SHORT(MIA_DISABLED, MIA_DISABLED));
              DosPostEventSem(hev);
              }
            return(MRESULT)TRUE;


          default:
            return WinDefWindowProc(hwnd, msg, mp1, mp2);
        }
      break;
    }


  /********************************************************/
  /* Let default routine process message and return. */
  /********************************************************/
  return WinDefWindowProc(hwnd, msg, mp1, mp2);
  }


/*************************************************************/
/* Background thread for random moves and undo functions. */
/*************************************************************/
VOID Background(ULONG dummy)
  {
  LONG i;
  SHORT x, y, toggle;
  HAB habt;


  /****************************************************************/
  /* Get an anchor block handle so thread can access PM functions. */
  /****************************************************************/
```

```
    habt=WinInitialize(0);
    for(;;){

      /************************************************/
      /* Wait for main process to clear semaphore. */
      /************************************************/
      DosWaitEventSem(hev,SEM_INDEFINITE_WAIT);


      /***********************************/
      /* See if we are to perform an undo. */
      /***********************************/
      if(sUndoFlag==1){

        /***************************************************************/
        /* This is a circular buffer so set index to last valid entry. */
        /***************************************************************/
        if(ulUndoIndex==0)
          ulUndoIndex=SIZEOFUNDO-1;
        else
          ulUndoIndex-;


        /************************************************************/
        /* Undo moves while valid move and stop is not indicated. */
        /************************************************************/
        while((backup[ulUndoIndex].x<30) && (!StopState)){
          DosEnterCritSec();        /* Keep control from main process. */
          Slide(habt, hwndClient,  /* Slide piece. */
            backup[ulUndoIndex].x, backup[ulUndoIndex].y);
          backup[ulUndoIndex].x=30;  /* Invalidate buffer location. */
          backup[ulUndoIndex].y=30;
          if(ulUndoIndex==0)         /* Adjust index to next entry. */
            ulUndoIndex=SIZEOFUNDO-1;
          else
            ulUndoIndex-;

          /************************************************************/
          /* Let main process and other have more processing time. */
          /************************************************************/
          DosExitCritSec();
          DosSleep(SLEEPTIME);
          }


        /*********************************************************/
        /* Bump index to next place an entry can be placed. */
        /*********************************************************/
        if(ulUndoIndex==SIZEOFUNDO-1)
          ulUndoIndex=0;
        else
          ulUndoIndex++;


        /************************************************************/
        /* Let slide routine know that move are no longer from undo. */
        /************************************************************/
```

```
          forward=TRUE;

          /*********************************************************/
          /* Enable random moves menu item and clear undo flag. */
          /*********************************************************/
          WinPostMsg(WinWindowFromID(hwndFrame, FID_MENU),
            MM_SETITEMATTR,
            MPFROM2SHORT(IDM_MOVES, TRUE),
            MPFROM2SHORT(MIA_DISABLED, 0));
          sUndoFlag=0;
          }


     /******************************************/
     /* See if we are to perform random moves. */
     /******************************************/
     if(sRandomFlag==1){

       /***********************************************************************/
       /* Initialized toggle.  This variable will be used to cause      */
       /* alternating moves in the horizontal and vertical directions. */
       /***********************************************************************/
       toggle=0;

       /****************************************************/
       /* Do sMoves random move until stop is indicated. */
       /****************************************************/
       for(i=0; (i<sMoves) && (!StopState); i++){
         toggle=toggle^1;
         if(toggle){

           /**********************************************/
           /* Set for random move in vertical direction. */
           /**********************************************/
           x=sGridx;
           y=Random_Range(0, puzzle.sGrid, sGridy, sGridy);
           }
         else {

           /**********************************************/
           /* Set for random move in horizontal direction. */
           /**********************************************/
           y=sGridy;
           x=Random_Range(0, puzzle.sGrid, sGridx, sGridx);
           }
           DosEnterCritSec();   /* Keep control from main process. */
           Slide(habt, hwndClient, x, y);  /* Slide piece. */

           /*********************************************************/
           /* Let main process and other have more processing time. */
           /*********************************************************/
           DosExitCritSec();
           DosSleep(SLEEPTIME);
         }
```

```
/***********************************************/
/* Enable Undo menu item and clear random flag. */
/***********************************************/
sRandomFlag=0;
WinPostMsg(WinWindowFromID(hwndFrame, FID_MENU),
  MM_SETITEMATTR,
  MPFROM2SHORT(IDM_UNDO, TRUE),
  MPFROM2SHORT(MIA_DISABLED, 0));
  }


/*****************************************************************/
/* Clear stop flag and set semaphore to block this thread. */
/*****************************************************************/
StopState=FALSE;
DosResetEventSem(hev, &ulPostCt);
  }
  }


/***************************************/
/* Random bug time background thread. */
/***************************************/
VOID Bugtime(ULONG dummy)
  {
  LONG i, random_time;
  for(;;) {

  /*****************************************/
  /* Get a random number between 1 and 10. */
  /*****************************************/
  random_time=Random_Range(1, 10, 10, 100);

  /*************************************************/
  /* Wait between 1 and 10 minutes before post. */
  /*************************************************/
  for(i=0; i<random_time; i++)
    DosSleep(60000);

  /*****************************************************************/
  /* Post BUGRUN message to cause animation in main process. */
  /*****************************************************************/
  WinPostMsg(hwndClient, BUGRUN, NULL, NULL);
  }
  }
```

Listing 8-2. Multiple threads of execution.

As you can see in Listing 8-2, the main procedure of the slide puzzle application uses a DosEnterCritSec function before dispatching a message to a window procedure. It also places a DosExitCritSec function after the window procedure finishes. This is done so drawing that occurs in the message processing thread and doesn't interfere with drawing that occurs in the Background thread. The Background thread also uses these same two functions so the message processing thread does not interfere with its drawing. By doing this in both threads, only one thread of execution is allowed to draw in the presentation page at a time. But, before worrying about a conflict with the Background thread drawing, the Background thread must be created.

By looking at the routine that processes the WM_CREATE message in the ClientWndProc procedure, you can see where the slide puzzle application creates the other threads used by this program. (Remember, the WM_CREATE message for this window procedure will only be executed once at the start of the slide puzzle application.) The WM_CREATE routine first creates an event semaphore with the DosCreateEventSem function. Note that this event semaphore is created in a way that causes the Background thread to wait when it uses the DosWaitEventSem function. Once the semaphore is set up, the Background and Bugtime threads are created by using the DosCreateThread function. As you can see from the parameters for this function, a stack for the thread is also created. The minimum stack size for a thread in OS/2 is 4096 bytes. As soon as these threads are created, they are eligible to execute.

If you look toward the end of Listing 8-2, you will find the Background function. The first thing this thread does is create its own PM anchor block. **This is important**! Even though a thread shares the resources of its parent, Presentation Manager requires each thread that uses its service to have its own anchor block. As soon as the anchor block is created, the Background thread loops forever.

At the very top of the FOR loop, the Background thread uses the DosWaitEventSem function to wait for something to do from the message processing thread. Because the WM_CREATE thread in the ClientWndProc procedure set this event semaphore before this thread was created, the Background thread waits at the DosWaitEventSem function on its first encounter. However, when the user requests to either undo moves or cause random moves, this thread is unblocked from the message processing thread and continues to execute. When this happens, the Background thread tests to see if it is to perform an undo or a random move operation. It checks for the undo operation first.

If the undo operation is being requested, the Background thread decrements the undo index by one position. Then, while there are valid moves to undo and the message processing thread has **not** signaled a stop condition, this thread moves pieces. It does this by first using the DosEnterCritSec function to block the message processing routine from drawing in the presentation page. It then gets the move coordinates from the backup circular buffer and calls the slide function to perform the move animation. To see how the move is performed with the slide function, refer to Chapter 6, Animation.

After the move is completed, the move coordinates are invalidated in the circular buffer, the backup index is decremented, and the DosExitCritSec function is used to allow the message processing thread to execute again. At the very bottom of the undo loop, a DosSleep function is used to give other threads and processes more of an opportunity to execute.

Once the undo loop completes, the undo index is incremented so it is ready for the next forward move. The global variable named **forward** is then set to TRUE, which causes the slide function to start placing move coordinates in the circular buffer again. (The global variable named forward is set to FALSE by the message processing thread right before the event semaphore is cleared. This causes the slide function to stop recording moves in the circular buffer.) Finally, the undo routine enables the Random Moves menu item on the Option pull-down menu and the global variable named **sUndoFlag** is reset. (This menu item was disabled by the message processing thread before event semaphore was cleared.) After the undo logic completes, the Background thread checks to see if it is to perform random moves.

If random moves are being requested, a variable named **toggle** is initialized to 0 and random moves are performed until either the number of random moves requested by the user has been completed or a stop condition is indicated. The number of random moves requested is found in a global variable named **sMoves** and is set in the dialog procedure for the Random Moves option. The random moves are performed by first changing the state of the toggle variable by exclusive OR'ing it with a value of 1. This causes the variable to toggle between a value of 0 and 1 each time this operation is performed.

Every other time through the random moves FOR loop, the toggle variable will be true and coordinates for a random move in a vertical direction are obtained. The other times through the FOR loop, coordinates for a random move in the horizontal direction are obtained. Then, just like the undo routine, the DosEnterCritSec function suspends the message processing thread from executing while this thread moves a piece with the slide function. After the move is completed, the DosExitCritSec function is used to let the message processing thread execute again and a DosSleep function is used to gives other processes and threads an opportunity to execute.

Once the random moves FOR loop completes, this routine enables the Undo menu item on the Option pull-down menu and the global variable named **sRandomFlag** is reset. (This menu item was disabled by the message processing thread before event semaphore was cleared.) After the random moves logic completes, the Background thread sets the event semaphore. This causes the thread to be suspended after it goes to the top of the FOR loop. This process continues until the slide puzzle program terminates.

If you look in the middle of Listing 8-2 for the WM_COMMAND routine in the ClientWndProc procedure, you can see where the event semaphores are cleared to let the Background thread execute. As you can see, when the Undo option is selected, the global variable named **forward** is set to FALSE. This variable is tested by the slide function and, when it is TRUE, the slide function places move coordinates in the undo circular buffer. Therefore, setting this variable to FALSE causes the slide routine not to record move coordinates.

After the forward variable is set, a message is sent to the Options menu window to disable the Random Moves option. By doing this, random moves are not allowed when the Undo option is operating in the background. Once the Undo menu item is disabled, the global variable named **sUndoFlag** is set. This variable is used by the Background thread to determine if it is to perform undo moves. Finally, the event semaphore is posted with the DosPostEventSem function so the Background thread can start processing.

When the Stop option is selected from the Options pull-down menu, a test is done to see if an Undo or Random Moves option is executing. If one of these options is executing, the global variable named **StopState** is set and messages are sent to the Options menu window to enable both the Random Moves option and the Undo option. By setting the StopState variable, the Background thread is notified to stop whatever it is processing. Notice that both options are indiscriminately enabled.

When the Random Moves option is selected, the RandomDlgProc dialog procedure is started to gather information from the user. If no errors are detected from this dialog, this routine sets a global variable named **sRandomFlag**. This variable is used by the Background thread to determine if it is to perform random moves. Once the flag is set, a message is sent to the Options menu window to disable the Undo option. By doing this, the user is not allowed to request the Undo option while random moves are operating in the background. Finally, the event semaphore is cleared so the Background thread can start processing.

To see how another thread causes the grasshopper to randomly run across the screen, look toward the end of Listing 8-2 for the function called Bugtime. The first thing this thread does is generate a random number between 1 and 10. This number is used as a counter for a FOR loop which generates a random time delay for the bug animation. Inside the FOR loop, a DosSleep function suspends the Bugtime thread for one minute at a time. Therefore, this FOR loop keeps control for at least one minute but for no longer than ten minutes. When this FOR loop is finished, a message is posted that causes the bug animation to occur. To see the routine that performs the bug animation, see Chapter 6, Animation.

Notice that the Bugtime thread only uses one PM function to post the bug animation message. Even though this is a PM function, it doesn't require an anchor block handle; Thus, because this thread doesn't call any functions requiring an anchor block handle, this thread does not need to obtain one.

As you can see from this exercise, the complexity in using threads is not in their creation or the mechanisms that control them, but rather, it is deciding how to use them and coordinating their processing. Once you become familiar with their capability and learn how to use them, you will find them extremely powerful and handy. This book has only given you a brief exposure to multitasking. OS/2 has much more to offer in terms of features that control threads of execution and communication between processes!

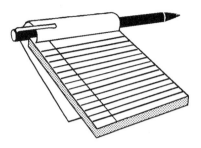

9

Notable OS/2 2.0 Enhancements

The slide puzzle program in this book is given as an example of a Presentation Manager program and has many of the basic features and structures that any PM program could have. Its purpose is to help you develop a solid understanding of a PM program structure and of the PM programming environment. The slide puzzle program is *not* designed to show you all the functions and features of Presentation Manager. That task would be huge and the complexity of such a program could overwhelm the beginner. Once you understand the slide puzzle program, however, many of the topics not covered by this example are easy to find, understand, and implement. For instance, your program may want to include support for things like the clipboard, printers, drag and drop, dynamic data exchange, and more advanced graphics functions. In many cases, you'll find the technical reference material that comes with the IBM OS/2 2.0 Developer's Toolkit has a brief explanation of these topics. Once you understand Presentation Manager basics, integrating these items is not difficult.

The slide puzzle program in this book is a 32-bit PM application and will only run in OS/2 2.0. This particular program, however, could be altered slightly and rebuilt as a 16-bit application. Once converted to a 16-bit application, the slide puzzle program could run in OS/2 1.3! There are new functions in OS/2 2.0, however, that can make your programming task easier, as well as make your application more appealing to the customer. Remember, because Presentation Manager can own many of the window procedures that actually draw to your application window, your application can have a very consistent looking interface and an enhanced look and style as OS/2 evolves! The following sections of this chapter highlight some new controls, standard dialogs, and window classes found in OS/2 2.0. You may find these new controls, standard dialogs, and window classes useful as you write your own application.

FILE DIALOG

Many applications need to request the name of a file used to retrieve information from or save information to. In the past, Presentation Manager programmers would create their own dialog boxes to open and save file services. Typically, these dialog boxes would look similar to the one shown in Screen 9-1. To support such a dialog box, the programmer would provide a dialog procedure that would operate with the OS/2 file system and interact with all the dialog box control windows. Because the programmer was providing the dialog box design and dialog procedure, the file dialog service could vary from application to application. In OS/2 2.0, there is a new PM function called *WinFileDlg* that provides the entire file dialog service for you!

To use the WinFileDlg function, you need to set up a FILEDLG data structure with information. The information you place in this structure lets you tailor the file dialog to meet your needs. For instance, this structure contains a pointer to a character string that indicates which drive and path to initialize the dialog fields

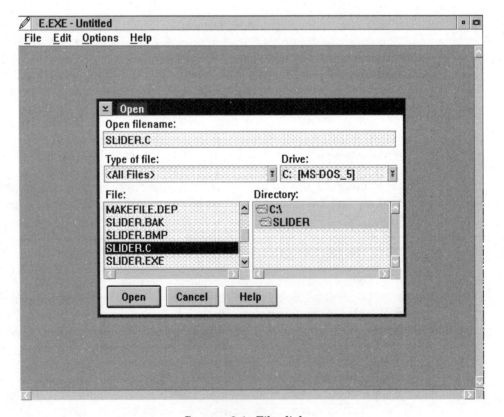

Screen 9-1. File dialog.

to. There also exists a style flag word in the FILEDLG structure that lets you further tailor the file dialog. These styles indicate things such as whether this is an Open dialog or SaveAs dialog, whether this dialog has a Help button, or whether this dialog is modal or modeless, and so on. These style flags have predefined definitions that all start with the prefix FDS_ and many of them can be OR'ed together. Once you have the FILEDLG structure initialized, pass the address of this structure as a parameter to the WinFileDlg function. On a successful return from the WinFileDlg function, a character string with the file name that the user selected will have been placed in the FILEDLG structure. Too easy!

FONT DIALOG

Just like the file dialog service, many applications want to allow the user to select one of several fonts that OS/2 has available. Also, just like the file dialog service, many programmers have designed and written their own dialog procedures to provide this service. With OS/2 2.0, a PM function called *WinFontDlg* exists that provides the select font service for you. Screen 9-2 shows an example of what this function can provide your application.

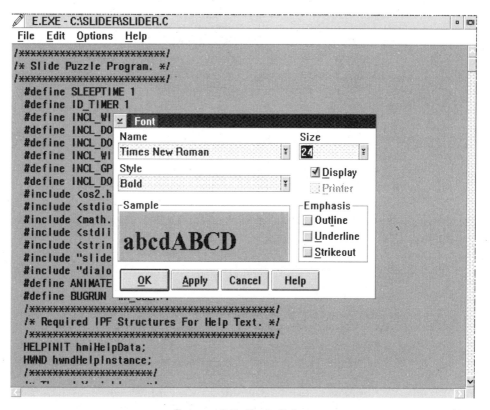

Screen 9-2. Font dialog.

To use the WinFontDlg function, you need to set up a the FONTDLG data structure type with information. The information you place in this structure allows you to tailor the font dialog. For instance, this structure has fields that let you specify initialization information for the dialog such as foreground color of the font, background color, point size, font family name, and so on. Like the FILEDLG structure, this structure also has a style flag word that allows you to further tailor the font dialog. These styles indicate things such as which type of fonts to list, whether this dialog will have a Help button, or whether this dialog is modal or not. These style flags have predefined values that all start with the prefix FNTS_. Many of these style flags can be OR'ed together.

Once you have the FONTDLG structure initialized, pass the address of this structure as a parameter to the WinFontDlg function. On a successful return from the WinFontDlg function, the font attributes for the font that the user selected are placed in the FONTDLG structure. Again, too easy!

VALUE SET CONTROL

Another new feature of OS/2 2.0 that you may find useful is the Value Set Control. This control is similar to the function available with radio buttons; however, the user actually makes a selection by clicking an object that is representative of the selection. For instance, if the user is selecting an art tool, he may click on an icon of a pencil, scissors, or a roller, and so on. If the user is selecting a fill pattern for an area, he may click on a pattern that represents the fill pattern. If a user wants to select a color for an object, he may click on a sample color. Screen 9-3 shows an example of where the Value Set function is used in a tool that you may have already used. This tool is the Dialog Editor and has options you can select by clicking on the image of the control window type that you want to add to your dialog box. These images are found on the right side of the Dialog Editor application window.

The Value Set Control is actually a new window class and has a predefined value of WC_VALUESET. So, like other windows, you can use a PM function called *WinCreateWindow* to create a Value Set window, give it a size and location, give it certain style attributes, and pass a pointer to information needed by the window class. The information pointed to for the Value Set window class is held in a VSCDATA data structure. The VSCDATA data structure contains information about the number of rows and columns the Value Set window will have for selection items.

The Value Set window class has several predefined styles from which you can choose. These styles all start with the prefix VS_ and indicate things such as whether the default attribute for each selection item is bit-map, or icon, or text, and so on. These styles can also indicate, for example, that each item will have a thin border placed around it or that bit-maps will be scaled to the size of an item's cell.

After the Value Set window is created, you can use a message called *VM_SETITEM* to initialize the content of Value Set items. You can also use a

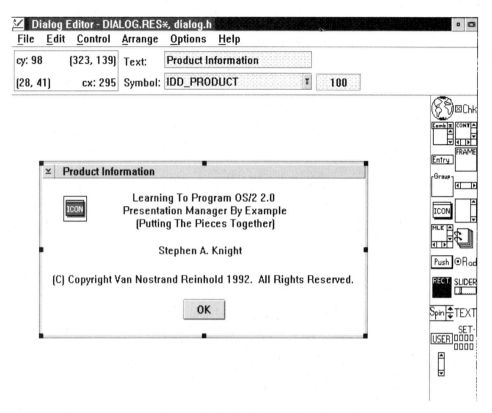

Screen 9-3. Value Set control.

message called *VM_SETMETRICS* to change the size and spacing between items. To set the initial selected item, use a message called *VM_SETSELECTEDITEM*. If you want to change the attribute of an item, use a message called *VM_SETITEMATTR*. All the valid attributes for Value Set items start with the prefix VIA_.

Once the Value Set window is created and initialized, your application will be notified whenever the user makes a selection. This notification comes via the WM_CONTROL message and has a notification value of *VN_SELECT*. Once you receive a notification from a Value Set window, you can use the *VM_QUERYSELECTEDITEM* message to find which item was selected. You can then use the *VM_QUERYITEM* message to get information stored at the items location.

SLIDER CONTROL

It isn't unusual to see scroll bars in PM applications. In fact, an application may use scroll bars in several places to aid in the scrolling of information. Many PM programmers have used scroll bars in other creative ways such as using scroll bars as a sliding instrument to adjust something other than a viewing area. The new Slider Control in OS/2 2.0 is ideal for this situation.

The Slider Control is similar to the scroll bar, but also has features that the standard scroll bar does not. Like the scroll bar, the Slider Control has a shaft and an object similar to a thumb within it. This object is called the slider arm. The slider arm, however, can not change its size like the thumb in a scroll bar. The shaft for the Slider Control can also have tick marks which represent incremental values for a scale on the slider shaft. Furthermore, the shaft can have detents. Detents are like tick marks because they represent a value on the scale, however, they do not have to be on increments of the scale. The Slider Control can also have slider buttons that can be used instead of the slider arm to adjust the control. These slider buttons can be located on either end of the slider shaft. Finally, the Slider Control has a ribbon strip associated with it. The ribbon strip is a color value that is different from the slider shaft and is used between the end of the slider shaft and the slider arm position. This ribbon highlights the location of the slider arm and resembles the look of mercury in a thermometer. To see some examples of Slider Controls, look at Screen 9-4. The Slider Controls shown in this screen represent controls on a stereo receiver.

Like the Value Set Control, the Slider Control is also a new window class and has a predefined value of WC_SLIDER. You can use the WinCreateWindow function to create a Slider Control window, give it a size and location, give it certain style attributes, and pass a pointer to information that is needed by the window class. This information is held in a SLDCDATA data structure. The SLDCDATA data structure contains information about the scales and increments that are applied to the Slider shaft. (The Slider Control can have a different scale on either side of the shaft.)

The Slider Control window class has several predefined styles from which you can choose. These styles all start with the prefix SLS_ and indicate things such as whether the control will be oriented horizontally or vertically, whether the home base for incrementing is at the top, bottom, left, or right of the slider shaft, or where the slider buttons will be located in relationship to the shaft.

After the Slider Control window is created, there are a series of messages you can send this window to customize it. All these messages start with the prefix SLM_ and do things like place tick marks on the shaft, set text beside tick marks, set detents, or set the slider arm position.

Once the Slider Control window is created and initialized, your application will be notified whenever the slider arm is manipulated. Notification comes via the WM_CONTROL message and two different notification values are possible. A notification value of SLN_SLIDERTRACK indicates the slider arm is being dragged by the user but not released. A notification value of SLN_CHANGE indicates the slider arm position is changed. Once you receive a notification from a Slider Control window, you can use the *SLM_QUERYSLIDERINFO* message to query for information about the current position of the slider arm.

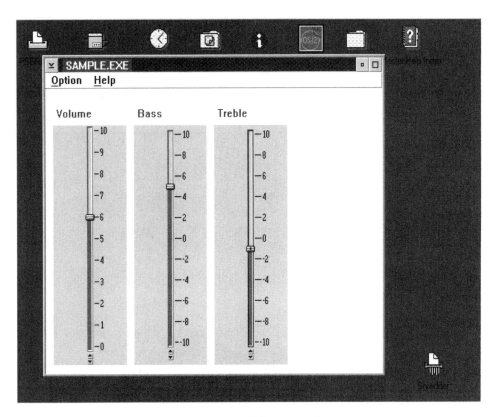

Screen 9-4. Slider controls.

As multimedia applications become more abundant, you will probably see a lot more of the Slider Control!

CONTAINER CONTROL

The user interface for OS/2 2.0 is designed to present information to the customer in a much more intuitive way than before. In many instances, this is done by representing data and functions as graphical objects and then presenting or manipulating these objects in different ways. The Container Control found in OS/2 2.0 is a mechanism that allows software developers to display their data objects in a variety of views. The views possible with the Container Control support are the icon view, the details view, the tree view, the name view, and the text view.

The icon view is probably the most familiar view to those that have used Presentation Manager before. This view is considered the *messy desk* paradigm and is represented by icons or bit-maps scattered across the client area with title information beneath them. Screen 9-5 shows an example of the icon view.

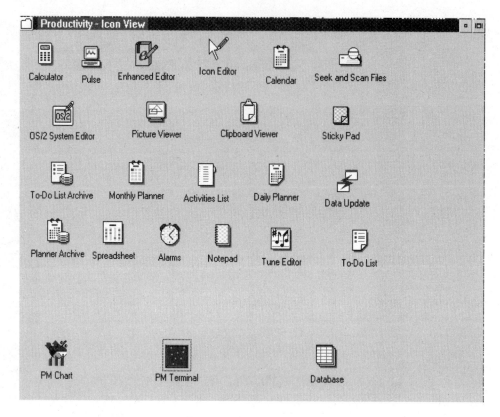

Screen 9-5. Icon view.

The icon view is appropriate to use when you wish to allow the user to move the objects around and leave them in locations of their own choice.

The details view provides a way to display detailed information about objects in an unlimited amount of columns. The columns can include bit-maps, icons, text, numbers, or date/time strings and can be scrolled both horizontally and vertically. Furthermore, the information can be split between two different windows that can be independently scrolled horizontally, but share a common vertical scroll bar. Screen 9-6 shows an example of the details view. The details view is a good choice for displaying information that fits best in a table or record format.

The tree view shows objects as they fit in a hierarchy. This is done by displaying the objects and their titles that are higher in the hierarchy on the left side of the display. The left-most object in this view is the root. The further an object is connected to the right, the deeper it is in the hierarchy. The right-most object is a leaf. Screen 9-7 shows an example of the tree view as it is applied to the file system. Another obvious use for this view, other than the one shown in Screen 9-7, is how it applies to most business organizations.

Icon	Title	Size	Last write date	Last write time	Last access date	Last access time	Creation date
	OS/2 2.0 Desktop	0	6-23-92	5:59:28 PM	0-0-80	12:00:00 AM	0-0-
	PATTERNS	0	7-10-92	7:16:32 PM	0-0-80	12:00:00 AM	0-0-
	OS2	0	6-23-92	5:15:08 PM	0-0-80	12:00:00 AM	0-0-
	PSFONTS	0	6-23-92	5:22:14 PM	0-0-80	12:00:00 AM	0-0-
	SPOOL	0	6-23-92	5:59:16 PM	0-0-80	12:00:00 AM	0-0-
	IBMWF	0	6-23-92	7:00:30 PM	0-0-80	12:00:00 AM	0-0-
	TOOLKT20	0	6-23-92	6:22:18 PM	0-0-80	12:00:00 AM	0-0-
	IBMC	0	6-23-92	7:04:50 PM	0-0-80	12:00:00 AM	0-0-
	CALC	0	6-24-92	3:27:52 PM	0-0-80	12:00:00 AM	0-0-
	WSE	0	6-25-92	4:32:46 PM	0-0-80	12:00:00 AM	0-0-
	DOSTOOLS	0	6-29-92	3:28:38 PM	0-0-80	12:00:00 AM	0-0-
	WPWIN	0	6-29-92	8:49:56 PM	0-0-80	12:00:00 AM	0-0-
	WPC	0	6-29-92	8:49:56 PM	0-0-80	12:00:00 AM	0-0-
	SLIDER	0	7-1-92	3:08:08 PM	0-0-80	12:00:00 AM	0-0-
	DRAW	0	7-10-92	4:19:20 PM	0-0-80	12:00:00 AM	0-0-
	JETFIGHT	0	8-9-92	5:21:58 PM	0-0-80	12:00:00 AM	0-0-
	GRAB	0	8-23-92	8:18:36 AM	0-0-80	12:00:00 AM	0-0-
	OS2LDR.MSG	8,440	3-30-92	12:00:00 PM	0-0-80	12:00:00 AM	0-0-
	AUTOEXEC.001	216	6-23-92	5:36:14 PM	0-0-80	12:00:00 AM	0-0-
	CONFIG.001	2,151	6-23-92	7:02:10 PM	0-0-80	12:00:00 AM	0-0-
	AUTOEXEC.BAK	216	7-7-92	4:29:20 PM	0-0-80	12:00:00 AM	0-0-
	CONFIG.BAK	1,939	7-7-92	4:41:50 PM	0-0-80	12:00:00 AM	0-0-
	CONFIG.002	2,272	7-6-92	8:55:38 PM	0-0-80	12:00:00 AM	0-0-
	AUTOEXEC.002	216	6-23-92	5:36:14 PM	0-0-80	12:00:00 AM	0-0-

Screen 9-6. Details view.

The name view and text view are not used as frequently as the other views. The name view basically places a text string to the right of icon or bit-map and the information is maintained in one or more columns. The text view is similar to the name view except it has no icon or bit-map associated with the text. Even though these views are not used as frequently as the other views, they do have their place and can help bridge older applications to a new environment. The name and text views are shown in Screens 9-8 and 9-9, respectively.

Often, software developers provide an option to let the customer select the type of view to present information. Of course, depending on the type of information that is being presented, not all views may make sense for a particular application. Whichever way you decide to present information, however, it is important to understand who you are developing the product for. Don't be trapped by assuming you understand the customer better than the customer! Look, listen, and learn!

The Container Control, like many of the other controls in this chapter, is implemented with a new window class. This window class has a predefined value of WC_CONTAINER. The item data for a container is stored in either a RECORDCORE or a MINIRECORDCORE data structure. Which of these two

Screen 9-7. Tree view.

data structure types you use depends on how you create the window and your requirements. But, whichever type of data structure you choose, you will find that the structures are chained together and have several data fields to fill in, depending on your view type. Once the window class is created, both the window class and your application have access to the information found in these data structures.

After the Container Control window is created, your application can maintain a dialog with the container by sending messages to its window and receiving notification messages from it. All messages to a Container Control window start with the predefined prefix of CM_. These messages allow you to do things such as insert records, remove records, search for a record, refresh the container, and change an item attribute. All notification messages received from a Container Control window arrive via the WM_CONTROL message. The notification values for Container Controls all have predefined values that start with the prefix CN_. These notification messages inform you of things such as change of input focus, scrolling, item selection, and drag and drop activities.

Screen 9-8. Name view.

As you can see, the Container Control is extremely powerful and useful; but, because of its additional flexibility and function, it is more complex to deal with than the other controls discussed in this chapter. The additional complexity suggested here is only relative to some other PM controls. If your application can make good use of containers, you will find that the cost of implementing them is very cheap for the added function you gain!

NOTEBOOK CONTROL

An obvious way to organize and present information is in a book. Using books to organize and present information is not a new concept to our society, but projecting the book paradigm onto the workstation is. Of course, workstations have been presenting information to users for years and a major function of a workstation has always been to present information. The way the workstation has traditionally accessed and presented information to the user, however, has not been strongly bound to the book scenario. This is the purpose of the Notebook Control.

```
┌──────────────────────────────────────────────────────────────────────────┐
│ ▣  OS2 - Icon View                                                   ▒▒ ▣ │
├──────────────────────────────────────────────────────────────────────────┤
│  IPMD.INI        RXQUEUE.EXE     CDFS.IFS         DOS.SYS         BITMAP     │
│  EPM.INI         RXSUBCOM.EXE    OS2.INI          DOSCALLS.LIB    APPS       │
│  TRACEFMT.EXE    CDROM.SYS       OS2SYS.INI       E.EXE           DRIVERS    │
│  CACHE.EXE       OS2_13.RC       TREE.COM         EAUTIL.EXE      UNPACK.EXE │
│  HPFS.IFS        OS2_20.RC       INI.RC           FIND.EXE        CHKDSK.COM │
│  FDISKPM.EXE     UPINI.RC        INISYS.RC        HELP.CMD        FORMAT.COM │
│  RECOVER.COM     PMSETUP.INF     POINTDD.SYS      HELPMSG.EXE     CLOCK01.SYS│
│  COM.SYS         SVGA.EXE        PRINT.COM        KEYB.COM        IBM1FLPY.ADD│
│  LABEL.COM       WIN_30.RC       REPLACE.EXE      KEYBOARD.DCP    IBM1S506.ADD│
│  TUTORIAL.EXE    XGA.RC          SETBOOT.EXE      MODE.COM        KBD01.SYS  │
│  BACKUP.EXE      PMDDE.EXE       SYSLEVEL.EXE     MOUSE.SYS       PRINT01.SYS│
│  LINK.EXE        ATTRIB.EXE      VIOTBL.DCP       MORE.COM        SCREEN01.SYS│
│  LINK386.EXE     FDISK.COM      ▐XCOPY.EXE▌       PCLOGIC.SYS     IBMINT13.I13│
│  CREATEDD.EXE    SAMPLE.SEP      EXTDSKDD.SYS     PMDD.SYS        OS2DASD.DMD│
│  LOG.SYS         SPOOL.EXE       PMCHKDSK.EXE     BOOK            OS2SCSI.DMD│
│  PATCH.EXE       STHR.EXE        PMFORMAT.EXE     PMREXX.EXE      TESTCFG.SYS│
│  PSTAT.EXE       UNDELETE.COM    PMSHELL.EXE      DISKCOMP.COM    ANSI.EXE   │
│  SYSLOG.EXE      VDISK.SYS       PSCRIPT.SEP      DLL             BOOT.COM   │
│  SYSLOGPM.EXE    VIEW.EXE        RC.EXE           HELP            CMD.EXE    │
│  TRACE.EXE       VIEWDOC.EXE     RCPP.ERR         INSTALL         COMP.COM   │
│  MAKEINI.EXE     RESTORE.EXE     RCPP.EXE         SYSTEM                     │
│  REXXTRY.CMD     SORT.EXE        DISKCOPY.COM     MDOS                       │
│ ◀                                                                         ▶ │
└──────────────────────────────────────────────────────────────────────────┘
```

Screen 9-9. Text view.

Screen 9-10 shows an example of the Notebook Control which is new in OS/2 2.0. Just by looking at this control, most users that have used a mouse will easily find their way through this interface. This isn't surprising because almost all users will recognize the notebook as a familiar object that they already know how to operate! This is not to say that all information should be presented with the Notebook Control. In fact, for many applications, other ways of presenting information may be much more appropriate and productive. Just remember that the Notebook Control is available and the notebook object may be very familiar and comfortable to your customer.

The Notebook Control can have tabs to separate the notebook into major sections. These major tabs are found on the opposite side of the notebooks binding, as shown in Screen 9-10. The Notebook control can also have minor tabs to separate major sections into even smaller sections. These minor tabs would be located orthogonal to the major tabs. Tabs may contain bit-maps or text. To get to these sections, simply click the mouse on the appropriate tab. Furthermore, if all the tabs don't fit on the Notebook Control, there are scroll button controls available to let you display more tab information.

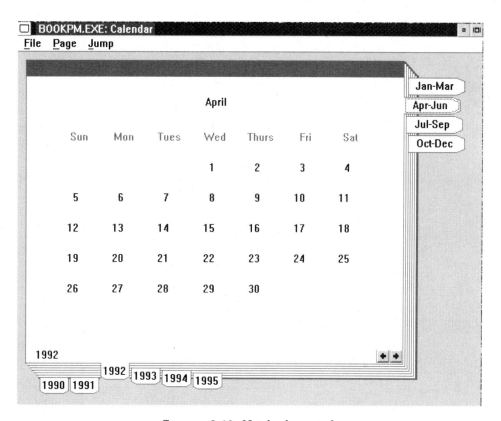

Screen 9-10. Notebook control.

Besides using tabs to get the user to the right area of the notebook, each page in the notebook can be accessed by navigating forward or backward a page at a time. Each page in the Notebook Control can then maintain a dialog with the user by way of your application code.

Like other controls explained in this chapter, the Notebook Control is made possible with a new window class. This window class has a predefined value of WC_NOTEBOOK. The Notebook Control window has style flags designed just for it that you can use to customize the look of the Notebook. All these style flags begin with the predefined prefix BKS_ and let you do things such as determine the orientation of the notebook, where the major tabs will be located, the shape of the tabs, the binding type, and so on.

Once the Notebook Control window is created, you can maintain a dialog with it by receiving notification messages from it and sending messages to it. All notification messages from the Notebook Control window are received via the WM_CONTROL message and have predefined notification values of BKN_. These notification values indicate events such as a page selection and new page size. All messages you send to the Notebook control window have predefined values that start with the prefix BKM_. These message allow your application to do things such as insert pages, delete pages, turn pages, query page ID, query tab text, set tab text, and set dimensions.

The new controls and features offered in OS/2 2.0 Presentation Manager help make OS/2 a consistent and powerful application platform for the customer. These features not only make the customer more productive because of the consistent and intuitive interface they provide, but they also help eliminate duplicate software that many developers would write to provide similar function.

As you become more advanced in the Presentation Manager programming environment, you will appreciate this powerful programming interface even more. Then, when you consider the true multitasking features, memory management features, interprocess communication mechanisms, and protection schemes of OS/2, you will see why OS/2 is in a class all its own!

Appendix A. Program Listings

SLIDER.H

```
#define   ID_SLIDEFRAME      1000

#define   IDI_MP1            100
#define   IDI_MP2            101
#define   IDI_MP3            102
#define   IDI_MP4            103
#define   IDI_MP5            104

#define   IDB_PIC1           105
#define   IDB_PIC2           106
#define   IDB_PIC3           107
#define   IDB_PIC4           108
#define   IDB_PIC5           109
#define   IDB_PIC6           110
#define   IDB_PIC7           101
#define   IDB_PIC8           112
#define   IDB_PIC9           113
#define   IDB_PIC10          114
#define   IDB_PIC11          115

#define   IDM_OPT            200
#define   IDM_UNDO           201
#define   IDM_NEW            202
#define   IDM_GRIDSTATE      203
#define   IDM_MOVES          204
#define   IDM_STOP           205
```

```
#define  IDM_PRODUCT       206
#define  IDM_EXIT          207
#define  IDM_HELP          208
#define  IDM_HELP_FOR_HELP 209


/*****************************************************/
/* Help Table Constants Definitions               */
/*****************************************************/
#define MAIN_HELPTABLE        501
#define MENU_SUBTABLE         502
#define DLG_SUBTABLE_PUZZLE   503
#define DLG_SUBTABLE_RANDOM   504


/*****************************************************/
/* Help Subtable Cross Reference Definition        */
/*****************************************************/
#define EXTENDED_HELP_PANEL_ID    1
#define KEYS_HELP_PANEL_ID        2
#define UNDO_PANEL_ID            10
#define NEW_PANEL_ID            11
#define GRIDSTATE_PANEL_ID      12
#define MOVES_PANEL_ID          13
#define STOP_PANEL_ID           14
#define PRODUCT_PANEL_ID        15
#define EXIT_PANEL_ID           16
#define PUZZLE_DLG_PANEL_ID     20
#define TIMEEDIT_PANEL_ID       21
#define GRIDEDIT_PANEL_ID       22
#define MOVEEDIT_PANEL_ID       30


#define SIZEOFUNDO        3000
#define STACKSIZE         4096
#define ALLOCFLAGS        0
#define ERROR_SEM_TIMEOUT 121
```

DIALOG.H

```
#define IDD_PRODUCT            100
#define IDD_RANDOM             200
#define IDD_MOVEEDIT           202
#define ID_HELP                203
#define IDD_NEWPUZZLE          300
#define IDD_TIMEEDIT           302
#define IDD_GRIDEDIT           304
```

SLIDER.C

```
/*************************/
/* Slide Puzzle Program. */
/*************************/
   #define SLEEPTIME 1
```

```
#define ID_TIMER 1
#define SLD_SFT 15
#define INCL_WINHELP
#define INCL_DOS
#define INCL_DOSPROCESS
#define INCL_WIN
#define INCL_GPI
#define INCL_DOSDEVICES
#include <os2.h>
#include <stdio.h>
#include <math.h>
#include <stdlib.h>
#include <string.h>
#include "slider.h"
#include "dialog.h"
#define ANIMATE WM_USER+0
#define BUGRUN  WM_USER+1


/*******************************************/
/* Required IPF Structures For Help Text. */
/*******************************************/
HELPINIT hmiHelpData;
HWND hwndHelpInstance;


/*********************/
/* Thread Variables. */
/*********************/
TID tidBack, tidBug;
USHORT usRC;
HEV hev;
ULONG ulPostCt;


/***************************/
/* Other Global Variables. */
/***************************/
HPOINTER hIptr1, hIptr2, hIptr3, hIptr4, hIptr5;
HAB hab;
HDC hdc, hdcMemory;
HPS hps, hpsMemory;
BITMAPINFOHEADER bmpSrc;
HBITMAP hbmSrc;
HWND hwndFrame, hwndClient, hwndMenu;
INT rc;
CHAR szError[80];
SHORT sGridy, sGridx;
LONG lcxMinMax, lcyMinMax;
SHORT sMoves, sRandomFlag=0, sUndoFlag=0;
ULONG ulUndoIndex;
BOOL forward;
POINTS backup[SIZEOFUNDO];
CHAR szClientClass[]="Slider";
CHAR szGrid[6]="5";
struct PUZZLEPARMS {
  SHORT sCapTime;
  SHORT sGrid;
```

```
      };
   struct PUZZLEPARMS puzzle;

   SHORT sMoveVar, sxPels, syPels;
   SHORT sGridState=0;
   BOOL StopState=FALSE, FirstTime=TRUE;
   LONG alBmpFormats[2];
   LONG lcxPelsPerMeter, lcyPelsPerMeter;
   LONG lcxPelsPerInch, lcyPelsPerInch;
   LONG lPointSize;
   PFNWP pfwnField1;
   PFNWP pfwnField2;

   /***********************/
   /* Function Prototypes. */
   /***********************/
   void FAR Slide(HAB habs, HWND hwnds, SHORT x, SHORT y);
   void FAR SetWidthsTable(HPS hps, LONG *alWidths,
      LONG *alWidthTable, CHAR *szStr, LONG *lTotal);
   void FAR Bug(void);
   BOOL FAR FindFont(HPS hps, LONG *lLcid, CHAR *szFontName);
   SHORT FAR Random_Range(SHORT lower_lim, SHORT upper_lim,
      SHORT lower_exc, SHORT upper_exc);
   LONG FAR GetSetID(HPS hps);
   BOOL FAR SetPtSize(HPS hps, LONG lLcid, LONG lPointSize,
      FIXED *width, FIXED *height);
   VOID _System Bugtime(ULONG );
   VOID _System Background(ULONG);

   /*************************************************/
   /* Window Procedure Entry Point Definitions. */
   /*************************************************/
   FNWP ClientWndProc;
   FNWP ProductDlgProc;
   FNWP RandomDlgProc;
   FNWP NewPuzzleDlgProc;
   FNWP NumberSubProc1;
   FNWP NumberSubProc2;

   /********************/
   /* Main Procedure. */
   /********************/
int main(int argc, char *argv[])
   {
   HDC hdcTemp;
   HPS hpsTemp;
   ULONG ulFrameFlags=FCF_TASKLIST | FCF_SIZEBORDER |
      FCF_TITLEBAR | FCF_MINMAX |
      FCF_SYSMENU | FCF_MENU | FCF_ICON | FCF_ACCELTABLE;
   HMQ hmq;
   QMSG qmsg;
   hab=WinInitialize(0);
   hmq=WinCreateMsgQueue(hab, 0);
```

```
/*********************************************/
/* Check to see if grid size was passed as */
/* a command line parameter.               */
/*********************************************/
if(argc==2){
  strcpy(szGrid, argv[1]);
  }


/*********************************************/
/* Convert parameter data from strings and */
/* initialize variables.                   */
/*********************************************/
puzzle.sGrid=atoi(szGrid);
puzzle.sCapTime=8;
sMoves=30;


/********************************/
/* IPF Initialization Structure. */
/********************************/
hmiHelpData.cb=sizeof(HELPINIT);
hmiHelpData.ulReturnCode=0;
hmiHelpData.pszTutorialName=NULL;
hmiHelpData.phtHelpTable=(PVOID)(0xffff0000 | MAIN_HELPTABLE);
hmiHelpData.hmodAccelActionBarModule=0;
hmiHelpData.idAccelTable=0;
hmiHelpData.idActionBar=0;
hmiHelpData.pszHelpWindowTitle=(PSZ)"Slide Puzzle Help";
hmiHelpData.hmodHelpTableModule=0;
hmiHelpData.fShowPanelId=0;
hmiHelpData.pszHelpLibraryName=(PSZ)"SLIDER.HLP";


/***************************/
/* Create instance of IPF. */
/***************************/
hwndHelpInstance=WinCreateHelpInstance(hab, &hmiHelpData);
if(!hwndHelpInstance)
  WinMessageBox(HWND_DESKTOP, HWND_DESKTOP,
    (PSZ)"Help Not Available", (PSZ)"Help Creation Error",
    1, MB_OK | MB_APPLMODAL | MB_MOVEABLE);
else {
  if(hmiHelpData.ulReturnCode){
    WinMessageBox(HWND_DESKTOP, HWND_DESKTOP,
      (PSZ)"Help Terminated Due to Error",
      (PSZ)"Help Creation Error",
      1, MB_OK | MB_APPLMODAL | MB_MOVEABLE);
    WinDestroyHelpInstance(hwndHelpInstance);
    }
  }
WinRegisterClass(hab, (PSZ)szClientClass, ClientWndProc,
  CS_SIZEREDRAW, 0);
hwndFrame=WinCreateStdWindow(HWND_DESKTOP, WS_VISIBLE,
  &ulFrameFlags, (PSZ)szClientClass, 0, 0L, 0,
  ID_SLIDEFRAME, &hwndClient);
```

```
/****************************************************/
/* Resolve the number of pels per inch in both the */
/* horizontal and vertical directions.             */
/****************************************************/
hpsTemp=WinGetPS(HWND_DESKTOP);
hdcTemp=GpiQueryDevice(hpsTemp);
if((hdcTemp!=0L) && (hdcTemp!=HDC_ERROR)){
  DevQueryCaps(hdcTemp, CAPS_VERTICAL_RESOLUTION, 1L,
    &lcyPelsPerMeter);
  DevQueryCaps(hdcTemp, CAPS_HORIZONTAL_RESOLUTION, 1L,
    &lcxPelsPerMeter);
  lcxPelsPerInch=(lcxPelsPerMeter*254)/10000;
  lcyPelsPerInch=(lcyPelsPerMeter*254)/10000;
  }


/******************************************************/
/* Set window position to be one half inch to right */
/* and one half inch up.  Make the window size       */
/* 7 inches by 6 inches.  Set input focus.           */
/******************************************************/
WinSetWindowPos(hwndFrame, 0L, (SHORT)lcxPelsPerInch/2,
  (SHORT)lcyPelsPerInch/2, (SHORT)lcxPelsPerInch*7,
  (SHORT)lcyPelsPerInch*6, SWP_SIZE | SWP_MOVE);
WinReleasePS(hpsTemp);
WinSetFocus(HWND_DESKTOP, hwndFrame);


/*****************************/
/* Associate instance of IPF. */
/*****************************/
  if(hwndHelpInstance)
    WinAssociateHelpInstance(hwndHelpInstance, hwndFrame);


/**************************************/
/* Get PM messages and dispatch them. */
/**************************************/
while(WinGetMsg(hab, &qmsg, 0, 0, 0)){
  DosEnterCritSec();
  WinDispatchMsg(hab, &qmsg);
  DosExitCritSec();
  }


/***************************/
/* Free resources obtained. */
/***************************/
  if(hwndHelpInstance)WinDestroyHelpInstance(hwndHelpInstance);
  GpiDeleteBitmap(hbmSrc);
  WinDestroyWindow(hwndFrame);
  WinDestroyMsgQueue(hmq);
  WinTerminate(hab);
  return 0;
  }

MRESULT EXPENTRY ClientWndProc(HWND hwnd, ULONG msg,
  MPARAM mp1, MPARAM mp2)
```

```
{
CHAR szProgName[]="SLIDER";
CHAR szStr1[]="Learning To Program";
CHAR szStr2[]="OS/2 2.0 Presentation Manager";
CHAR szStr3[]="By Example";
CHAR szStr4[]="(Putting the Pieces Together)";
CHAR szFontName[]="Courier";
CHAR szFontName1[]="Times New Roman";
LONG alWidths[80];
LONG alWidthTable[256];
SIZEF sizefxCharBox;
FIXED width, height;
BOOL fRet=FALSE;
float fPitch;
BITMAPINFOHEADER2 bmp;
HBITMAP hbmt;
ULONG ulMouse;
HDC hdcbm;
HPS hpsd;
POINTL apt1[4];
LONG  lRow, lCol, lTotal, lLcid;
SIZEL sizl;
SHORT x, y, i;
POINTL shear, ptl;
MATRIXLF matlfModel;
RECTL rclInvalid;
LONG pattern[]={
    PATSYM_DEFAULT, PATSYM_DENSE1, PATSYM_DENSE2,
    PATSYM_DENSE3, PATSYM_DENSE4, PATSYM_DENSE5,
    PATSYM_DENSE6, PATSYM_DENSE7, PATSYM_DENSE8,
    PATSYM_NOSHADE};

switch(msg){
  /*******************************************************/
  /* Process the animate message.  This will only occur */
  /* once after the first WM_PAINT message.          */
  /*******************************************************/
  case ANIMATE:
    WinSetPointer(HWND_DESKTOP,
      WinQuerySysPointer(HWND_DESKTOP, SPTR_WAIT, FALSE));
    GpiResetPS(hps, GRES_ALL);
    apt1[0].x=0;            /* Target left. */
    apt1[0].y=0;
    apt1[1].x=sxPels;       /* Target right. */
    apt1[1].y=syPels;
    GpiBitBlt(hps, hps, 2L, apt1, ROP_ONE, BBO_AND);


    /*******************************************************/
    /* Get key bit-map and adjust for an inch square. */
    /*******************************************************/
    hbmt=GpiLoadBitmap(hps, 0, IDB_PIC1,
      (LONG)(lcxPelsPerInch), (LONG)(lcyPelsPerInch));
    for(x=1; x<6; x++){     /* Put 5 keys wide. */
      for(y=1; y<5; y++){   /* Put 4 keys high. */
```

```
        ptl.x=x*lcxPelsPerInch;
        ptl.y=y*lcyPelsPerInch;
        WinDrawBitmap(hps, hbmt, NULL, &ptl, CLR_NEUTRAL,
          CLR_BACKGROUND, DBM_NORMAL);
        }
     }

  /***********************************************/
  /* Find font by name, else any outline font. */
  /***********************************************/
  if(!FindFont(hps, &lLcid, szFontName))
    FindFont(hps, &lLcid, NULL);
  lPointSize=80;  /* Set font size to 80 points. */
  fRet=SetPtSize(hps, lLcid, lPointSize, &width, &height);
  if(fRet){
    sizefxCharBox.cy=height;
    sizefxCharBox.cx=width;
    fRet=GpiSetCharBox(hps, &sizefxCharBox);
    }

  /*********************************************/
  /* Set width table and get width of string. */
  /*********************************************/
  SetWidthsTable(hps, alWidths, alWidthTable,
    szProgName, &lTotal);

  /******************************************************/
  /* Calculate pitch factor based on 5 inch space. */
  /******************************************************/
  fPitch=(float)(5*lcxPelsPerInch)/(float)lTotal;
  sizefxCharBox.cx=width*fPitch;  /* Adjust width. */
  fRet=GpiSetCharBox(hps, &sizefxCharBox);
  SetWidthsTable(hps, alWidths, alWidthTable,
    szProgName, &lTotal);

  /***************************************************/
  /* Rotate 30 degrees and put up SLIDER in red. */
  /***************************************************/
  ptl.x=(LONG)(((float)lcxPelsPerInch)*1.5);
  ptl.y=(LONG)(((float)lcyPelsPerInch)*1.5);
  GpiRotate(hps, &matlfModel, TRANSFORM_REPLACE,
  MAKEFIXED(30, 0), &ptl);
  GpiSetModelTransformMatrix(hps, 9L, &matlfModel,
    TRANSFORM_ADD);
  GpiMove(hps, &ptl);
  GpiSetColor(hps, CLR_RED);
  GpiCharStringPos(hps, NULL, CHS_VECTOR,
    (LONG)strlen(szProgName), (PSZ)szProgName, alWidths);
  DosSleep(3000);   /* Wait 3 seconds */

  /*****************************************************/
  /* Slide one inch square out of presentation page. */
  /*****************************************************/
  for(lRow=4; lRow>0; lRow--){
```

```
for(lCol=5; lCol>0; lCol-){
  aptl[0].y=lRow*lcyPelsPerInch;          /* Target bottom */
  aptl[1].y=(lRow+1)*lcyPelsPerInch;      /* Target top */
  aptl[2].y=lRow*lcyPelsPerInch;          /* Source bottom */
  for(x=lCol*lcxPelsPerInch; x<7*lcxPelsPerInch; x=x+SLD_SFT){

    /***************/
    /* Slide right. */
    /***************/
    aptl[0].x=x+SLD_SFT;                          /* Target left */
    aptl[1].x=x+SLD_SFT+lcxPelsPerInch;       /* Target right */
    aptl[2].x=x;                              /* Source left */
    GpiBitBlt(hps, hps, 3L, aptl, ROP_SRCCOPY, BBO_AND);

    /***************/
    /* Erase bits. */
    /***************/
    aptl[0].x=x;                             /* Target left */
    aptl[1].x=x+SLD_SFT;                          /* Target right */
    GpiBitBlt(hps, hps, 2L, aptl, ROP_ONE, BBO_AND);
    DosSleep(SLEEPTIME);
    }
  lCol=lCol-1;
  if(lCol>0){
    aptl[0].x=lCol*lcyPelsPerInch;        /* Target left */
    aptl[1].x=(lCol+1)*lcyPelsPerInch;    /* Target right */
    aptl[2].x=lCol*lcyPelsPerInch;        /* Source left */
    for(y=lRow*lcyPelsPerInch; y<6*lcyPelsPerInch; y=y+SLD_SFT){

      /*************/
      /* Slide up. */
      /*************/
      aptl[0].y=y+SLD_SFT;                        /* Target bottom */
      aptl[1].y=y+SLD_SFT+lcyPelsPerInch;      /* Target top */
      aptl[2].y=y;                             /* Source bottom */
      GpiBitBlt(hps, hps, 3L, aptl, ROP_SRCCOPY, BBO_AND);

      /***************/
      /* Erase bits. */
      /***************/
      aptl[0].y=y;                           /* Target bottom */
      aptl[1].y=y+SLD_SFT;                        /* Target top */
      GpiBitBlt(hps, hps, 2L, aptl, ROP_ONE, BBO_AND);
      DosSleep(SLEEPTIME);
      }
    }
  }
}


/*******************************************************/
/* Reset presentation spaces, then get it again and   */
/* animate with shearing.                             */
/*******************************************************/
GpiResetPS(hps, GRES_ALL);
```

```
GpiResetPS(hpsMemory, GRES_ALL);
GpiQueryDeviceBitmapFormats(hpsMemory, 2L, alBmpFormats);
memset(&bmp, 0, sizeof(bmp));
bmp.cbFix=sizeof bmp;
bmp.cx=sxPels;
bmp.cPlanes=(USHORT)alBmpFormats[0];
bmp.cBitCount=(USHORT)alBmpFormats[1];
bmp.cy=syPels;
hbmt=GpiCreateBitmap(hpsMemory, &bmp, 0L, NULL, NULL);
GpiSetBitmap(hpsMemory, hbmt);


/********************************/
/* Clear out presentation pages. */
/********************************/
aptl[0].x=0; aptl[0].y=0;
aptl[1].x=sxPels; aptl[1].y=syPels;
aptl[2].x=0; aptl[2].y=0;
GpiBitBlt(hps, hps, 2L, aptl, ROP_ZERO, BBO_AND);
GpiBitBlt(hpsMemory, hpsMemory, 2L, aptl, ROP_ZERO, BBO_AND);


/*****************************************************/
/* Look for font by name else find any outline font. */
/*****************************************************/
if(!FindFont(hpsMemory, &lLcid, szFontName1))
  FindFont(hpsMemory, &lLcid, NULL);
lPointSize=30;  /* Set font to 30 points. */
fRet=SetPtSize(hpsMemory, lLcid, lPointSize, &width, &height);
if(fRet){
  sizefxCharBox.cy=height;
  sizefxCharBox.cx=width;
  }
fRet=GpiSetCharBox(hpsMemory, &sizefxCharBox);


/*****************************************************/
/* Set color and shear for memory presentation space. */
/* Then put all text in this presentation page.       */
/*****************************************************/
GpiSetColor(hpsMemory, CLR_CYAN);
shear.x=10; shear.y=25;
GpiSetCharShear(hpsMemory, &shear);
SetWidthsTable(hpsMemory, alWidths,
  alWidthTable, szStr1, &lTotal);
ptl.x=((7*lcxPelsPerInch)-lTotal)/2; /* Center text 4 */
ptl.y=lcyPelsPerInch*4;             /* inches from bottom */
GpiMove(hpsMemory, &ptl);
GpiCharStringPos(hpsMemory, NULL, CHS_VECTOR,
  (LONG)strlen(szStr1), (PSZ)szStr1, alWidths);


/*****************************************************/
/* Change point size of font and get rid of shear. */
/*****************************************************/
lPointSize=18;
```

```
fRet=SetPtSize(hpsMemory, lLcid, lPointSize, &width, &height);
if(fRet){
  sizefxCharBox.cy=height;
  sizefxCharBox.cx=width;
  }
fRet=GpiSetCharBox(hpsMemory, &sizefxCharBox);
shear.x=0; shear.y=1;
GpiSetCharShear(hpsMemory, &shear);


/****************************************************************/
/* Center next 2 lines of text in memory presentation page. */
/****************************************************************/
SetWidthsTable(hpsMemory, alWidths,
  alWidthTable, szStr2, &lTotal);
ptl.x=((7*lcxPelsPerInch)-lTotal)/2;  /* Center text */
ptl.y=lcyPelsPerInch*3;         /* 3 inches from bottom */
GpiMove(hpsMemory, &ptl);
GpiCharStringPos(hpsMemory, NULL, CHS_VECTOR,
  (LONG)strlen(szStr2), (PSZ)szStr2, alWidths);
SetWidthsTable(hpsMemory, alWidths,
  alWidthTable, szStr3, &lTotal);
ptl.x=((7*lcxPelsPerInch)-lTotal)/2;  /* Center text */
ptl.y=lcyPelsPerInch*2.5;  /* 2.5 inches from bottom */
GpiMove(hpsMemory, &ptl);
GpiCharStringPos(hpsMemory, NULL, CHS_VECTOR,
  (LONG)strlen(szStr3), (PSZ)szStr3, alWidths);


/*********************************************/
/* Change color and center last             */
/* line of text in memory presentation page. */
/*********************************************/
GpiSetColor(hpsMemory, CLR_YELLOW);
SetWidthsTable(hpsMemory, alWidths,
  alWidthTable, szStr4, &lTotal);
ptl.x=((7*lcxPelsPerInch)-lTotal)/2;  /* Center text */
ptl.y=lcyPelsPerInch*1;         /* 1 inches from bottom */
GpiMove(hpsMemory, &ptl);
GpiCharStringPos(hpsMemory, NULL, CHS_VECTOR,
  (LONG)strlen(szStr4), (PSZ)szStr4, alWidths);


/*******************************************/
/* Fade in top 3 text lines with Bit Blt. */
/*******************************************/

aptl[0].x=0; aptl[0].y=lcyPelsPerInch*2;
aptl[1].x=lcxPelsPerInch*7; aptl[1].y=lcyPelsPerInch*5;
aptl[2].x=0; aptl[2].y=lcyPelsPerInch*2;
for(x=1; x<10; x++){
  GpiSetPattern(hps, pattern[x]);
  GpiBitBlt(hps, hpsMemory, 3L, aptl, ROP_MERGECOPY, BBO_AND);
  DosSleep(SLEEPTIME);
  }
```

```
    DosSleep(2500);   /* Wait 2.5 seconds. */

    /*****************************************/
    /* Fade in last text line with Bit Blt. */
    /*****************************************/
    aptl[0].x=0; aptl[0].y=lcyPelsPerInch*.5;
    aptl[1].x=lcxPelsPerInch*7; aptl[1].y=lcyPelsPerInch*2;
    aptl[2].x=0; aptl[2].y=lcyPelsPerInch*.5;
    for(x=1; x<10; x++){
      GpiSetPattern(hps, pattern[x]);
      GpiBitBlt(hps, hpsMemory, 3L, aptl, ROP_MERGECOPY, BBO_AND);
      DosSleep(SLEEPTIME);
      }
    DosSleep(3000);     /* Wait 3 seconds */

    /**********************************************/
    /* Fade out all text from screen with Bit Blt. */
    /**********************************************/
    aptl[0].x=0; aptl[0].y=lcyPelsPerInch*.5;
    aptl[1].x=lcxPelsPerInch*7; aptl[1].y=lcyPelsPerInch*5;
    aptl[2].x=0; aptl[2].y=lcyPelsPerInch*.5;
    for(x=9; x>1; x-){
      GpiSetPattern(hps, pattern[x]);
      GpiBitBlt(hps, hpsMemory, 3L, aptl, ROP_MERGECOPY, BBO_AND);
      DosSleep(SLEEPTIME);
      }
    GpiDeleteBitmap(hbmt);

    /*************************************/
    /* Get master bit-map from memory. */
    /*************************************/
    GpiResetPS(hpsMemory, GRES_ALL);
    GpiQueryBitmapParameters(hbmSrc, &bmpSrc);
    GpiSetBitmap(hpsMemory, hbmSrc);

    /*****************************************/
    /* Clear out screen presentation page. */
    /*****************************************/
    aptl[0].x=0; aptl[0].y=0;
    aptl[1].x=sxPels; aptl[1].y=syPels;
    GpiBitBlt(hps, hps, 2L, aptl, ROP_ZERO, BBO_AND);
    DosSleep(500);   /* Wait .5 seconds. */

    /***********************************************/
    /* Randomly blt in tenth inch squares of master */
    /* bit-map.  Do 8000 squares then stop.        */
    /***********************************************/
    for(i=0; i<8000; i++){
      aptl[0].x=Random_Range(0,
        (7*lcxPelsPerInch)-(lcxPelsPerInch/10), 0, 0);
      aptl[0].y=Random_Range(0,
        (6*lcyPelsPerInch)-(lcyPelsPerInch/10), 0, 0);
      aptl[1].x=aptl[0].x+(lcxPelsPerInch/7);
      aptl[1].y=aptl[0].y+(lcyPelsPerInch/7);
```

```
      aptl[2].x=aptl[0].x; aptl[2].y=aptl[0].y;
      GpiBitBlt(hps, hpsMemory, 3L, aptl, ROP_SRCCOPY, BBO_AND);
      }
  WinInvalidateRect(hwnd, NULL, FALSE);   /* Cause full paint. */
  WinSetPointer(HWND_DESKTOP,
    WinQuerySysPointer(HWND_DESKTOP, SPTR_APPICON, FALSE));
  return(MRESULT)TRUE;

/***********************/
/* Process bug request. */
/***********************/
case BUGRUN:
  Bug();
  return(MRESULT)TRUE;


/*********************************/
/* Process window create message. */
/*********************************/
case WM_CREATE:
  hdc=WinOpenWindowDC(hwnd);   /* Create window device context. */
  sizl.cx=0;                   /* Create Micro-PS.  Keep as global. */
  sizl.cy=0;
  hps=GpiCreatePS(hab, hdc, &sizl, PU_PELS | GPIT_MICRO |
    GPIA_ASSOC | GPIF_DEFAULT);

  /**********************************************************/
  /* Set semaphore before thread is created so it will wait */
  /* right away.  This semaphore is used by the background  */
  /* thread.                                                */
  /**********************************************************/
  DosCreateEventSem(NULL, &hev, 0, 0);

  /*******************/
  /* Create threads. */
  /*******************/
  DosCreateThread(&tidBack, Background, 0UL, 0UL, 4096);
  DosCreateThread(&tidBug, Bugtime, 0UL, 0UL, 4096);


  /*******************************************/
  /* Load pointers and save their handles. */
  /*******************************************/
  hIptr1=WinLoadPointer(HWND_DESKTOP, 0, IDI_MP1);   /* Up. */
  hIptr2=WinLoadPointer(HWND_DESKTOP, 0, IDI_MP2);   /* Right. */
  hIptr3=WinLoadPointer(HWND_DESKTOP, 0, IDI_MP3);   /* Down. */
  hIptr4=WinLoadPointer(HWND_DESKTOP, 0, IDI_MP4);   /* Left. */
  hIptr5=WinLoadPointer(HWND_DESKTOP, 0, IDI_MP5);   /* X. */

  /***********************/
  /* Initialize undo array. */
  /***********************/
  ulUndoIndex=0;
  for(i=0; i<SIZEOFUNDO; i++){
    backup[i].x=30;
    backup[i].y=30;
```

```
  }
forward=TRUE;

/**********************************************************/
/* Create memory device context for our screen bit-map. */
/**********************************************************/
hdcMemory=DevOpenDC(hab, OD_MEMORY, (PSZ)"*", OL, OL, OL);
sizl.cx=0;    /* Create presentation space for screen bit-map. */
sizl.cy=0;
hpsMemory=GpiCreatePS(hab, hdcMemory, &sizl,
  PU_PELS | GPIF_DEFAULT | GPIT_MICRO | GPIA_ASSOC);


/*****************************************************/
/* Get the screen dimension in pels and save it. */
/*****************************************************/
sxPels=WinQuerySysValue(HWND_DESKTOP, SV_CXSCREEN);
syPels=WinQuerySysValue(HWND_DESKTOP, SV_CYSCREEN);


/*********************************************/
/* Set up bit-map header for correct size. */
/*********************************************/
GpiQueryDeviceBitmapFormats(hpsMemory, 2L, alBmpFormats);
memset(&bmp, 0, sizeof(bmp));
bmp.cbFix=sizeof bmp;
bmp.cx=sxPels;
bmp.cPlanes=(USHORT)alBmpFormats[0];
bmp.cBitCount=(USHORT)alBmpFormats[1];
bmp.cy=syPels;
hbmSrc=GpiCreateBitmap(hpsMemory, &bmp, OL, NULL, NULL);
GpiSetBitmap(hpsMemory, hbmSrc);
aptl[0].x=0; aptl[0].y=0;
aptl[1].x=bmp.cx; aptl[1].y=bmp.cy;
aptl[2].x=0; aptl[2].y=0;


/************************************************/
/* Copy the desktop image to our memory device. */
/************************************************/
hpsd=WinGetScreenPS(HWND_DESKTOP);
GpiBitBlt(hpsMemory, hpsd, 3L, aptl, ROP_SRCCOPY, BBO_AND);


/***********************************************/
/* Calculate a piece size in pels and save it. */
/***********************************************/
lcxMinMax=bmp.cx/puzzle.sGrid;
lcyMinMax=bmp.cy/puzzle.sGrid;


/********************************************/
/* Blank out bottom right piece of puzzle. */
/********************************************/
aptl[0].x=(puzzle.sGrid-1)*lcxMinMax; aptl[0].y=0;
aptl[1].x=aptl[0].x+lcxMinMax; aptl[1].y=lcyMinMax;
GpiBitBlt(hpsMemory, hpsMemory, 2L, aptl, ROP_ZERO, BBO_AND);
```

```
/****************************************************/
/* Set blank piece location and release resource. */
/****************************************************/
sGridy=0; sGridx=puzzle.sGrid-1;
WinReleasePS(hpsd);
return(MRESULT)FALSE;


/***************************/
/* Process keyboard items. */
/***************************/
case WM_CHAR:
  if((sRandomFlag==1) || (sUndoFlag==1))return 0;
  if(CHARMSG(&msg)->fs & KC_KEYUP)
    return(MRESULT)FALSE;
  if(CHARMSG(&msg)->fs & KC_VIRTUALKEY){
    switch (CHARMSG(&msg)->vkey){
      case VK_LEFT:     /* Check for left arrow. */
        x=sGridx+1; y=sGridy;
        Slide(hab, hwnd, x, y);
        return(MRESULT)TRUE;
      case VK_RIGHT:    /* Check for right arrow. */
        if(sGridx>0){
          x=sGridx-1; y=sGridy;
          Slide(hab, hwnd, x, y);
          }
        return(MRESULT)TRUE;
      case VK_DOWN:     /* Check for down arrow. */
        y=sGridy+1; x=sGridx;
        Slide(hab, hwnd, x, y);
        return(MRESULT)TRUE;
      case VK_UP:       /* Check for up arrow. */
        if(sGridy>0){
          y=sGridy-1; x=sGridx;
          Slide(hab, hwnd, x, y);
          }
        return(MRESULT)TRUE;
      }
    }
  return(MRESULT)FALSE;


/*********************************/
/* Process pull-down menu items. */
/*********************************/
case WM_COMMAND:
  switch (COMMANDMSG(&msg)->cmd){


    /********************************/
    /* Process undo pull-down option. */
    /********************************/
    case IDM_UNDO:
      forward=FALSE;
      WinSendMsg(WinWindowFromID(hwndFrame, FID_MENU),
```

```
          MM_SETITEMATTR,
            MPFROM2SHORT(IDM_MOVES, TRUE),
            MPFROM2SHORT(MIA_DISABLED, MIA_DISABLED));
        sUndoFlag=1;
        DosPostEventSem(hev);
        return(MRESULT)TRUE;


    /*********************************/
    /* Process stop pull-down option. */
    /*********************************/
    case IDM_STOP:
      if((sUndoFlag==1) || (sRandomFlag==1)){
        StopState=TRUE;
        WinSendMsg(WinWindowFromID(hwndFrame, FID_MENU),
          MM_SETITEMATTR,
          MPFROM2SHORT(IDM_UNDO, TRUE),
          MPFROM2SHORT(MIA_DISABLED, 0));
        WinSendMsg(WinWindowFromID(hwndFrame, FID_MENU),
          MM_SETITEMATTR,
          MPFROM2SHORT(IDM_MOVES, TRUE),
          MPFROM2SHORT(MIA_DISABLED, 0));
        }
      return(MRESULT)TRUE;


    /*******************************************/
    /* Process random move pull-down option. */
    /*******************************************/
    case IDM_MOVES:
      if(WinDlgBox(HWND_DESKTOP, hwnd, RandomDlgProc,
        0, IDD_RANDOM, &sMoves)){
        sRandomFlag=1;
        WinSendMsg(WinWindowFromID(hwndFrame, FID_MENU),
          MM_SETITEMATTR,
          MPFROM2SHORT(IDM_UNDO, TRUE),
          MPFROM2SHORT(MIA_DISABLED, MIA_DISABLED));
        DosPostEventSem(hev);
        }
      return(MRESULT)TRUE;


    /*****************************************/
    /* Process new puzzle pull-down option. */
    /*****************************************/
    case IDM_NEW:
      if(WinDlgBox(HWND_DESKTOP, hwnd, NewPuzzleDlgProc,
        0, IDD_NEWPUZZLE, &puzzle))
        WinStartTimer(hab, hwnd, ID_TIMER, puzzle.sCapTime*1000);
      return(MRESULT)TRUE;


    /************************************/
    /* Process product pull-down option. */
    /************************************/
    case IDM_PRODUCT:
      WinDlgBox(HWND_DESKTOP, hwnd, ProductDlgProc,
        0, IDD_PRODUCT, 0);
```

```
      return(MRESULT)TRUE;

/*********************************/
/* Process exit pull-down option. */
/*********************************/
case IDM_EXIT:
    WinPostMsg(hwnd, WM_QUIT, NULL, NULL);
  return(MRESULT)TRUE;

/******************************************/
/* Process grid state pull-down option. */
/******************************************/
case IDM_GRIDSTATE:
  sGridState=sGridState^1; /* Change grid state flag. */

  /*************************************************/
  /* Check or uncheck menu item as appropriate. */
  /*************************************************/
  if(!sGridState){
    WinSendMsg(WinWindowFromID(hwndFrame, FID_MENU),
      MM_SETITEMATTR,
      MPFROM2SHORT(IDM_GRIDSTATE, TRUE),
      MPFROM2SHORT(MIA_CHECKED, 0));
    }
  else {
    WinSendMsg(WinWindowFromID(hwndFrame, FID_MENU),
      MM_SETITEMATTR,
      MPFROM2SHORT(IDM_GRIDSTATE, TRUE),
      MPFROM2SHORT(MIA_CHECKED, MIA_CHECKED));
    }

  /***********************************/
  /* Get the master memory bit-map. */
  /***********************************/
  GpiResetPS(hpsMemory, GRES_ALL);
  GpiQueryBitmapParameters(hbmSrc, &bmpSrc);
  GpiSetBitmap(hpsMemory, hbmSrc);

  /*************************************************/
  /* Set the mix to invert all pixels drawn and */
  /* then draw grid lines.                       */
  /*************************************************/
  GpiSetMix(hpsMemory, FM_INVERT);
  for(lRow=0; lRow<=syPels/lcyMinMax; lRow++){
    ptl.x=0; ptl.y=lRow*lcyMinMax;
    GpiMove(hpsMemory, &ptl);
    ptl.x=sxPels;
    GpiLine(hpsMemory, &ptl);
    }
  for(lCol=0; lCol<=sxPels/lcxMinMax; lCol++){
    ptl.y=0; ptl.x=lCol*lcxMinMax;
    GpiMove(hpsMemory, &ptl);
    ptl.y=syPels;
    GpiLine(hpsMemory, &ptl);
```

```
            }
          WinInvalidateRect(hwnd, NULL, FALSE);
          return(MRESULT)TRUE;


        /***************************/
        /* Display HELP_FOR_HELP. */
        /***************************/
        case IDM_HELP_FOR_HELP:
          if(hwndHelpInstance)
            WinSendMsg(hwndHelpInstance, HM_DISPLAY_HELP, OL, OL);
          break;

        default:
          return WinDefWindowProc(hwnd, msg, mp1, mp2);
      }
      break;


    /******************************/
    /* Process help error message. */
    /******************************/
    case HM_ERROR:
      if((hwndHelpInstance && (ULONG)mp1)==HMERR_NO_MEMORY){
        WinMessageBox(HWND_DESKTOP, HWND_DESKTOP,
          (PSZ)"Help Terminated Due to Error",
          (PSZ)"Help Error",
          1, MB_OK | MB_APPLMODAL | MB_MOVEABLE);
        WinDestroyHelpInstance(hwndHelpInstance);
        }
      else {
        WinMessageBox(HWND_DESKTOP, HWND_DESKTOP,
          (PSZ)"Help Error Occurred",
          (PSZ)"Help Error",
          1, MB_OK | MB_APPLMODAL | MB_MOVEABLE);
        }
      break;


    /***********************************/
    /* Process query keys help message. */
    /***********************************/
    case HM_QUERY_KEYS_HELP:
      return((MRESULT)KEYS_HELP_PANEL_ID);
      break;


    /******************************/
    /* Process timer create message. */
    /******************************/
    case WM_TIMER:

      /*********************************************************/
      /* Only one timer is started so assume that timer caused */
      /* this message to occur and delete old bitmap.         */
      /*********************************************************/
      WinStopTimer(hab, hwnd, ID_TIMER);  /* Stop the time. */
      Gpi Delte Bitmap (hbm Src);
```

```
/*******************************************************/
/* Reset presentation space for master bit-map image. */
/*******************************************************/
GpiResetPS(hpsMemory, GRES_ALL);
GpiQueryDeviceBitmapFormats(hpsMemory, 2L, alBmpFormats);
memset(&bmp, 0, sizeof(bmp));
bmp.cbFix=sizeof bmp;
bmp.cx=sxPels;
bmp.cPlanes=(USHORT)alBmpFormats[0];
bmp.cBitCount=(USHORT)alBmpFormats[1];
bmp.cy=syPels;
hbmSrc=GpiCreateBitmap(hpsMemory, &bmp, 0L, NULL, NULL);
GpiSetBitmap(hpsMemory, hbmSrc);


/*******************************************************/
/* Copy desktop image into memory presentation page. */
/*******************************************************/
aptl[0].x=0; aptl[0].y=0;              /* Target lower left. */
aptl[1].x=bmp.cx; aptl[1].y=bmp.cy; /* Target upper right. */
aptl[2].x=0; aptl[2].y=0;              /* Source lower left. */
hpsd=WinGetScreenPS(HWND_DESKTOP);
GpiBitBlt(hpsMemory, hpsd, 3L, aptl, ROP_SRCCOPY, BBO_AND);


/*********************************************************/
/* Calculate the number of pels for the width and height */
/* of a puzzle piece.                                    */
/*********************************************************/
lcxMinMax=bmp.cx/puzzle.sGrid;
lcyMinMax=bmp.cy/puzzle.sGrid;


/**********************************************************/
/* Create blank puzzle piece in lower right puzzle corner. */
/**********************************************************/
aptl[0].x=(puzzle.sGrid-1)*lcxMinMax; aptl[0].y=0;
aptl[1].x=aptl[0].x+lcxMinMax; aptl[1].y=lcyMinMax;
GpiBitBlt(hpsMemory, hpsMemory, 2L, aptl, ROP_ZERO, BBO_AND);


/************************************************/
/* Turn on the grid if the grid state is set. */
/************************************************/
if(sGridState) {
  GpiSetMix(hpsMemory, FM_INVERT);
  for(lRow=0; lRow<=syPels/lcyMinMax; lRow++){
    ptl.x=0; ptl.y=lRow*lcyMinMax;
    GpiMove(hpsMemory, &ptl);
    ptl.x=sxPels;
    GpiLine(hpsMemory, &ptl);
    }
  for(lCol=0; lCol<=sxPels/lcxMinMax; lCol++){
    ptl.y=0; ptl.x=lCol*lcxMinMax;
    GpiMove(hpsMemory, &ptl);
    ptl.y=syPels;
    GpiLine(hpsMemory, &ptl);
    }
```

```
       }

   /**********************************************************/
   /* Initialize undo index, buffer, and blank location. */
   /**********************************************************/
   ulUndoIndex=0;
   for(i=0; i<SIZEOFUNDO; i++){
     backup[i].x=30;
     backup[i].y=30;
     }
   forward=TRUE;
   sGridy=0;
   sGridx=puzzle.sGrid-1;

   /**********************************************************/
   /* Release resources and cause beep to let user know a */
   /* screen has been captured.                           */
   /**********************************************************/
   WinReleasePS(hpsd);
   WinInvalidateRect(hwnd, NULL, FALSE);  /* Cause full paint. */
   DosBeep(523, 100);
   return(MRESULT)TRUE;

/********************************/
/* Process mouse button 1 down. */
/********************************/
case WM_BUTTON1DOWN:
  if((sRandomFlag==1) || (sUndoFlag==1))return 0;
  x=MOUSEMSG(&msg)->x; /* Convert to grid coordinate. */
  y=MOUSEMSG(&msg)->y;
  x=x/lcxMinMax;
  y=y/lcyMinMax;

  /**************************************/
  /* Check for mouse pointer in bounds. */
  /**************************************/
  if((x<puzzle.sGrid) && (y<puzzle.sGrid)){

    /***************************************************/
    /* Check for in pointer in valid row or column. */
    /***************************************************/
    if((y==sGridy) || (x==sGridx))
      Slide(hab, hwnd, x, y);
    else DosBeep(523, 100);
  }
  return(MRESULT)TRUE;

/*******************************/
/* Process mouse move messages. */
/*******************************/
case WM_MOUSEMOVE:
  x=MOUSEMSG(&msg)->x;
  y=MOUSEMSG(&msg)->y;
```

```
      x=x/lcxMinMax;
      y=y/lcyMinMax;

      /**************************************************/
      /* Set correct pointer icon based on position. */
      /**************************************************/
      if((y==sGridy) || (x==sGridx)){
        if((y<sGridy) && (x==sGridx))
          WinSetPointer(HWND_DESKTOP, hIptr1);
        if((y>sGridy) && (x==sGridx))
          WinSetPointer(HWND_DESKTOP, hIptr3);
        if((x<sGridx) && (y==sGridy))
          WinSetPointer(HWND_DESKTOP, hIptr2);
        if((x>sGridx) && (y==sGridy))
          WinSetPointer(HWND_DESKTOP, hIptr4);
        if((x==sGridx) && (y==sGridy))
          WinSetPointer(HWND_DESKTOP, hIptr5);
        }
      else
        WinSetPointer(HWND_DESKTOP, hIptr5);
      return(MRESULT)TRUE;

/**************************/
/* Process paint message. */
/**************************/
case WM_PAINT:
  if(FirstTime){    /* This only gets processed once. */
    FirstTime=FALSE;
    WinSendMsg(hwnd, ANIMATE, NULL, NULL);
    }
  else {

    /**************************************************/
    /* Paint the invalid region with the contents of */
    /* the master bit-map in memory.               */
    /**************************************************/
    WinBeginPaint(hwnd, hps, &rclInvalid);
    GpiSetBitmap(hpsMemory, hbmSrc);
    aptl[0].x=rclInvalid.xLeft;  /* Target lower left. */
    aptl[0].y=rclInvalid.yBottom;
    aptl[1].x=rclInvalid.xRight; /* Target upper right. */
    aptl[1].y=rclInvalid.yTop;
    aptl[2].x=rclInvalid.xLeft;  /* Source lower left. */
    aptl[2].y=rclInvalid.yBottom;
    aptl[3].x=rclInvalid.xRight; /* Source upper right. */
    aptl[3].y=rclInvalid.yTop;
    GpiBitBlt(hps, hpsMemory, 4L, aptl, ROP_SRCCOPY, BBO_AND);
    WinEndPaint(hps);
    }
  return(MRESULT)TRUE;

/***********************************/
/* Destory resources accumulated.  */
/***********************************/
```

```
      case WM_DESTROY:
        WinDestroyPointer(hIptr1);
        WinDestroyPointer(hIptr2);
        WinDestroyPointer(hIptr3);
        WinDestroyPointer(hIptr4);
        WinDestroyPointer(hIptr5);
        GpiDestroyPS(hpsMemory);
        DevCloseDC(hdcMemory);
        GpiDestroyPS(hps);
        return(MRESULT)NULL;
    }


  /****************************************************/
  /* Let default routine process message and return. */
  /****************************************************/
  return WinDefWindowProc(hwnd, msg, mp1, mp2);
  }


/*******************************************/
/* Product information dialog procedure. */
/*******************************************/
MRESULT EXPENTRY ProductDlgProc(HWND hwnd, ULONG msg,
  MPARAM mp1, MPARAM mp2){
  switch(msg) {
    case WM_COMMAND:
      switch(COMMANDMSG(&msg)->cmd){
        case DID_OK:
          WinDismissDlg(hwnd, TRUE);
          return(MRESULT)TRUE;
        }
      break;
    }
  return WinDefDlgProc(hwnd, msg, mp1, mp2);
  }


/*********************************/
/* Random moves dialog procedure. */
/*********************************/
MRESULT EXPENTRY RandomDlgProc(HWND hwnd, ULONG msg,
  MPARAM mp1, MPARAM mp2)
  {
  static SHORT FAR *prandom;
  CHAR szTemp[6];
  SHORT sTemp;
  switch (msg) {

    /*********************/
    /* Initialize dialog. */
    /*********************/
    case WM_INITDLG:
      prandom=PVOIDFROMMP(mp2);
      pfwnField1=WinSubclassWindow(
        WinWindowFromID(hwnd, IDD_MOVEEDIT), NumberSubProc1);
```

```
                sprintf(szTemp, "%d\0", *prandom);
                WinSetDlgItemText(hwnd, IDD_MOVEEDIT, (PSZ)szTemp);
                return(MRESULT)0L;

            /**************************/
            /* Process notifications. */
            /**************************/
            case WM_COMMAND:
              switch (COMMANDMSG(&msg)->cmd) {

                /*************************/
                /* Process OK pushbutton. */
                /*************************/
                case DID_OK:
                  WinQueryDlgItemText(hwnd, IDD_MOVEEDIT, 5, (PSZ)szTemp);
                  sTemp=atoi(szTemp);
                  if((sTemp<1) || (sTemp>1000)){
                    WinMessageBox(HWND_DESKTOP, hwnd,
                    (PSZ)"Moves value needs to be between 1 and 1000.",
                    (PSZ)"Random Moves", 0,
                    MB_MOVEABLE | MB_OK | MB_ICONEXCLAMATION);
                    }
                  else {
                    *prandom=sTemp;
                    WinSubclassWindow(
                      WinWindowFromID(hwnd, IDD_MOVEEDIT), pfwnField1);
                    WinDismissDlg(hwnd, TRUE);
                    }
                  return(MRESULT)TRUE;

                /*****************************/
                /* Process Cancel pushbutton. */
                /*****************************/
                case DID_CANCEL:
                  WinSubclassWindow(
                    WinWindowFromID(hwnd, IDD_MOVEEDIT), pfwnField1);
                  WinDismissDlg(hwnd, FALSE);
                  return(MRESULT)TRUE;
                }
              break;
            }
        return WinDefDlgProc(hwnd, msg, mp1, mp2);
        }

/******************************/
/* New puzzle dialog procedure. */
/******************************/
MRESULT EXPENTRY NewPuzzleDlgProc(HWND hwnd, ULONG msg,
    MPARAM mp1, MPARAM mp2)
    {
    static struct PUZZLEPARMS FAR *pnew;
    CHAR szTemp[5];
    SHORT sTemp;
```

```
    switch (msg) {

        /**********************/
        /* Initialize dialog. */
        /**********************/
        case WM_INITDLG:
          pnew=PVOIDFROMMP(mp2);
          pfwnField1=WinSubclassWindow(
            WinWindowFromID(hwnd, IDD_GRIDEDIT), NumberSubProc1);
          pfwnField2=WinSubclassWindow(
            WinWindowFromID(hwnd, IDD_TIMEEDIT), NumberSubProc2);
          sprintf(szTemp, "%d\0", pnew->sCapTime);
          WinSetDlgItemText(hwnd, IDD_TIMEEDIT, (PSZ)szTemp);
          sprintf(szTemp, "%d\0", pnew->sGrid);
          WinSetDlgItemText(hwnd, IDD_GRIDEDIT, (PSZ)szTemp);
          WinSetFocus(HWND_DESKTOP, WinWindowFromID(hwnd, IDD_GRIDEDIT));
          return(MRESULT)1L;

        /***************************/
        /* Process notifications. */
        /***************************/
        case WM_COMMAND:
          switch (COMMANDMSG(&msg)->cmd){

            /***************************/
            /* Process OK pushbutton. */
            /***************************/
            case DID_OK:
              WinQueryDlgItemText(hwnd, IDD_TIMEEDIT, 5, (PSZ)szTemp);
              sTemp=atoi(szTemp);
              if((sTemp<1) || (sTemp>60)){
                WinMessageBox(HWND_DESKTOP, hwnd,
                (PSZ)"Time value needs to be between 1 and 60.",
                (PSZ)"New Puzzle", 0,
                MB_MOVEABLE | MB_OK | MB_ICONEXCLAMATION);
                return(MRESULT)TRUE;
                }
              pnew->sCapTime=sTemp;
              WinQueryDlgItemText(hwnd, IDD_GRIDEDIT, 5, (PSZ)szTemp);
              sTemp=atoi(szTemp);
              if((sTemp<4) || (sTemp>25)){
                WinMessageBox(HWND_DESKTOP, hwnd,
                (PSZ)"Grid value needs to be between 4 and 25.",
                (PSZ)"New Puzzle", 0,
                MB_MOVEABLE | MB_OK | MB_ICONEXCLAMATION);
                return(MRESULT)TRUE;
                }
              pnew->sGrid=sTemp;
              WinSubclassWindow(
                WinWindowFromID(hwnd, IDD_GRIDEDIT), pfwnField1);
              WinSubclassWindow(
                WinWindowFromID(hwnd, IDD_TIMEEDIT), pfwnField2);
              WinDismissDlg(hwnd, TRUE);
              return(MRESULT)TRUE;
```

```
              /*****************************/
              /* Process Cancel pushbutton. */
              /*****************************/
              case DID_CANCEL:
                WinSubclassWindow(
                  WinWindowFromID(hwnd, IDD_GRIDEDIT), pfwnField1);
                WinSubclassWindow(
                  WinWindowFromID(hwnd, IDD_TIMEEDIT), pfwnField2);
                WinDismissDlg(hwnd, FALSE);
                return(MRESULT)TRUE;
            }
          break;
        }
      return WinDefDlgProc(hwnd, msg, mp1, mp2);
    }


/*****************************/
/* Window subclass procedure. */
/*****************************/
MRESULT EXPENTRY NumberSubProc1(HWND hwnd, ULONG msg,
  MPARAM mp1, MPARAM mp2)
  {
  switch(msg){
    /*****************************/
    /* Filter keyboard messages. */
    /*****************************/
    case WM_CHAR:
      if((CHARMSG(&msg)->fs & KC_KEYUP) ||
        (CHARMSG(&msg)->fs & KC_VIRTUALKEY))
        return ((*pfwnField1) (hwnd, msg, mp1, mp2));
      if(CHARMSG(&msg)->fs & KC_CHAR)
        if(isdigit(CHARMSG(&msg)->chr))
          return ((*pfwnField1) (hwnd, msg, mp1, mp2));
      return(MRESULT)NULL;
    default:
      return ((*pfwnField1) (hwnd, msg, mp1, mp2));
    }
  }


/*****************************/
/* Window subclass procedure. */
/*****************************/
MRESULT EXPENTRY NumberSubProc2(HWND hwnd, ULONG msg,
  MPARAM mp1, MPARAM mp2)
  {
  switch(msg) {
    /*****************************/
    /* Filter keyboard messages. */
    /*****************************/
    case WM_CHAR:
      if((CHARMSG(&msg)->fs & KC_KEYUP) ||
        (CHARMSG(&msg)->fs & KC_VIRTUALKEY))
        return ((*pfwnField2) (hwnd, msg, mp1, mp2));
      if(CHARMSG(&msg)->fs & KC_CHAR)
```

```
        if(isdigit(CHARMSG(&msg)->chr))
          return ((*pfwnField2) (hwnd, msg, mp1, mp2));
      return(MRESULT)NULL;
    default:
      return ((*pfwnField2)(hwnd, msg, mp1, mp2));
    }
  }

/************************************/
/*  Random number in range function. */
/************************************/
SHORT FAR Random_Range(SHORT lower_lim, SHORT upper_lim,
  SHORT lower_exc, SHORT upper_exc)
  {
  int i;
getrand:
    i=(((((double)rand())/32767)*(upper_lim-lower_lim))+lower_lim;
    if(i>=lower_exc && i<=upper_exc)
      goto getrand;
    return(i);
  }

/*****************************/
/* Get a set ID for our font. */
/*****************************/
LONG FAR GetSetID(HPS hps)
  {
  #define MAXSETID 254L
  INT i;
  LONG lLcid=GPI_ERROR;
  LONG lCount;
  BOOL fRet=FALSE;
  PLONG alLcids=NULL;
  PLONG alTypes;
  PSTR8 aNames;

  /*************************************************/
  /* See if any local set IDs have been used yet. */
  /*************************************************/
  lCount=GpiQueryNumberSetIds(hps);
  if(lCount==0)
    return(1L);

  /*********************************/
  /* Find first unused local set ID. */
  /*********************************/
  if(lCount!=GPI_ALTERROR){
    alLcids=malloc((SHORT)(16*lCount));
    alTypes=(PLONG)(alLcids+lCount);
    aNames=(PSTR8)(alTypes+lCount);
    if(alLcids!=NULL)
      fRet=GpiQuerySetIds(hps, lCount, alTypes, aNames, alLcids);
    if(fRet){
      for(lLcid=1; lLcid<(MAXSETID+1); lLcid++){
```

```
            for(i=0; (i<(INT)lCount) && (alLcids[i]!=lLcid); i++);
            if(i==(INT)lCount)break;
            }
         if(lLcid==MAXSETID+1)lLcid=GPI_ERROR;
         }
      free(alLcids);
      }
   return(lLcid);
   }


/***********************************/
/* Set point size for outline font. */
/***********************************/
BOOL FAR SetPtSize(HPS hps, LONG lLcid, LONG lPointSize,
   FIXED *width, FIXED *height)
   {
   #define POINTSPERINCH 72L
   HDC hdc;
   BOOL fRet=FALSE;
   LONG lYDevResFont;
   POINTL aptlPoints[2];
   LONG lYSizeInPels;
   LONG lYSizeInWC;


   /*******************************************/
   /* Query current font vertical resolution. */
   /*******************************************/
   hdc=GpiQueryDevice(hps);
   DevQueryCaps(hdc, CAPS_VERTICAL_FONT_RES, 1L, &lYDevResFont);


   /*************************************************************/
   /* Calculate point size and convert to world coordinates. */
   /*************************************************************/
   lYSizeInPels=((lYDevResFont*lPointSize)/POINTSPERINCH);
   aptlPoints[0].x=0L; aptlPoints[0].y=0L;
   aptlPoints[1].x=0L; aptlPoints[1].y=lYSizeInPels;
   GpiConvert(hps, CVTC_DEVICE, CVTC_WORLD, 2L, aptlPoints) ;
   lYSizeInWC=aptlPoints[1].y-aptlPoints[0].y;


   /*********************************************************/
   /* Set the font for the presentation space and make the */
   /* width and height value type fixed.                   */
   /*********************************************************/
   fRet=GpiSetCharSet(hps, lLcid);
   *width=lYSizeInWC*0x10000;
   *height=lYSizeInWC*0x10000;
   return(fRet);
   }


/**************************************************/
/* Set width table and calculate string length. */
/**************************************************/
void FAR SetWidthsTable(HPS hps, LONG *alWidths,
   LONG *alWidthTable, CHAR *szStr, LONG *lTotal)
```

```
   {
   FONTMETRICS fm;
   PKERNINGPAIRS akpairs=NULL;
   LONG i, j;

   /*********************************************/
   /* Get width table for all 256 codepoints. */
   /*********************************************/
   GpiQueryWidthTable(hps, 0L, 256L, alWidthTable);

   /*****************************************************/
   /* Check for kerning font and get pair if needed. */
   /*****************************************************/
   GpiQueryFontMetrics(hps, (LONG)sizeof(FONTMETRICS), &fm);
   if(fm.sKerningPairs){
     akpairs=malloc(fm.sKerningPairs*sizeof(KERNINGPAIRS));
     GpiQueryKerningPairs(hps, fm.sKerningPairs, akpairs);
     }

   /***************************************************************/
   /* Set widths for each character in string before kerning. */
   /***************************************************************/
   for(i=0; i<(LONG)strlen(szStr); i++)
     alWidths[i]=alWidthTable[szStr[i]];

   /***************************************************/
   /* Modify widths array with kerning adjustments. */
   /***************************************************/
   if(fm.sKerningPairs){
     for(i=0; i<(LONG)strlen(szStr); i++){
       for(j=0; j<fm.sKerningPairs; j++){
         if(szStr[i]==(UCHAR)akpairs[j].sFirstChar &&
           szStr[i+1]==(UCHAR)akpairs[j].sSecondChar){
           alWidths[i]+=akpairs[j].lKerningAmount;
           break;
           }
         }
       }
     }
   if(fm.sKerningPairs)free(akpairs);  /* Free kerning values. */
   /*******************************/
   /* Calculate total string width. */
   /*******************************/
   *lTotal=0;
   for(i=0; i<(LONG)strlen(szStr); i++)
   *lTotal=*lTotal+alWidths[i];
   return;
   }

/*****************************/
/* Find outline font by name. */
/*****************************/
BOOL FAR FindFont(HPS hps, LONG *lLcid, CHAR *szFontName)
   {
```

```
PFONTMETRICS afmMetrics=NULL;
LONG lNumFonts, lReqFonts, i, lRemFonts=GPI_ALTERROR;
BOOL fRet=FALSE;
HDC hdc=0L;
USHORT usCodepage=GPI_ERROR;
FATTRS fatAttrs;

/**********************************************************/
/* Query number of public fonts known by PM and allocate */
/* memory in which to read their metrics information.     */
/**********************************************************/
lReqFonts=0;
if(szFontName!=NULL)
  lNumFonts=GpiQueryFonts(hps, QF_PUBLIC, (PSZ)szFontName, &lReqFonts,
    0L, NULL);
else lNumFonts=GpiQueryFonts(hps, QF_PUBLIC, NULL, &lReqFonts,
  0L, NULL);

/***********************************************/
/* Get memory for font metrics if any exist. */
/***********************************************/
if((lNumFonts!=GPI_ALTERROR) && (lNumFonts!=0L))
  afmMetrics=malloc((SHORT)(lNumFonts*sizeof(FONTMETRICS)));

/*************************************/
/* Query font information into array. */
/*************************************/
if(afmMetrics!=NULL)
  if(szFontName!=NULL)
    lRemFonts=GpiQueryFonts(hps, QF_PUBLIC, (PSZ)szFontName,
      &lNumFonts, (LONG)sizeof(FONTMETRICS), afmMetrics);
  else
    lRemFonts=GpiQueryFonts(hps, QF_PUBLIC, NULL, &lNumFonts,
      (LONG)sizeof(FONTMETRICS), afmMetrics);

/******************************************/
/* Search for outline font and create it. */
/******************************************/
if(lRemFonts!=GPI_ALTERROR){
  for(i=0; i<(INT)lNumFonts; i++){
    if(afmMetrics[i].fsDefn&FM_DEFN_OUTLINE){
      *lLcid=GetSetID(hps);   /* Get a set ID for the font. */

      /*******************************/
      /* Set the attribute of the font. */
      /*******************************/
      if(*lLcid!=GPI_ERROR)usCodepage=GpiQueryCp(hps);
      fatAttrs.usRecordLength=sizeof(FATTRS);
      fatAttrs.fsSelection=0;
      fatAttrs.lMatch=0L;
      strcpy(fatAttrs.szFacename, afmMetrics[i].szFacename);
      fatAttrs.idRegistry=afmMetrics[i].idRegistry;
      fatAttrs.usCodePage=usCodepage;
      fatAttrs.lMaxBaselineExt=0L;
```

```
         fatAttrs.lAveCharWidth=0L;
         fatAttrs.fsType=0;
         fatAttrs.fsFontUse=(FATTR_FONTUSE_OUTLINE |
           FATTR_FONTUSE_TRANSFORMABLE);

         /************************/
         /* Create logical font. */
         /************************/
         if(usCodepage!=GPI_ERROR){
           fRet=GpiCreateLogFont(hps, NULL,
           *lLcid, &fatAttrs)!=GPI_ERROR;
           }
         break ;
         }
       }
     }
   if(afmMetrics!=NULL) free(afmMetrics); /* Free memory from array. */
   return(fRet);
   }


/**************************/
/* Perform bug animation. */
/**************************/
void FAR Bug(void)
   {
   BITMAPINFOHEADER2 bmp;
   HBITMAP hbmBug, hbmbm1, hbmbmMask1;
   HDC hdcBug;
   HPS hpsBug, hpsDesk;
   POINTL aptl[4];
   SIZEL sizl;
   POINTL ptl;
   LONG frames=5, xsize=128, ysize=80, shift=12, lRow, x, xlag, i;
   INT sBitMapID[]={IDB_PIC2, IDB_PIC3,
                    IDB_PIC4, IDB_PIC5,
                    IDB_PIC6, IDB_PIC7,
                    IDB_PIC8, IDB_PIC9,
                    IDB_PIC10, IDB_PIC11};

   /*****************************************************/
   /* Get memory device context and presentation space. */
   /*****************************************************/
   hdcBug=DevOpenDC(hab, OD_MEMORY, (PSZ)"*", 0L, 0L, 0L);
   sizl.cx=0; sizl.cy=0;
   hpsBug=GpiCreatePS(hab, hdcBug, &sizl,
     PU_PELS | GPIF_DEFAULT | GPIT_MICRO | GPIA_ASSOC);
   GpiQueryDeviceBitmapFormats(hpsBug, 2L, alBmpFormats);
   memset(&bmp, 0, sizeof(bmp));
   bmp.cbFix=sizeof bmp;
   if(sxPels<xsize*frames)bmp.cx=xsize*frames;
   else bmp.cx=sxPels;
   bmp.cPlanes=(USHORT)alBmpFormats[0];
   bmp.cBitCount=(USHORT)alBmpFormats[1];
   bmp.cy=ysize*4;
```

```
    hbmBug=GpiCreateBitmap(hpsBug, &bmp, OL, NULL, NULL);
    GpiSetBitmap(hpsBug, hbmBug);

    /*********************************************/
    /* Put bit-maps in memory presentation page. */
    /*********************************************/
    for (x=0; x<5 ; x++){
      hbmbm1=GpiLoadBitmap(hpsBug, 0, sBitMapID[x*2],
        (LONG)xsize, (LONG)ysize);
      hbmbmMask1=GpiLoadBitmap(hpsBug, 0, sBitMapID[(x*2)+1],
        (LONG)xsize, (LONG) ysize);
      ptl.y=ysize*2; ptl.x=xsize*x;
      WinDrawBitmap(hpsBug, hbmbm1, NULL, &ptl, CLR_NEUTRAL,
        CLR_BACKGROUND, DBM_NORMAL);
Gpi Delete Bitmap(hbmbm1)
Gpi Delete Bitmap(hbmbmMask1)
      ptl.y=ysize*3; ptl.x=xsize*x;
      WinDrawBitmap(hpsBug, hbmbmMask1, NULL, &ptl, CLR_NEUTRAL,
        CLR_BACKGROUND, DBM_NORMAL);
      }

    /*********************/
    /* Copy the bug path. */
    /*********************/
    lRow=Random_Range(0, syPels-ysize, 0, 0);
    aptl[0].x=0; aptl[0].y=0;              /* Target bottom left. */
    aptl[1].x=sxPels; aptl[1].y=ysize; /* Target upper right. */
    aptl[2].x=0;                          /* Source bottom left. */
    aptl[2].y=lRow;
    hpsDesk=WinGetScreenPS(HWND_DESKTOP);
    GpiBitBlt(hpsBug, hpsDesk, 3L, aptl, ROP_SRCCOPY, BBO_AND);

    /***********************/
    /* Make a bug work area. */
    /***********************/
    aptl[0].x=0; aptl[0].y=ysize;           /* Target bottom left. */
    aptl[1].x=sxPels; aptl[1].y=ysize*2; /* Target upper right. */
    aptl[2].x=0;                          /* Source bottom left. */
    aptl[2].y=lRow;
    GpiBitBlt(hpsBug, hpsDesk, 3L, aptl, ROP_SRCCOPY, BBO_AND);

    /****************/
    /* Do animation. */
    /****************/
    for (x=0; x<sxPels+shift; i=0){

      /***************************************************/
      /* Cut hole in bug work area with correct bug mask. */
      /***************************************************/
      for(i=0; i<frames; i++){
        aptl[0].x=x; aptl[0].y=ysize;           /* Target bottom left. */
        aptl[1].x=xsize+x; aptl[1].y=ysize*2; /* Target upper right. */
        aptl[2].x=xsize*i; aptl[2].y=ysize*3; /* Source bottom left. */
        GpiBitBlt(hpsBug, hpsBug, 3L, aptl, ROP_SRCAND, BBO_AND);
```

```
      /*********************************/
      /* Copy bug into hole in work area. */
      /*********************************/
      aptl[2].y=ysize*2;              /* Change source bottom left. */
      GpiBitBlt(hpsBug, hpsBug, 3L, aptl, ROP_SRCPAINT, BBO_AND);


      /************************************************/
      /* Copy bug frame from work area to screen. */
      /************************************************/
      if(x==0)xlag=0;
      else xlag=x-shift;
      aptl[0].x=xlag; aptl[0].y=lRow;              /* Target bottom left. */
      aptl[1].x=xsize+x; aptl[1].y=ysize+lRow; /* Target upper right. */
      aptl[2].x=xlag; aptl[2].y=ysize;              /* Source bottom left. */
      GpiBitBlt(hpsDesk, hpsBug, 3L, aptl, ROP_SRCCOPY, BBO_AND);


      /*********************************/
      /* Restore work area from save area. */
      /*********************************/
      aptl[0].x=x; aptl[0].y=ysize;              /* Target bottom left. */
      aptl[1].x=x+xsize; aptl[1].y=ysize*2; /* Target upper right. */
      aptl[2].x=x; aptl[2].y=0;              /* Source bottom left. */
      GpiBitBlt(hpsBug, hpsBug, 3L, aptl, ROP_SRCCOPY, BBO_AND);
      DosSleep(SLEEPTIME);
      x=x+shift;
      }
    }
  WinReleasePS(hpsDesk);
  GpiDestroyPS(hpsBug);
  DevCloseDC(hdcBug);
  GpiDeleteBitmap(hbmBug);
  WinInvalidateRect(HWND_DESKTOP, NULL, TRUE); /* Cause full paint. */
  return;
  }


/*****************************/
/* Slide animation function. */
/*****************************/
void FAR Slide(HAB habs, HWND hwnds, SHORT x, SHORT y)
  {
  POINTL aptl[4], aptlb[4], aptlc[4];
  SIZEL sizl;

  /***********************************/
  /* Record move if this is not an undo. */
  /***********************************/
  if(forward){
    backup[ulUndoIndex].x=sGridx;
    backup[ulUndoIndex].y=sGridy;
    ulUndoIndex++;
    if(ulUndoIndex==SIZEOFUNDO)ulUndoIndex=0;
    }
```

```
/***********************/
/* Get master bit-map. */
/***********************/
GpiQueryBitmapParameters(hbmSrc, &bmpSrc);
GpiSetBitmap(hpsMemory, hbmSrc);

/*****************************/
/*  Check for slide to right. */
/*****************************/
if((y==sGridy) && (x<sGridx)){

  /*****************************/
  /* Rectangles for image copy. */
  /*****************************/
  aptl[0].y=y*lcyMinMax;                       /* Target bottom. */
  aptl[1].y=aptl[0].y+lcyMinMax;               /* Target top. */
  aptl[2].y=y*lcyMinMax;                       /* Source bottom. */
  aptl[0].x=(x*lcxMinMax)+SLD_SFT;             /* Target left. */
  aptl[1].x=(sGridx*lcxMinMax)+SLD_SFT;        /* Target right. */
  aptl[2].x=x*lcxMinMax;                       /* Source left. */

  /*****************************/
  /* Rectangles for blank copy. */
  /*****************************/
  aptlb[0].y=y*lcyMinMax;              /* Target bottom. */
  aptlb[1].y=aptl[0].y+lcyMinMax;      /* Target top. */
  aptlb[0].x=x*lcxMinMax;             /* Target left. */
  aptlb[1].x=(x*lcxMinMax)+SLD_SFT;   /* Target right. */

  /*******************************************/
  /* Rectangles for memory to display copy. */
  /*******************************************/
  aptlc[0].y=y*lcyMinMax;                        /* Target bottom. */
  aptlc[1].y=aptl[0].y+lcyMinMax;                /* Target top. */
  aptlc[2].y=y*lcyMinMax;                        /* Source bottom. */
  aptlc[0].x=x*lcxMinMax;                        /* Target left. */
  aptlc[1].x=(sGridx*lcxMinMax)+SLD_SFT;  /* Target right. */
  aptlc[2].x=x*lcxMinMax;                        /* Source left. */

  /******************/
  /* Do slide right. */
  /******************/
  for(sMoveVar=SLD_SFT; sMoveVar<lcxMinMax;
    sMoveVar=sMoveVar+SLD_SFT){
    GpiBitBlt(hpsMemory, hpsMemory, 3L, aptl,  /* Shift image. */
      ROP_SRCCOPY, BBO_AND) ;
    aptl[0].x=aptl[0].x+SLD_SFT;
    aptl[1].x=aptl[1].x+SLD_SFT;
    aptl[2].x=aptl[2].x+SLD_SFT;
    GpiBitBlt(hpsMemory, hpsMemory, 2L, aptlb,  /* Insert blank. */
      ROP_ZERO, BBO_AND);
    aptlb[0].x=aptlb[0].x+SLD_SFT;
```

```
        aptlb[1].x=aptlb[1].x+SLD_SFT;

        /*************************************************/
        /* Copy from memory to display presentation page. */
        /*************************************************/
        GpiBitBlt(hps, hpsMemory, 3L, aptlc,
          ROP_SRCCOPY, BBO_AND);
        aptlc[0].x=aptlc[0].x+SLD_SFT;
        aptlc[1].x=aptlc[1].x+SLD_SFT;
        aptlc[2].x=aptlc[2].x+SLD_SFT;
        DosSleep(SLEEPTIME);
        }

    /*****************************/
    /* Shift remainder of image. */
    /*****************************/
    aptl[0].x=(x*lcxMinMax)+lcxMinMax;    /* Image rectangle. */
    aptl[1].x=(sGridx*lcxMinMax)+lcxMinMax;
    aptlb[0].x=(x*lcxMinMax);              /* Blank rectangle. */
    aptlb[1].x=(x*lcxMinMax)+lcxMinMax;
    GpiBitBlt(hpsMemory, hpsMemory, 3L, aptl, ROP_SRCCOPY, BBO_AND);
    GpiBitBlt(hpsMemory, hpsMemory, 2L, aptlb, ROP_ZERO,BBO_AND);
    aptl[0].x=x*lcxMinMax;
    aptl[1].x=(sGridx*lcxMinMax)+lcxMinMax;
    aptl[2].x=x*lcxMinMax;
    GpiBitBlt(hps, hpsMemory, 3L, aptl, ROP_SRCCOPY, BBO_AND);
    DosSleep(SLEEPTIME);
    }

/*****************************/
/*  Check for slide to left. */
/*****************************/
if((y==sGridy) && (x>sGridx)){

    /*****************************/
    /* Rectangles for image copy. */
    /*****************************/
    aptl[0].y=y*lcyMinMax;                            /* Target bottom. */
    aptl[1].y=aptl[0].y+lcyMinMax;                    /* Target top. */
    aptl[2].y=y*lcyMinMax;                            /* Source bottom. */
    aptl[0].x=(sGridx*lcxMinMax)+
      (lcxMinMax-SLD_SFT);                            /* Target left. */
    aptl[1].x=(x*lcxMinMax)+(lcxMinMax-SLD_SFT); /* Target right. */
    aptl[2].x=(sGridx*lcxMinMax)+lcxMinMax;          /* Source left. */

    /*****************************/
    /* Rectangles for blank copy. */
    /*****************************/
    aptlb[0].y=y*lcyMinMax;                           /* Target bottom. */
    aptlb[1].y=aptl[0].y+lcyMinMax;                   /* Target top. */
    aptlb[0].x=(x*lcxMinMax)+(lcxMinMax-SLD_SFT);  /* Target left. */
    aptlb[1].x=(x*lcxMinMax)+lcxMinMax;               /* Target right. */

    /*****************************************/
    /* Rectangles for memory to display copy. */
    /*****************************************/
```

```
      aptlc[0].y=y*lcyMinMax;                             /* Target bottom. */
      aptlc[1].y=aptl[0].y+lcyMinMax;                     /* Target top. */
      aptlc[2].y=y*lcyMinMax;                             /* Source bottom. */
      aptlc[0].x=(sGridx*lcxMinMax)+(lcxMinMax-SLD_SFT); /* Target left. */
      aptlc[1].x=(x*lcxMinMax)+lcxMinMax;                 /* Target right. */
      aptlc[2].x=(sGridx*lcxMinMax)+(lcxMinMax-SLD_SFT); /* Source left. */

      /*******************/
      /* Do slide left. */
      /*******************/
      for(sMoveVar=SLD_SFT; sMoveVar<lcxMinMax;
        sMoveVar=sMoveVar+SLD_SFT){
        GpiBitBlt(hpsMemory, hpsMemory, 3L, aptl,    /* Shift image. */
          ROP_SRCCOPY, BBO_AND);
        aptl[0].x=aptl[0].x-SLD_SFT;
        aptl[1].x=aptl[1].x-SLD_SFT;
        aptl[2].x=aptl[2].x-SLD_SFT;
        GpiBitBlt(hpsMemory, hpsMemory, 2L, aptlb,  /* Insert blank. */
          ROP_ZERO, BBO_AND);
        aptlb[0].x=aptlb[0].x-SLD_SFT;
        aptlb[1].x=aptlb[1].x-SLD_SFT;

        /****************************************************/
        /* Copy from memory to display presentation page. */
        /****************************************************/
        GpiBitBlt(hps, hpsMemory, 3L, aptlc,
          ROP_SRCCOPY, BBO_AND);
        aptlc[0].x=aptlc[0].x-SLD_SFT;
        aptlc[1].x=aptlc[1].x-SLD_SFT;
        aptlc[2].x=aptlc[2].x-SLD_SFT;
        DosSleep(SLEEPTIME);
        }

      /*****************************/
      /* Shift remainder of image. */
      /*****************************/
      aptl[0].x=sGridx*lcxMinMax;
      aptlb[0].x=x*lcxMinMax;
      aptl[1].x=x*lcxMinMax;
      aptlb[1].x=(x*lcxMinMax)+lcxMinMax;
      GpiBitBlt(hpsMemory, hpsMemory, 3L, aptl, ROP_SRCCOPY, BBO_AND);
      GpiBitBlt(hpsMemory, hpsMemory, 2L, aptlb, ROP_ZERO, BBO_AND);
      aptl[0].x=sGridx*lcxMinMax;
      aptl[1].x=(x*lcxMinMax)+lcxMinMax;
      aptl[2].x=sGridx*lcxMinMax;
      GpiBitBlt(hps, hpsMemory, 3L, aptl, ROP_SRCCOPY, BBO_AND);
      }

  /**************************/
  /*  Check for slide down. */
  /**************************/
  if((x==sGridx) && (y>sGridy)){

    /*****************************/
    /* Rectangles for image copy. */
    /*****************************/
```

```
        aptl[0].y=(sGridy*lcyMinMax)+
          (lcyMinMax-SLD_SFT);                       /* Target bottom. */
        aptl[1].y=(y*lcyMinMax)+(lcyMinMax-SLD_SFT); /* Target top. */
        aptl[2].y=(sGridy*lcyMinMax)+lcyMinMax;      /* Source bottom. */
        aptl[0].x=x*lcxMinMax;                       /* Target left. */
        aptl[1].x=(x*lcxMinMax)+lcxMinMax;           /* Target right. */
        aptl[2].x=x*lcxMinMax;                       /* Source left. */


        /******************************/
        /* Rectangles for blank copy. */
        /******************************/
        aptlb[0].y=(y*lcyMinMax)+(lcyMinMax-SLD_SFT); /* Target bottom. */
        aptlb[1].y=(y*lcyMinMax)+lcyMinMax;          /* Target top. */
        aptlb[0].x=x*lcxMinMax;                      /* Target left. */
        aptlb[1].x=(x*lcxMinMax)+lcxMinMax;          /* Target right. */


        /*****************************************/
        /* Rectangles for memory to display copy. */
        /*****************************************/
        aptlc[0].y=(sGridy*lcyMinMax)+(lcyMinMax-SLD_SFT); /* Target bottom. */
        aptlc[1].y=(y*lcyMinMax)+lcyMinMax;               /* Target top. */
        aptlc[2].y=(sGridy*lcyMinMax)+(lcyMinMax-SLD_SFT); /* Source bottom. */
        aptlc[0].x=x*lcxMinMax;                           /* Target left. */
        aptlc[1].x=(x*lcxMinMax)+lcxMinMax;               /* Target right. */
        aptlc[2].x=x*lcxMinMax;                           /* Source left. */


        /******************/
        /* Do slide down. */
        /******************/
        for(sMoveVar=SLD_SFT; sMoveVar<lcyMinMax;
          sMoveVar=sMoveVar+SLD_SFT){
          GpiBitBlt(hpsMemory, hpsMemory, 3L, aptl,    /* Shift image. */
            ROP_SRCCOPY, BBO_AND);
          aptl[0].y=aptl[0].y-SLD_SFT;
          aptl[1].y=aptl[1].y-SLD_SFT;
          aptl[2].y=aptl[2].y-SLD_SFT;
          GpiBitBlt(hpsMemory, hpsMemory, 2L, aptlb,  /* Insert blank. */
            ROP_ZERO, BBO_AND);
          aptlb[0].y=aptlb[0].y-SLD_SFT;
          aptlb[1].y=aptlb[1].y-SLD_SFT;


          /****************************************************/
          /* Copy from memory to display presentation page. */
          /****************************************************/
          GpiBitBlt(hps, hpsMemory, 3L, aptlc,
            ROP_SRCCOPY, BBO_AND) ;
          aptlc[0].y=aptlc[0].y-SLD_SFT;
          aptlc[1].y=aptlc[1].y-SLD_SFT;
          aptlc[2].y=aptlc[2].y-SLD_SFT;
          DosSleep(SLEEPTIME);
          }


        /****************************/
        /* Shift remainder of image. */
        /****************************/
```

```
    apt1[0].y=sGridy*lcyMinMax;
    apt1b[0].y=y*lcyMinMax;
    apt1[1].y=y*lcyMinMax;
    apt1b[1].y=(y*lcyMinMax)+lcyMinMax;
    GpiBitBlt(hpsMemory, hpsMemory, 3L, apt1, ROP_SRCCOPY, BBO_AND);
    GpiBitBlt(hpsMemory, hpsMemory, 2L, apt1b, ROP_ZERO, BBO_AND);
    apt1[0].y=sGridy*lcyMinMax;
    apt1[1].y=(y*lcyMinMax)+lcyMinMax;
    apt1[2].y=sGridy*lcyMinMax;
    GpiBitBlt(hps, hpsMemory, 3L, apt1, ROP_SRCCOPY, BBO_AND);
    }


/************************/
/*  Check for slide up. */
/************************/
if((x==sGridx) && (y<sGridy)){

    /*****************************/
    /* Rectangles for image copy. */
    /*****************************/
    apt1[0].y=(y*lcyMinMax)+SLD_SFT;        /* Target bottom. */
    apt1[1].y=(sGridy*lcyMinMax)+SLD_SFT; /* Target top. */
    apt1[2].y=y*lcyMinMax;                   /* Source bottom. */
    apt1[0].x=x*lcxMinMax;                   /* Target left. */
    apt1[1].x=(x*lcxMinMax)+lcxMinMax;       /* Target right. */
    apt1[2].x=x*lcxMinMax;                   /* Source left. */


    /*****************************/
    /* Rectangles for blank copy. */
    /*****************************/
    apt1b[0].y=y*lcyMinMax;                  /* Target bottom. */
    apt1b[1].y=(y*lcyMinMax)+SLD_SFT;    /* Target top. */
    apt1b[0].x=x*lcxMinMax;                  /* Target left. */
    apt1b[1].x=(x*lcxMinMax)+lcxMinMax; /* Target right. */


    /******************************************/
    /* Rectangles for memory to display copy. */
    /******************************************/
    apt1c[0].y=y*lcyMinMax;                      /* Target bottom. */
    apt1c[1].y=(sGridy*lcyMinMax)+SLD_SFT; /* Target top. */
    apt1c[2].y=y*lcyMinMax;                      /* Source bottom. */
    apt1c[0].x=x*lcxMinMax;                      /* Target left. */
    apt1c[1].x=(x*lcxMinMax)+lcxMinMax;          /* Target right. */
    apt1c[2].x=x*lcxMinMax;                      /* Source left. */


    /***************/
    /* Do slide up. */
    /***************/
    for(sMoveVar=SLD_SFT; sMoveVar<lcyMinMax;
      sMoveVar=sMoveVar+SLD_SFT){
      GpiBitBlt(hpsMemory, hpsMemory, 3L, apt1,    /* Shift image. */
        ROP_SRCCOPY, BBO_AND) ;
      apt1[0].y=apt1[0].y+SLD_SFT;
      apt1[1].y=apt1[1].y+SLD_SFT;
      apt1[2].y=apt1[2].y+SLD_SFT;
```

```
        GpiBitBlt(hpsMemory, hpsMemory, 2L, aptlb,   /* Insert blank. */
          ROP_ZERO, BBO_AND);
        aptlb[0].y=aptlb[0].y+SLD_SFT;
        aptlb[1].y=aptlb[1].y+SLD_SFT;
        aptlb[2].y=aptlb[2].y+SLD_SFT;

        /****************************************************/
        /* Copy from memory to display presentation page. */
        /****************************************************/
        GpiBitBlt(hps, hpsMemory, 3L, aptlc,
          ROP_SRCCOPY, BBO_AND) ;
        aptlc[0].y=aptlc[0].y+SLD_SFT;
        aptlc[1].y=aptlc[1].y+SLD_SFT;
        aptlc[2].y=aptlc[2].y+SLD_SFT;
        DosSleep(SLEEPTIME);
        }
      aptl[0].y=(y*lcyMinMax)+lcyMinMax;
      aptlb[0].y=y*lcyMinMax;
      aptl[1].y=(sGridy*lcyMinMax)+lcyMinMax;
      aptlb[1].y=(y*lcyMinMax)+lcyMinMax;
      GpiBitBlt(hpsMemory, hpsMemory, 3L, aptl, ROP_SRCCOPY, BBO_AND);
      GpiBitBlt(hpsMemory, hpsMemory, 2L, aptlb, ROP_ZERO, BBO_AND);
      aptl[0].y=y*lcyMinMax;
      aptl[1].y=(sGridy*lcyMinMax)+lcyMinMax;
      aptl[2].y=y*lcyMinMax;
      GpiBitBlt(hps, hpsMemory, 3L, aptl, ROP_SRCCOPY, BBO_AND);
      }
  /****************************************************/
  /* Update global variables and release resources. */
  /****************************************************/
  sGridx=x;
  sGridy=y;
  return;
  }


/**************************************************************/
/* Background thread for random moves and undo functions. */
/**************************************************************/
VOID Background(ULONG dummy)
  {
  LONG i;
  SHORT x, y, toggle;
  HAB habt;

  /****************************************************************/
  /* Get an anchor block handle so thread can access PM functions. */
  /****************************************************************/
  habt=WinInitialize(0);
  for(;;){

    /**********************************************/
    /* Wait for main process to clear semaphore. */
    /**********************************************/
    DosWaitEventSem(hev,SEM_INDEFINITE_WAIT);
```

```
/**********************************/
/* See if we are to perform an undo. */
/**********************************/
if(sUndoFlag==1){

  /************************************************************/
  /* This is a circular buffer so set index to last valid entry. */
  /************************************************************/
  if(ulUndoIndex==0)
    ulUndoIndex=SIZEOFUNDO-1;
  else
    ulUndoIndex-;

  /*********************************************************/
  /* Undo moves while valid move and stop is not indicated. */
  /*********************************************************/
  while((backup[ulUndoIndex].x<30) && (!StopState)){
    DosEnterCritSec();        /* Keep control from main process. */
    Slide(habt, hwndClient,   /* Slide piece. */
      backup[ulUndoIndex].x, backup[ulUndoIndex].y);
    backup[ulUndoIndex].x=30;  /* Invalidate buffer location. */
    backup[ulUndoIndex].y=30;
    if(ulUndoIndex==0)         /* Adjust index to next entry. */
      ulUndoIndex=SIZEOFUNDO-1;
    else
      ulUndoIndex-;

    /*********************************************************/
    /* Let main process and other have more processing time. */
    /*********************************************************/
    DosExitCritSec();
    DosSleep(SLEEPTIME);
    }

  /*****************************************************/
  /* Bump index to next place an entry can be placed. */
  /*****************************************************/
  if(ulUndoIndex==SIZEOFUNDO-1)
    ulUndoIndex=0;
  else
    ulUndoIndex++;

  /*********************************************************/
  /* Let slide routine know that move are no longer from undo. */
  /*********************************************************/
  forward=TRUE;

  /*******************************************************/
  /* Enable random moves menu item and clear undo flag. */
  /*******************************************************/
  WinPostMsg(WinWindowFromID(hwndFrame, FID_MENU),
    MM_SETITEMATTR,
    MPFROM2SHORT(IDM_MOVES, TRUE),
    MPFROM2SHORT(MIA_DISABLED, 0));
```

```
        sUndoFlag=0;
        }


    /******************************************/
    /* See if we are to perform random moves. */
    /******************************************/
    if(sRandomFlag==1){

      /*************************************************************/
      /* Initialized toggle.  This variable will be used to cause    */
      /* alternating moves in the horizontal and vertical directions. */
      /*************************************************************/
      toggle=0;

      /***************************************************/
      /* Do sMoves random move until stop is indicated. */
      /***************************************************/
      for(i=0; (i<sMoves) && (!StopState); i++){
        toggle=toggle^1;
        if(toggle){

          /*********************************************/
          /* Set for random move in vertical direction. */
          /*********************************************/
          x=sGridx;
          y=Random_Range(0, puzzle.sGrid, sGridy, sGridy);
          }
        else {

          /***********************************************/
          /* Set for random move in horizontal direction. */
          /***********************************************/
          y=sGridy;
          x=Random_Range(0, puzzle.sGrid, sGridx, sGridx);
          }
          DosEnterCritSec();    /* Keep control from main process. */
          Slide(habt, hwndClient, x, y);  /* Slide piece. */

          /*********************************************************/
          /* Let main process and other have more processing time. */
          /*********************************************************/
          DosExitCritSec();
          DosSleep(SLEEPTIME);
        }

      /***********************************************/
      /* Enable Undo menu item and clear random flag. */
      /***********************************************/
      sRandomFlag=0;
      WinPostMsg(WinWindowFromID(hwndFrame, FID_MENU),
        MM_SETITEMATTR,
        MPFROM2SHORT(IDM_UNDO, TRUE),
        MPFROM2SHORT(MIA_DISABLED, 0));
```

```
        }

    /**********************************************************/
    /* Clear stop flag and set semaphore to block this thread. */
    /**********************************************************/
    StopState=FALSE;
    DosResetEventSem(hev, &ulPostCt);
    }
  }

/**************************************/
/* Random bug time background thread. */
/**************************************/
VOID Bugtime(ULONG dummy)
  {
  LONG i, random_time;
  for(;;) {

    /****************************************/
    /* Get a random number between 1 and 10. */
    /****************************************/
    random_time=Random_Range(1, 10, 10, 100);

    /**********************************************/
    /* Wait between 1 and 10 minutes before post. */
    /**********************************************/
    for(i=0; i<random_time; i++)
      DosSleep(60000);

    /**********************************************************/
    /* Post BUGRUN message to cause animation in main process. */
    /**********************************************************/
    WinPostMsg(hwndClient, BUGRUN, NULL, NULL);
    }
  }
```

SLIDER.RC

```
#include <os2.h>
#include "slider.h"
#include "dialog.h"

ICON    ID_SLIDEFRAME slider.ico
POINTER IDI_MP1       slider1.ptr
POINTER IDI_MP2       slider2.ptr
POINTER IDI_MP3       slider3.ptr
POINTER IDI_MP4       slider4.ptr
POINTER IDI_MP5       slider5.ptr
BITMAP  IDB_PIC1      slider1.bmp
BITMAP  IDB_PIC2      bug1.bmp
BITMAP  IDB_PIC3      bug1mask.bmp
BITMAP  IDB_PIC4      bug2.bmp
BITMAP  IDB_PIC5      bug2mask.bmp
```

```
BITMAP    IDB_PIC6        bug3.bmp
BITMAP    IDB_PIC7        bug3mask.bmp
BITMAP    IDB_PIC8        bug4.bmp
BITMAP    IDB_PIC9        bug4mask.bmp
BITMAP    IDB_PIC10       bug5.bmp
BITMAP    IDB_PIC11       bug5mask.bmp


MENU  ID_SLIDEFRAME
  BEGIN
  SUBMENU "~Options", IDM_OPT
    BEGIN
    MENUITEM "~Undo \tCtrl+U",                IDM_UNDO
    MENUITEM "~New Puzzle... \tCtrl+N",       IDM_NEW
    MENUITEM "~Grid On \tCtrl+G",             IDM_GRIDSTATE
    MENUITEM "~Random Moves... \tCtrl+R",  IDM_MOVES
    MENUITEM SEPARATOR
    MENUITEM "~Stop \tCtrl+S",                IDM_STOP
    MENUITEM SEPARATOR
    MENUITEM "~Product Information... \tCtrl+P", IDM_PRODUCT
    MENUITEM SEPARATOR
    MENUITEM "E~xit \tAlt+F4",                IDM_EXIT
    END
  SUBMENU "~Help", IDM_HELP, MIS_HELP
    BEGIN
    MENUITEM "~Help for help...", IDM_HELP_FOR_HELP
    MENUITEM "~Extended help...", SC_HELPEXTENDED,MIS_SYSCOMMAND
    MENUITEM "~Keys help...",     SC_HELPKEYS,MIS_SYSCOMMAND
    MENUITEM "Help ~index...",    SC_HELPINDEX,MIS_SYSCOMMAND
    END
  END


ACCELTABLE ID_SLIDEFRAME
  BEGIN
  VK_F4, IDM_EXIT, VIRTUALKEY, ALT
  "^U", IDM_UNDO
  "^N", IDM_NEW
  "^G", IDM_GRIDSTATE
  "^R", IDM_MOVES
  "^S", IDM_STOP
  "^P", IDM_PRODUCT
  "^u", IDM_UNDO
  "^n", IDM_NEW
  "^g", IDM_GRIDSTATE
  "^r", IDM_MOVES
  "^s", IDM_STOP
  "^p", IDM_PRODUCT
  END


rcinclude dialog.dlg


/*************************/
/* Help Table Definition */
/*************************/
HELPTABLE MAIN_HELPTABLE
```

```
      BEGIN
      HELPITEM ID_SLIDEFRAME, MENU_SUBTABLE, EXTENDED_HELP_PANEL_ID
      HELPITEM IDD_NEWPUZZLE, DLG_SUBTABLE_PUZZLE, PUZZLE_DLG_PANEL_ID
      HELPITEM IDD_RANDOM, DLG_SUBTABLE_RANDOM, MOVEEDIT_PANEL_ID
      END


/*****************************/
/* Help Sub Table Definitions */
/*****************************/
HELPSUBTABLE MENU_SUBTABLE
   BEGIN
   HELPSUBITEM IDM_UNDO,      UNDO_PANEL_ID
   HELPSUBITEM IDM_NEW,       NEW_PANEL_ID
   HELPSUBITEM IDM_GRIDSTATE, GRIDSTATE_PANEL_ID
   HELPSUBITEM IDM_MOVES,     MOVES_PANEL_ID
   HELPSUBITEM IDM_STOP,      STOP_PANEL_ID
   HELPSUBITEM IDM_PRODUCT,   PRODUCT_PANEL_ID
   HELPSUBITEM IDM_EXIT,      EXIT_PANEL_ID
   END

HELPSUBTABLE DLG_SUBTABLE_PUZZLE
   BEGIN
   HELPSUBITEM IDD_GRIDEDIT,  GRIDEDIT_PANEL_ID
   HELPSUBITEM IDD_TIMEEDIT,  TIMEEDIT_PANEL_ID
   END

HELPSUBTABLE DLG_SUBTABLE_RANDOM
   BEGIN
   HELPSUBITEM IDD_MOVEEDIT,  MOVEEDIT_PANEL_ID
   END
```

DIALOG.DLG

```
DLGINCLUDE 1 "C:\SLIDER\dialog.h"

DLGTEMPLATE IDD_RANDOM LOADONCALL MOVEABLE DISCARDABLE
BEGIN
    DIALOG    "Random Moves", IDD_RANDOM, 39, 22, 202, 61, WS_VISIBLE,
              FCF_SYSMENU | FCF_TITLEBAR
    BEGIN
        LTEXT            "Enter Number of Random Moves. (1-1000)", 201, 9,
                         47, 182, 8
        ENTRYFIELD       "1234", IDD_MOVEEDIT, 11, 36, 25, 8, ES_MARGIN
        PUSHBUTTON       "OK", DID_OK, 15, 14, 40, 14
        PUSHBUTTON       "Cancel", DID_CANCEL, 78, 14, 40, 14
        PUSHBUTTON       "Help", ID_HELP, 140, 14, 40, 14, BS_HELP |
                         BS_NOPOINTERFOCUS
    END
END


DLGTEMPLATE IDD_NEWPUZZLE LOADONCALL MOVEABLE DISCARDABLE
BEGIN
```

```
    DIALOG  "New Puzzle", IDD_NEWPUZZLE, 80, 64, 191, 84, WS_VISIBLE,
        FCF_SYSMENU | FCF_TITLEBAR
    BEGIN
        LTEXT           "Enter Time Delay In Seconds.  (1-60)", 301, 7, 71,
                        159, 8
        ENTRYFIELD      "12", IDD_TIMEEDIT, 10, 60, 18, 8, ES_MARGIN
        LTEXT           "Grid Number.  (4-25)", 303, 7, 41, 96, 8, NOT
                        WS_GROUP
        ENTRYFIELD      "12", IDD_GRIDEDIT, 10, 30, 18, 8, ES_MARGIN
        PUSHBUTTON      "OK", DID_OK, 15, 6, 40, 14, WS_GROUP
        PUSHBUTTON      "Cancel", DID_CANCEL, 75, 6, 40, 14
        PUSHBUTTON      "Help", ID_HELP, 137, 6, 40, 14, BS_HELP |
                        BS_NOPOINTERFOCUS
    END
END


DLGTEMPLATE IDD_PRODUCT LOADONCALL MOVEABLE DISCARDABLE
BEGIN
    DIALOG  "Product Information", IDD_PRODUCT, 10, 9, 295, 98, WS_VISIBLE,
        FCF_SYSMENU | FCF_TITLEBAR
    BEGIN
        ICON            ID_SLIDEFRAME, ID_SLIDEFRAME, 19, 71, 21, 16, WS_GROUP
        LTEXT           "Learning To Program OS/2 2.0", 101, 82, 82, 135, 8
        LTEXT           "Presentation Manager By Example", 102, 73, 74, 152,
                        8
        LTEXT           "(Putting The Pieces Together)", 103, 85, 66, 128, 8
        LTEXT           "(C) Copyright Van Nostrand Reinhold 1992.  All Righ"
                        "ts Reserved.", 104, 9, 31, 278, 8
        PUSHBUTTON      "OK", DID_OK, 128, 9, 40, 14
        LTEXT           " Stephen A. Knight", 106, 103, 49, 86, 8
    END
END
```

Appendix B. Help Information

```
.**********************************************************
.* This file contains the help panel definitions for  *
.* the Slide Puzzle program.                           *
.**********************************************************
:userdoc.
.*
:h1 res=1.  Extended Help for Slider
:hp2.Slide Puzzle Overview:ehp2.
.*
:artwork align=left name='slider.bmp'.
.*
:p.The Slide Puzzle program is designed to demonstrate basic concepts
about Presentation Manager.  It does this by using basic PM functions that
beginning PM application writers need to know.  It also uses some PM
functions in ways many programmers find interesting.  An explanation of the
PM functions used in this program and how they are used is in the text of
the book :hp2.Learning To Program OS/2 2.0 Presentation
Manager By Example:ehp2.. C source code for this
program is distributed with the book on a diskette.
This source code is intended to be a model PM program that you can change.
By changing this code, you will begin to understand and learn more about
Presentation Manager.
.*
```

:p.Playing the Slide Puzzle game is fairly easy. The puzzle is a matrix
of pieces that form a larger image. One puzzle piece is black or blank
and can be considered a hole in the puzzle. Puzzle pieces can slide into
the hole from either a horizontal or vertical direction. This results in
the hole being filled but causes another hole to be created from where the
piece was slid. After several random moves have been made, the puzzle
will be scrambled. The objective of the game is to return the pieces to
the correct positions to form the whole image again.
.*
:p.To cause a puzzle piece to move, use the mouse or the keyboard.
If you are using the mouse, simply click mouse botton 1 on the piece you
want to slide toward the hole. With the mouse, you can slide multiple
pieces in the same row or column toward the hole. If you are using the
keyboard, press the arrow key that corresponds to the direction you want
to move the piece to fill the hole. The keyboard can only move a
single puzzle piece toward the hole.
.*
:p.After you start the slide puzzle, a bug will run across the screen at
random. This bug is a grasshopper and has the following appearance:
.*
:artwork align=left name='bug1mask.bmp'.
.*
:p.Several options are available in the :hp2.Options:ehp2. pull-down menu
to make this game more interesting. These game options are as follows:
.*
:ol.
:li.Undo
:li.New Puzzle
:li.Grid On
:li.Random Moves
:li.Stop
:li.Product Information
:eol.
.*
:p.To get more information about any one of these options, double click on
one of the following highlighted words (or press the Tab key until the
highlighted word is selected and then press Enter).
.*
:p.
:link reftype=hd res=10.
Undo
:elink.
:link reftype=hd res=11.
    New Puzzle
:elink.
:link reftype=hd res=12.
    Grid On
:elink.
:link reftype=hd res=13.
    Random Moves
:elink.
:link reftype=hd res=14.
    Stop
:elink.
:link reftype=hd res=15.

```
      Product Information
:elink.
:link reftype=hd res=16.
    Exit
:elink.
.*
:h1 res=10.  Undo Option
:p.This pull-down option is used to restore the Slide Puzzle back to its
original state.  It can only :hp1.undo:ehp1. a total of 3000 previous
moves.  Therefore, if more than 3000 moves have been performed before this
option is selected, the puzzle may not be solved with this feature.
.*
:p.To stop the Undo option, select the
:hp2.Stop:ehp2. option from the :hp2.Options:ehp2. pull-down.
Note that the
:hp2.Random Moves:ehp2. option can not be performed while this option is
executing.
:i1.undo
.*
:h1 res=11.  New Puzzle Option
:p.This pull-down option is used to capture a new desktop image to be
used as a new puzzle.  Once you select this option, a dialog box
will prompt you for a time value and a grid size.
.*
:p.The time value is used as a delay before the screen is captured.  This
time delay allows you to arrange the desktop before the
screen is captured.  The Slide Puzzle Application will beep when the
capture of the new puzzle image is completed.  The value for this time
delay is in seconds.
.*
:p.The grid size determines the number of puzzle pieces.  The
puzzle is always a matrix with the same number of pieces on each size.
Therefore, if you use a value of 8 for the grid size, 63 pieces are
created for the puzzle.  (The blank piece makes it 64!)
:i1.new puzzle
.*
:h1 res=12. Grid On Option
:p.This pull-down option will toggle the grid lines on or off.  These
lines show the puzzle piece boundaries.  You may find this option very
helpful for some images.
:i1.grid on
.*
:h1 res=13.  Random Moves Option
:p.This pull-down option will cause random moves of the puzzle pieces to
occur.  Once you select this option, a dialog box will prompt you for the
number of random moves you'd like this option to perform.
.*
:p.Anytime you would like to stop this option, you can select the
:hp2.Stop:ehp2. option from the :hp2.Options:ehp2. pull-down.  Note that
the
:hp2.Undo:ehp2. option can not be performed while this option is
executing.
:i1.random moves
.*
:h1 res=14.  Stop Option
```

```
:p.This pull-down option will stop either the :hp2.Random Moves:ehp2. or
:hp2.Undo:ehp2. options if they are in process.
:il.stop
.*
:h1 res=15.  Product Information Option
:p.This pull-down option will cause a dialog box to appear.  This dialog
box contains the Slide Puzzle book title and copyright statement.
:il.product information
.*
:h1 res=16.  Exit Option
:p.This pull-down option will cause the Slide Puzzle application to
terminate.
:il.exit
.*
.********************
.* Key Assignments. *
.********************
:h1 res=2. Help for Key Assignments
:p.:hp2.PUZZLE ACCELERATOR KEYS:ehp2.
:dl tsize=5 break=all.
:dt.Ctrl+U
:dd.Undo
:dt.Ctrl+N
:dd.New Puzzle
:dt.Ctrl+G
:dd.Grid On Toggle
:dt.Ctrl+R
:dd.Random Moves
:dt.Ctrl+S
:dd.Stop
:dt.Ctrl+P
:dd.Product Information
:dt.Alt+F4
:dd.Exit
:edl.
.*
:p.:hp2.HELP KEYS:ehp2.
:dl tsize=5 break=all.
:dt.F1
:dd.Get help
:dt.F2
:dd.Get extended help (from within any help window)
:dt.Alt+F4
:dd.End help
:dt.F9
:dd.Go to a list of keys (from within any help window)
:dt.F11
:dd.Go to the help index (from within any help window)
:dt.Esc
:dd.Previous Help Panel, or End help if only one panel
:dt.Alt+F6
:dd.Go to/from help and programs
:dt.Shift+F10
:dd.Get help for help
:edl.
```

```
.*
:p.:hp2.SYSTEM KEYS:ehp2.
:dl tsize=5 break=all.
:dt.Alt+Esc
:dd.Switch to the next program
:dt.Ctrl+Esc
:dd.Switch to the Task List
:edl.
.*
:p.:hp2.WINDOW KEYS:ehp2.
:dl tsize=5 break=all.
:dt.F10
:dd.Go to/from the action bar
:dt.Arrow keys
:dd.Move among choices
:dt.End
:dd.Go to the last choice in a pull-down
:dt.Esc
:dd.Cancel a pull-down or the system menu
:dt.Home
:dd.Go to the first choice in a pull-down
:dt.Underlined letter
:dd.Move among the choices on the action bar and pull-downs
:dt.Alt+F4
:dd.Close the window
:dt.Alt+F5
:dd.Restore the window
:dt.Alt+F7
:dd.Move the window
:dt.Alt+F8
:dd.Size the window
:dt.Alt+F9
:dd.Minimize the window
:dt.Alt+F10
:dd.Maximize the window
:dt.Shift+Esc or Alt+Spacebar
:dd.Go to/from the system menu
:dt.Shift+Esc or Alt
:dd.Go to/from the system menu of a text window
:edl.
.*
:h1 res=20.  New Puzzle Dialog
:p.The New Puzzle Dialog allows you to specify a time delay and
the grid number for a new puzzle.  The time delay is the number of
seconds the slide puzzle will wait before
it captures the desktop image.
This new image will be used as the new puzzle image.  This time
delay can be between 1 and 60 seconds.  During this time, you may
want to arrange or hide objects on the desktop so the puzzle
image is more interesting.
.*
:p.The grid number is used to determine the number of puzzle
pieces for the new puzzle.  This number can be between 1 and 25
and represents the number of puzzle pieces on each side of the
puzzle.  Hence, a grid number of 8 will cause the puzzle to
```

have 64 pieces minus 1 for the blank piece.
.*
:h1 res=21. Time Delay Field
:p.The time delay field represents the number of seconds the
slide puzzle will wait before it captures the desk-top image.
This new image will be used as the new puzzle image. This time
delay can be between 1 and 60 seconds.
.*
:h1 res=22. Grid Number Field
:p.The grid number is used to determine the number of puzzle
pieces for the new puzzle. This number can be between 1 and 25
and represents the number of puzzle pieces on each side of the
puzzle. Hence, a grid number of 8 will cause the puzzle to
have 64 pieces minus 1 for the blank piece.
.*
:h1 res=30. Random Moves
:p.The Random Moves Dialog allows you to specify the number
of moves the slide puzzle will perform in the background to mixup
the puzzle. This number can range from 1 to 1000. If you want
to stop the random moves before they complete, use the
stop option from the Options pull-down menu.
.*
:index.
:euserdoc.

INDEX